The Jeweled Path

The Jeweled Path

*The Biography of the Diamond Approach
to Inner Realization*

KAREN JOHNSON

Foreword by A. H. Almaas

SHAMBHALA
Boulder
2018

Shambhala Publications, Inc.
4720 Walnut Street
Boulder, Colorado 80301
www.shambhala.com

9 8 7 6 5 4 3 2 1

First Edition
Printed in the United States of America

♾This edition is printed on acid-free paper that meets the
American National Standards Institute z39.48 Standard.
♻This book was printed on 30% postconsumer recycled paper.
For more information please visit www.shambhala.com.
Distributed in the United States by Penguin Random House LLC
and in Canada by Random House of Canada Ltd

Library of Congress Cataloging-in-Publication Data
Names: Johnson, Karen (Codeveloper of the Diamond Approach), author.
Title: The jeweled path: the biography of the Diamond Approach to inner
realization / Karen Johnson; foreword by A. H. Almaas.
Description: First edition. | Boulder: Shambhala, 2018. | Includes
bibliographical references.
Identifiers: LCCN 2017013586 | ISBN 9781611804355 (pbk.: alk. paper)
Subjects: LCSH: Ridhwan Foundation—History. | Ridhwan Foundation—
Doctrines. | Johnson, Karen (Codeveloper of the Diamond Approach) |
Almaas, A. H.
Classification: LCC BP605.R53 J64 2018 | DDC 204—dc23
LC record available at https://lccn.loc.gov/2017013586

A Deep Bow

To the miraculous river of wisdom,
which imparts itself in many ways.

To the venerable sages of all faiths and views
spanning all times and places,
who offer us tools for tapping into the Good,
our deepest nature,
for the benefit of all humanity.

To the jeweled emissaries that deliver
the Path of the Diamond Approach from the invisible realm,
and the beings—past, present, and future—
who are vessels of their divine knowledge.

And to the messenger
the master
the man—
Hameed Ali

Contents

Foreword

The book you have in your hands might be the first of its kind. It is not simply a biography of the individuals closely associated with a spiritual path but rather the story of the genesis and growth of that path as expressed through the lives of those individuals. And the story is told by an insider present at the path's inception—by a true, living vehicle of the teaching who remains central to its ongoing development.

The Jeweled Path is not the story of a single awakening or epiphany from which a path arose, as happens in many teachings. Spanning many years, it is an unfolding tale of a path that simply erupted on the scene and unpacked itself in our lifetime rather than over the course of generations. It is the story of a logos that reveals a heartfelt knowledge and a discriminating intelligence that I believe the world is now ready for.

Since 1984, when the earliest Diamond Approach writings appeared, there has been much speculation about what this teaching is, how it came about, and what kind of person writes the books that represent the body of the teaching. The Diamond Approach has been called a philosophy, a spiritual psychology, a transpersonal psychology or philosophy, a synthesis of Western psychology and Eastern teachings, a synthesis of Buddhist teachings with other paths such as Sufism, and various other characterizations. I have been referred to as a Sufi, a Buddhist, a Vedantist, a philosopher, a scholar, a psychologist, and so on.

None of these descriptions are accurate, yet it is understandable that such ideas are put forward by individuals who were not close to the genesis of the teaching. It did not matter that I said many times that the Diamond Approach is not a synthesis of any kind, and that this path is quite different from other well-known teachings, ancient or modern. Even now, it does not make sense to most people when I tell them that I am not the source of this path because no human being could have developed it on his or her own. I thought of writing an autobiography, as some people suggested, partly to help dispel these well-meaning ideas and speculations. But I realized many years ago that it would be a monumental task, for this journey is a long series of awakenings and describing in detail the discovery of such a vast spiritual terrain would have taken me years and filled many volumes. My books detail some of the unpacking of the teaching and the secrets of reality, but *The Jeweled Path* tells how it all happened, filling a gap that my writings cannot.

Karen Johnson was a friend of mine before this path even began. As it unfolded, we became closer and deeper friends, spiritual friends. If anybody is qualified to present the truth of how the Diamond Approach originated and how it developed, she is. Karen knows this path from the inside out and has done a masterful job condensing in one small volume a rich and multifaceted story, replete with details of an inner process that included many births, deaths, and rebirths.

You will find *The Jeweled Path* readable and human, personal and intimate, even as Karen is narrating experiences of transcendence and sharing deep spiritual mysteries. She writes with spacious elegance and a compelling, often humorous, descriptive power that together communicate the feel of how things transpired. In showing the marvelous and sometimes miraculous ways this teaching has developed, she goes beyond describing the events themselves to discuss what it means to live out the various realizations that arise in the Diamond Approach.

Karen is a superb storyteller. She does not simply write *about* the knowledge and realizations that came through; she puts everything in context, as an unfolding of unusual occurrences in the midst of ordinary living. Although this book is in no way a comprehensive account of the Diamond Approach, you will be transported into the midst of a wide range of inquiries, awakenings, discoveries, and revelations—as well as the struggles and perplexities we faced—as this path intelligently unfolded through my consciousness, Karen's, and the consciousness of others who have been on this journey.

In addition to relating her personal experiences, Karen also talks about a number of my inquiries, awakenings, and insights, many of which we participated in together. I made available to her the approximately six thousand pages of my journals: thirty-six notebooks of handwritten entries, followed by more than twenty years of computer files. Excerpts throughout her book offer an additional sense of the texture and feel of what was happening at various junctures on this path.

I have read and reread the chapters of this book and had discussions with Karen to review and sometimes clarify various events, as well as to understand some of the implications that were not evident in the journal entries. I can attest to the authenticity and truth of Karen's writing about me, the Ridhwan School, and the teachings of the Diamond Approach.

I am grateful that Karen undertook this task. It is a service not only to readers who want to know the story of the Diamond Approach and the students who are the beneficiaries of this teaching but also to the teaching itself. It is an expression of the reality behind the teaching, and this will hopefully guard against the mythologies, conjectures, and imaginings that usually occur when the story is told after the characters are long dead.

Both Karen and I are thankful for the many individuals who have confirmed the universality of the discoveries of the teaching through their participation in the Diamond Approach. Many have also helped the development of the teaching through their service in establishing and growing the Ridhwan School—the worldly home of this teaching—and by working with the many students who have become travelers on this path.

A. H. ALMAAS (HAMEED ALI)
October 2016
Berkeley, California

Author's Preface

Hameed Ali did not set out to deliberately create a spiritual path. He didn't know for some time that his experiences, and those of others around him, would evolve into a teaching. But what began as a personal investigation of inner truth gradually revealed itself as having many of the markings of a spiritual path in its own right. At some point, it became obvious that the journey we were on was not only for our own discovery, it was also showing us foundational principles of the human soul and its relationship to essential nature that would apply to and benefit many people.

The inspiration for *The Jeweled Path* arose in part from a wish to answer the many questions asked by individuals who have become interested in how the Diamond Approach unfolded. As our work has become more well known throughout the world, it was obvious that a chronicle of the development of the Diamond Approach was needed, both for those who have been involved with the Ridhwan School and people who have only heard about it or have limited familiarity with the teachings.

It also became clear that the teaching would outlive the initial teachers, so we realized that we had a rare opportunity to write about the genesis of a teaching while the original founders are still alive. Yet this book became more than just a useful idea; it became an inner dictate that wouldn't leave me alone. I found myself carving out days and weeks to study Hameed's journals, rummage through my own papers and memories, and then begin. As I delved into the project, the process of writing took on a life of its own—vivid, intense, elaborate. It was as though I were rediscovering each experience anew. I could feel, sense, *be* in the atmosphere of each scene. It was like holographic time travel. The events of the past came alive with the vibrant joy of exploration and discovery of universes we had not heard of; the painful conditions of despair, loss, and disillusionment that are also part of our human soul; and the learning and loving and growing that happened. The then became a living now.

This served my purpose well, since what is most important is to convey an authentic sense of the people, places, and events that led to our breakthroughs, bringing you right into the midst of them with me. I would love for you to get a sense of the rich and textured experiences that were part of the remarkable organic process that parted the veil to reveal wondrous and beautiful treasures. I want to tell you how the Diamond Approach work was born. And I want to put you in direct touch with the beating pulse of it as it continues to grow and flourish as a living teaching.

The Jeweled Path covers mainly the first fifteen years or so of the path's unfolding, referring only briefly in the last two chapters to the two and a half decades that followed. I chose to focus on what kinds of processes and dynamics were involved in the emergence of the Diamond Approach and its initial stages of development instead of detailing the content of the teaching and the path in full.

In the course of our journey, we moved through many endings, many deaths. Along the way, specific turning points marked distinct passages to new realms of consciousness, exposing radical shifts in perception and the experience of reality. Each one revealed even more of the mystery of Being, giving birth to a continuing series of transformations of our sense of self. And every experience opened the way to a deeper understanding of True Nature without dismissing what had come before. An elegant system was divulging itself, presenting its wisdom for the road inward by reorienting our minds, hearts, bodies, and souls. Step by step, we followed.

Meditation had always played a supportive role in our inner practice, but awakenings most often arose out of a growing practice of Inquiry as we moved through each day of joys and sorrows, tasks and opportunities—whenever we approached our experience and life with openness and a sense of adventure. Perhaps the central aspect of our process that many people are unaware of is that much of this happened while we were watching TV, sitting in a café, strolling along a sidewalk, shopping, or riding in the car. From within these ordinary circumstances a teaching emerged about the realization of our nature and how to live that realization.

Although a great deal of understanding and synthesis occurred spontaneously as the experiences were revealing themselves, much of what developed into the formal teaching was synthesized, systematized, and refined in hindsight by looking back at the copious notes that Hameed made along the way in his journals. The thoroughness of his record keeping is remarkable. Tracking the detailed, interlacing threads of our processes would have been impossible without them. Rereading those journals as I wrote this book gave me the opportunity to follow the timeline of the teaching as it displayed itself through our experiences. I saw relationships between segments of the teaching I'd never noticed before, and when Hameed and I discussed them, new details of the teaching were unpacked.

Hameed's journals, and the nineteen books he has written thus far (one of which—*Divine Eros: The Illuminating Force of Love in Everyday Life*—was coauthored with me), are considered to be the canon of the teaching. Thirteen of his books are edited transcriptions of new teachings, which are given mainly at his yearly Asilomar retreats. The first nine books were published under his own imprint, which he named Diamond Books. Beginning with *Spacecruiser Inquiry: True Guidance for the Inner Journey* in 2002, Shambhala Publications took over the publications of his books.

Three of the teachers in the Ridhwan School have published related works: Byron Brown's *Soul without Shame: A Guide to Liberating Yourself from the Judge Within*; John Davis's *The Diamond Approach: An Introduction to the Teachings of A. H. Almaas* (both published by Shambhala); and Sandra Maitri's *The Spiritual Dimension of the Enneagram: Nine Faces of the Soul* (Tarcher) and *The Enneagram of Passions and Virtues* (Power Moves Entertainment).

The purpose of this book is to begin the tale of how that teaching arose through unsuspecting, adventurous spirits and settled into the spiritual discipline it is known as today. It is a love story of truth-seeking and truth-finding, of the knowledge of love and the love of knowledge, and of a topsy-turvy magical ride penetrating uncharted universes. It is replete with the difficulties and delights of moving into the deep unknown. It is also a tale of friendship and spiritual companionship, of life, adventure, mystery, and the beauty of the invisible world manifesting its secrets.

Of course, mine is only one voice, one vantage point, among many. Each teacher, each student, and anyone who has been touched by or involved in this work in some way has something important to add. Many people, events, experiences, and understandings are left unmentioned but are no less worthy of inclusion. However, to write in more detail about what transpired in the first fifteen years would take at least another volume. And it would take many more to tell the story of the twenty-five years since then.

Gratitude consistently arose as I wrote, and I am deeply in touch with it as I complete this preface. I am honored to be the vehicle through which this tale is told and feel moved by the opportunity to tell it. If by the time you finish reading this book, I have given you a sense of the fertile context in which the teaching emerged and illuminated itself, and if I have answered some questions and given you a feel for how this precious work evolved, then my job will have been done well enough. Better yet, if you feel the twinkling of liquid light moving within, perhaps the journey is alive in your own heart—quietly, secretly waiting for you to notice.

This is an invitation to enter the adventure. I hope you enjoy it.

KAREN JOHNSON
November 30, 2016

The Jeweled Path

1 ❖ The Journey Begins

LIFE CHANGED FOREVER the day I set out in my sky-blue VW Bug heaving with everything I owned. An old carpenter's chest, a gift from my mother and stepfather, had been carefully packed with watercolors, paintbrushes, and other art paraphernalia and small, cherished belongings. A single suitcase that easily held all of my clothes cordially rubbed sides with it. Add a futon and a sleeping bag—purple, of course—neatly tucked into the back, and I was ready to go.

My mother, June, did not bid me goodbye that morning. Instead, she wished me well. Love encompassed us. Tears welled. She was sad to see me go but was excited for me too. I was embarking on the adventure of a lifetime and she knew it, maybe even more than I did at the time.

She waved big as I drove off, and I caught a glimpse of her in my rearview mirror. She leaned long and to her left, stretching to capture the last hint of me. The view shrank until all I could see was a shock of white hair glowing in the distance like a star. I turned my sights to the road before me.

As I rounded the first corner, a strand of memory connected the fading star of white to the vivid mental picture of making my announcement that I was leaving: "Mom, Sandra is going to Colorado with a friend to work there. She's asked me if I want to come along. I've decided to go with her."

I had no particular reason to leave. The comfort and opportunities of the Bay Area in California were plentiful in the early 1970s when Silicon Valley was booming, but it was empty for me. I had hoped she would understand without my having to explain why I wanted to go, and I felt anxious that she might not let me off the hook.

The yielding, soft intensity of her sea-green eyes had set the tone for our conversation. After a time, she looked away briefly, then returned her attention to me. Quietly but in her usual forthright manner she simply asked, "Why are you going?" She held her gaze steady, slightly squinting. The question hung in the space between us.

Beyond the brief explanation I had just given, I couldn't articulate any reason for this unprecedented departure. No job plan and an uncertain living situation made me cautious about telling her that I felt a deep feeling of rightness about it. Above all, I did not want her to feel I was abandoning her. I wanted her blessings, her support. I desperately wanted her to know that I was moving toward something important.

This mysterious pull I wanted to follow was not strange to her. She had known such a feeling, and it had guided her in her own life. From the time I was young, my mother had welcomed the unknown, taking risks that challenged convention. June embodied the conservative and wild creative spirit, with Doris Day looks and an artsy, beatnik take on life—and a bit of Mary Poppins thrown in. Her sense of adventure had instilled in her four children the lust for life. I was hoping this out-of-the-blue idea would appeal to her daring side.

"I don't know. It just really feels right for me, Mom," I answered her.

Her eyes moistened just enough to increase the wattage of her eyes. She smiled with sweet acknowledgment. No judgment. I felt she knew exactly what I meant. I relaxed into her loving embrace.

"Follow your heart, honey," she said with a breathy whisper in my ear. And three weeks later, that is exactly what I did.

❖ ❖ ❖

I was an average kid in most respects. A relatively happy child at home, I was quick to laugh and vigorously engaged with my siblings as we played games and teased one another. But my first years in elementary school were awkward; I became ever more shy and quiet, finding it sometimes difficult to connect with other kids. This may have been due to something that no one else I knew seemed to experience or understand: I saw energy around things. People, plants, and animals, mostly.

One day, I asked my mother about it. I must have been about six or seven because as I write this I can see myself looking a long way up to catch her attention. "Mommy, why do people have lights around them?" She kneeled down next to me, and her eyes softened as they narrowed to probe and console at the same time.

"I don't know."

When I saw her expression of wonder and mild concern, I realized that although she didn't know what was going on with me, she did not think I was strange or bad for it. She just didn't want me to feel even more out of place at school. I was a chubby girl, and this, combined with my unusual vision, made me a target for ridicule. The title "class cootie" had been bestowed on me and was flung at me on more than one occasion.

I remember coming home numerous times at the end of the school day, hurt, confused, and even frightened by what I had seen. It was not uncommon for me to arrive at our front door red-eyed, my cheeks flushed and wet with tears. I often felt like I was from another planet. Still, one advantage of this alien capacity was that I could tell whether someone was telling the truth or not. This was handy.

I had no way to communicate about any of this. Mommy wanted to help and didn't know how. This was painful for me at times, but her love for me was never in question. As I became more and more distressed, she found a psychologist who helped children to cope with these sorts of experiences. She specialized in sensitives, as they were called at the time, but that term also implied being psychic.[1]

I have vivid memories of much of my childhood, but I can barely remember these meetings with the therapist. My mother claims that after the third and last session, I felt protected from having to see and feel so much. I vaguely recall the psychologist guiding me to visualize a protective shield around me.

By the fifth grade, I no longer saw the colors and forms around people; I got to know my peers by interacting with them. I had multiple friends for the first time and was eager to go to school each morning to see them and learn new things. I felt normal. I *liked* myself. I wasn't looking for any more than that. But something happened one day that reminded me of the realms I had glimpsed before.

It happened on a very normal day as I was reading the very normal *Palo Alto Times*. I was not yet in puberty but was no longer a little girl, so I must have been around eleven years old. Sprawled out on my soft belly, soaking up the heat from the cork floor in our Eichler house in Palo Alto, I was leafing through a section of the newspaper to find an article for current events class. I was dimly aware of my father and mother discussing an article about a girl who had just died in a car accident.

My attention zoomed in when I heard my mother reading aloud to my father—as best as I can remember it: "As she lay on the ground, dying, with her father holding her hand, she looked up at him and said, 'Don't worry, Daddy. I know where I am going.'"

An intense need to understand the meaning of birth, death, and the events in between these two inescapable markers burst out of me. "Where was she going?" I asked with all the passion of my little heart, not addressing anyone in particular. My eyes searched the air but found nowhere to land. I was entranced with the question itself; at the same time, I wondered about Mom and Dad—what were they thinking and feeling? Half-audible comments sputtered out of them, then dissipated like puffs of smoke. No satisfying answer came from above either.

The question of death and the hereafter dropped into my chest like a rock and wedged itself next to my heart as an unopened secret. It haunted me for months.

I guess you could say that this was my first existential crisis, although that would be too fancy a word for a kid that age. The death of that young girl, coupled with my early experiences of the energetic universe, propelled me into a search for meaning beyond this physical world. I knew there was more to it than meets the eye. The urgency to meet that "more," to *know* it, only became stronger. A significant shift had occurred: I was no longer afraid of the unknown or unexplained. I was *curious*.

It is natural for children of that age to become aware that life ends, people die. Questions come, questions fade away, as explanations are given to a child to fill the void. Often those explanations so fill the space of wonder that the queries disappear entirely. In some children, the curiosity is channeled in all manner of creative and interesting ways. My dissatisfaction with the usual explanations persisted. I kept my antennae up for anything that might offer clues.

Religion began to play a role in my search for answers. The religious influences in my early years were varied. My mother and father, both of Scandinavian descent, had a fairly traditional Lutheran upbringing but didn't bring up their children with the same rigor. There were several reasons for this lax attitude. Some dark stories regarding the church had left them ambivalent about whether and how much to involve us in a strict religious training. In spite of its shortcomings, however, they felt that religion could be a positive influence—in small doses.

On a more positive note, my great-grandmother on my mother's side—from County Cork, Ireland—married a Chippewa Indian chief and lived on a reservation in northern Wisconsin for about ten years. She had left her first husband by whom she had three sons, one of whom was my grandfather.

Chippewa legends and beliefs are passed down from generation to generation through pictures and stories, and although as a child, my mother went to church regularly like her mother did, she eagerly drank these stories in. She learned very young that everything is alive and filled with spirit—the stream she sat by with her grandfather to receive the sacred teachings, the trees that listened in as they spoke, even the big rock she was sitting on. So it was probably not the big surprise it might have been to the average mother in the fifties when I reported seeing spirit all around me.

Even so, my parents would get on kicks about providing a consistent churchgoing experience for us kids; every few years, they would resolve to find a place to land that would give us a solid ethical focus. We finally settled on a progressive Unitarian church in Palo Alto, where the Sunday school teachers encouraged independent thinking in the kids and taught us about many different religions.

At one of the book sales that were held after every Sunday service, I was drawn to *The Diary of Anne Frank*. I became fascinated for two reasons. First, in addition to having seen the camps right after the end of World War II, my father had also been at the Nuremberg Trials of the major war criminals. Mother said he came back a changed man after both experiences. He told us stories about the atrocities he had seen and frequently used them to point out what human beings can do to one another.

Second, Anne Frank's diary presented me with a perspective of someone near my age—I saw a whole other face of that war. Anne's bravery and faith in the face of adversity inspired me. She had suffered far beyond what I had experienced and somehow managed to find something she could be certain of beyond the physical world of appearances. This added more fuel to the flame lit by the newspaper story about the death of the young stranger.

These two girls had met with such a tragic end, but they seemed to have had some kind of magic key. Two vibrant lives cut short. I had mine to live. What gave them such courage and strength, so much love and kindness? Even though Anne faced fear every day, she never lost faith in the good in people or in her God. She sought answers and searched herself for them. Did Anne also know where she was going? Did she know about the realm beyond this world that the girl dying in the accident was so sure would welcome her? What did they know? What did it mean? More important, how could *I* know?

Our family always said grace before dinner, and Mother always said prayers with us before bed. I began to pray on my own, and it became a way to feel my heart's yearning for God, for love, for companionship. I looked forward to praying every day. The form my prayer took depended on whether I was feeling joyous gratitude and celebration, yearning for something or someone, or sad about an event in my own life or someone else's that made me want to ask for help. Sometimes, while praying, I sensed love mingling with my salty tears, melting the rock that had wedged itself in my chest when I read about the little girl.

In hindsight, I could say I felt a sense of devotion, though over time, God had changed from the familiar Sistine Chapel image to a presence with no specific form or face. I didn't know how Anne and the girl in the newspaper understood God, but I began to sense what they might have known: I felt that I, too, would be okay, no matter what. Deep in me were goodness and strength. Not in an I-am-a-good-girl kind of way—just plain goodness. I felt lucky, too. I had found a doorway to my heart. I opened it.

This explicit sense of underlying goodness arrived just in time. Circumstances in my life forced me to grow up rapidly. My mother left the family when I was twelve to join the man who would become my stepfather. This was a painful, empty time for me. I was often overcome by loss and inner chaos. Although the years immediately following her departure held deep hurts, the void eventually opened to blessings.

The timing of these events is rather a blur for me. I can still feel the fuzzy sense of myself as a teenage girl gobsmacked by the loss of my mother and being left in the care of my emotionally devastated father. It felt like I was the one who needed to take care of him, as well as my younger sister and brother. My big brother had gone off to college, so I became the I-can-do-it-all girl. Cooking, cleaning, laundry—whatever needed doing, I found a way to manage it. This, of course, left all the mess underneath the strength, which would have to be dealt with later. Meanwhile, I kept pulling it together.

To top it off, my sister left to be with our mother a few months afterward. She and I had shared a bedroom for most of our lives. A piece of my heart went numb with pain that day, shot through to the core with the loss of her and scabbed over with guilt. I had failed to provide her with what she needed emotionally and in probably every other way. The family was torn asunder. I felt responsible for that and was trying to make it right.

The blessings? June found her true love, Russ—yes, he had the same name as my father—and he was a good match for her, and when I moved in with them later on, Russ became a sturdy, loving stepfather for me.

Meanwhile, junior high school became a haven for me. It gave me structure. I didn't miss a single day during the entire three years. Much to my surprise, I found I had a passion for science. Maybe my need for more structure stimulated the interest. Also, I had one of those teachers who is so inspiring that it was difficult not to catch his exuberance for the subject matter. He turned the complex world of scientific theory into a fascinating playground of discovery. He saw my enthusiasm and encouraged me to pursue the sciences, but I chose to continue with what I had loved and felt most confident in for as long as I could remember, which was art.

Mother was an artist, so we had always had a place at home for painting and playing with all types of creative media. She taught me art as self-exploration. One of my first lessons was to color outside the lines in the coloring book. I resisted that initially. But art quickly became a language I easily understood; I could express myself with it more directly than with words. Once you learn the basic nature of the medium and have the correct tools to apply it with, my mother would say, you can just let it be part of you. Let it speak. And then listen.

At fifteen, I found my way back to my mother when I resolved to leave my father and move in with her. It was the first difficult decision of my adult life. My father was deeply wounded by Mother's leaving and then mine. But leaving the wreckage behind seemed necessary for my survival. I just couldn't look back. An inner sense of correctness and right action was coming through with strength and certainty. This was rare, for I was desperately unassertive at the time. Now I could make a choice for a real life and let go of the weight of responsibility that was far beyond what I could manage. You could say that a healthy dose of adolescent rebelliousness was rearing up and coming to the rescue.

My new stepfather gave me the great gift of bringing the dimension of the numinous into my world. He became what my father could not be—someone who could help me find the answers I was looking for. A great blessing hidden in a lot of pain, but before it could be received, we had a lot to work through. At first, I hated him. He had taken my mother from me and deeply hurt my father. But when he took me by the shoulders one day, looked me straight in the eye, and said, "You can hate me all you want, but you can't treat me like shit in my own house," a sliver of light came through. From then on, I felt I could begin to talk to him about my feelings. He sat, he listened, and he understood. I could hate him for what he did, but I also saw that my negative feelings toward him weren't the only truth of the matter.

Russ also helped me to see that I had potential in many areas and taught me how to tap into it. I became excited by challenges instead of being frightened by them. He introduced my high school friends and me to self-hypnosis, which became a vehicle for exploration along with the yoga and meditation he also turned me on to. By age sixteen, I was teaching yoga in my physical education classes at school. I spent many an afternoon at the East West Bookstore, which was then in Menlo Park, poring over books on virtually every religious and spiritual path. On my sixteenth birthday, Russ gave me Paramahansa Yogananda's *Autobiography of a Yogi*. I devoured it and immediately joined the Self-Realization Fellowship.

Some of our weekends were spent on trips to West Coast centers of art and counterculture activities—Big Sur, Monterey, Carmel, Sausalito. Russ and June attended workshops at Esalen Institute with Fritz Perls and some of the early consciousness pioneers. They ate it all up and brought the knowledge home for me and my friends to taste.

I made trips north with my siblings and our friends just to hang out in Haight-Ashbury or at City Lights Bookstore in North Beach or to see the great performers' outdoor concerts—not to mention those at the Fillmore Auditorium and the Avalon Ballroom. And we wouldn't have missed for anything the Be-In at Golden Gate Park during the Summer of Love in '67.

With the guidance of my mother and stepfather, my friends and I would spend many evenings and weekends engaged in astral traveling, shamanic journeying, self-hypnosis, healing, past-life regression, and meditation. I began to have dreams about energy fields around people. The dreams came more frequently and I became anxious. When I told my mother about them, she reminded me that as a child I used to see these fields and wondered what the connection might be. With some trepidation, we began to investigate this phenomenon together.

The memories flooded back in. I began to *see* the energy fields again and discovered they had a name—auras. I found out that other people, some of whom had been experimenting with hallucinatory drugs, had similar experiences. As my understanding of myself increased, so did my capacity to perceive. My perception developed over time to include a greater empathic sensitivity—I could feel in my own body the sensations of other people's experiences.

In high school, I had many opportunities to refine my artistic capacities and express what I was learning about myself. Though I focused on painting and printmaking, I also discovered the world of theater through new friends who were deeply engaged in classical and contemporary productions. I had so much fun with these brilliant, creative people, and we immersed ourselves in a direct mode of learning. Instead of only reading about the Renaissance, for instance, we would make period costumes and stage big feasts in the backyard. We found out how to build a roaring fire pit and went about roasting a well-fatted pig on a spit. Interspersed among a few lusty songs, a dance or two, and some conversation in iambic pentameter, you could see me chomping on a hefty turkey leg with one hand and downing a pint of mead in the other, with a gleam in my eye.

So many things came together for me in those years. And I had friends, really close friends. We all cared for and loved one another. I belonged.

When the time came to go to college, I was reluctant. Not because I didn't want to learn and be enriched but because I was happy to have found a home where so many interesting things were happening, where I felt loved, nourished, encouraged to question and seek answers, to communicate my feelings and ideas. I wanted to linger just a while more, nestled in the arms of the loving household that had become the womb of my spirit.

Alongside my hesitancy, the urge to try out my own wings was burgeoning. It was time to fledge.

2 ⋄ Growing Up in Kuwait

HAMEED AND I WERE an unlikely pair to become good friends. The first eighteen years of our respective lives provide a study in contrasts. The dry, primitive desert of Kuwait in the 1940s was light-years from the lush apricot orchards of the university town of Palo Alto where I lived in the '50s and early '60s. Our neighborhood was a colorful mix of races, religions, and cultures, but I was least familiar with Middle Eastern culture. My childhood fantasy of "Arabia" was of an exotic land of magic: crowds funneling through narrow streets and flooding into noisy marketplaces . . . haughty camels crossing burning sands . . . folding tents made of tapestry . . . the obligatory shimmering oasis.

Completing the picture were musicians playing beautiful unknown instruments and dark-haired girls in silk and jewels, dancing in a cloud of the sweet scents of frankincense and myrrh. I was obviously under the influence of fairy tales and Hollywood, but the particulars were not entirely off—merely glamorized and blown out of proportion. The more I heard about daily life in Hameed's homeland, the more fascinated I became.

I learned that before the big oil boom in Kuwait, there were no phones. No TV! No *sidewalks*. For some time, the only vehicle around was the old yellow school bus that Hameed's uncle drove, picking up children from various areas in the city and safely delivering them to elementary school. The first car in the neighborhood was purchased by Hameed's father. "It was a black Mercedes," Hameed told me. "I am not sure why my father was the first to own a car, since he was not one of the more well-off."

Bread was baked in a ceramic oven in the courtyard of the family's rustic mud-brick house, even in the searing 120-degree desert heat. Within the conglomeration of small neighborhoods in Kuwait City, extended families lived close to one another, giving each area a feeling of village life. Though primitive in many ways, Kuwait City in the 1950s was already a bustling city 150,000 strong. It did not yet have every advantage of the West, but it did benefit in many respects from becoming a British colony after World War I. Even so, everyday life for the Ali family was unlike anything I had imagined.

Hameed speaks of being carried for miles astride his mother's hip until they reached the ocean, where they would spend the day washing clothes in the salty water. For someone like me, who enjoyed padding around on heated floors in a four-bedroom home, was driven to swim-team practice in a state-of-the art Rambler station wagon, and had her clothes washed and dried in machines, Hameed's modest beginnings produced a feeling of awe and an appreciation for the simplicity of the environment he was reared in.

Hameed's father, Muhsen, was a merchant. His mother, Hameeda, was a woman whose main work in life was to raise children—she eventually had eight—and care for the household. The marriage had been arranged through family, which was protocol; even so, the two seemed to love each other very much. According to Hameed, expressions of his parents' love were subtle. It was, and still is, considered impolite to be publicly demonstrative in that culture, yet the affection between them was strong, and the family was held within its field.

Mama Hameeda was from Karbala, Iraq. At the tender age of seventeen, she said goodbye to her home, family, friends, and culture and left to marry Muhsen. Hameed was born the following year and was welcomed with much love and pride into the family. He felt Hameeda as an ocean of kindness and tender love. His grandmother, Latifa, lived with the family and was a second mother to him. He speaks of her as a bright and happy presence who was always overjoyed to see him and selflessly gave of what she had. If there was food to be shared between them, he would be given the bigger piece, and she would enjoy watching him eat it. These two women who loved him with such profound tenderness and delight offered him a rare opportunity: to be loved and cherished at the most vulnerable time in his life. I believe that this benevolent beginning was a major contributing factor in supporting him to be who and what he is today.

When Hameed was an infant, the family of three moved to Iraq for a couple of years, where Muhsen worked with Hameed's uncle to start a business. When Hameed was twenty months old, the polio virus struck the neighborhood, and Hameed was one among several of his playmates who fell ill. He ran a high fever for weeks. Fear that he would die consumed the family, and Muhsen gave blood daily for transfusions to aid his son's recovery, which Hameed did not know about until his adult years. The story of his father's response to this devastating illness only ratified the feeling in the household of Muhsen's fierce love and care.

The debilitating illness crippled Hameed's right leg. His only "handicap" was not being able to do many chores around the house. He was able to run and play games with the other children by holding his knee so that his leg wouldn't collapse, but as he grew taller, this was no longer viable and he needed a crutch.

The crutch is part of him now. I never think of him as handicapped, and neither does he—the result of many years of deeply working through the self-images and feelings about the physical condition he has had for nearly all of his walking life.

Hameed's father was a strong figure in the household. He was also generous and protective and took his father role and responsibility for the family very seriously. Daily, he would go off to eke out the small sum he could earn for sheltering, feeding, and clothing his rapidly growing brood. Though Muhsen could be stern and was known to have angry outbursts on rare occasions, it was a felt understanding in the family that under all the blustery tone was a good man. This probably accounts for the fact that Hameed never seemed to suffer any long-term effects from his father's temperament.

A family of eight children is enormous by my standards—I thought my family of four children was big!—though not unheard of in the United States. As it was in my family, spats and skirmishes in the Ali household broke out here and there—"but nothing unusual," Hameed says. His siblings loved and respected him, and he especially remembers enjoying wrestling with his brothers. He never knew the two youngest girls very well because they were born just about the time he was leaving for college in the United States.

On lazy afternoons, Hameed would read as many books as he could—he was particularly fond of mysteries and detective stories. He also liked to gather other children together to play school, reading to them and taking the role of the teacher. Hameed enjoyed both teaching and telling stories, and he reports that his "students" loved it. This role seemed to come naturally to him.

As a young teen, he fell in love with the girl across the street. He never spoke to her, but they communicated with an occasional smile or friendly glance. According to Hameed, dating, as such, was not prohibited—it simply was not done. In fact, males and females did not socialize in public or at school, and kids did not attend dances or concerts as I did as a teenager.

Instead, youngsters would befriend one another at family gatherings. One of Hameed's friends, Hameed Qabazard, had a father with an eight-millimeter projector, so several families would gather together at their home to watch old movies before television became more common. As for marriage, it was, and still is, allowed between cousins, first or second. Although this is a foreign concept to many in the United States, I was surprised to find out that it is still legal in some states.

Hameed doesn't describe himself as having any unusual powers or perceptions as he was growing up. He claims that his childhood was about as normal as a childhood could be: "I didn't have any special talents or capacities; nothing stood out as unusual or different, other than my obvious physical condition." His schooling was also "normal and average," as he puts it.

Nothing significant distinguished his experience from that of his peers or foreshadowed what would later transpire. However, he does remember occasional times of utter simplicity and clarity, of great depth and ease, very similar to some of the spiritual states he experienced later. "They may be natural for a child," he told me once. "I didn't see these feelings and sensations as anything unusual; I did not think of them as exalted states. Just simple." Later on, he realized that what was different was not the state he was in—most children might experience that state at some point—what was different was that he recognized what it was at the time.

Not only did he feel and see the depth and openness of his own experience, he also didn't question it, for he thought it was normal for everyone. This is actually one of the difficulties Hameed had along the way—he assumed that everyone was like him. This view remained largely unquestioned, diminishing only slowly over time. The advantages and difficulties of this attitude would emerge later on as he worked with students.

One example of his early wisdom is an insight that came to him one day when he was twelve years old: *Idha ja'atkum addunia fakhuthuha, wala tredduha*—"When the world comes to you, take it in, embrace it, and do not turn it away." This became a foundational principle of the Work, which emphasizes encountering the everyday experiences exactly where and as we are and using them as access routes to the world of spirit.

In high school, it became apparent that Hameed had a good mind and was excelling in his studies. When this came to light, his parents neither discouraged nor encouraged him. But a teacher who noticed that his young student "had a good eye and a good sense of design" was supportive of his talent for drawing and painting and encouraged him to go into the arts. It soon became obvious that both sides of his brain were functioning quite well and with enthusiasm. Hameed did as well in the sciences as in the arts. Ever the curious one, he did experiments at home, occasionally setting his clothes on fire and making messes with chemical concoctions.

Hameed's religious upbringing was not strict. Mama Hameeda was religiously Muslim and faithfully followed the tradition of praying five times a day, but his father was secular. When Hameed was born, his grandfather and great-grandfather on his mother's side bestowed formal blessings on the couple's first son. This was an auspicious and happy occasion for the family, especially because as ayatollahs,[1] they both were respected as religious leaders and authorities.

Hameed, like his father, was more Muslim in culture than in practice. He did not respond to the calls to prayer as his mother did and tended to take more of a backseat view of the religion. But he was part of a culture heavily influenced by Muslim rules and traditions, such as the segregation of the sexes in virtually every setting except the home, the prohibition of alcohol, and the observance of certain religious state-sanctioned holidays, much the way Christmas and Easter holidays are observed in the States. They are simply regarded as time set apart from the usual daily tasks, and those who are interested participate in the rituals connected with religious holy days. School requirements for learning the precepts of Islam and the history of Muslim religion and culture steeped him in studies that were akin to catechism classes taught in Catholic schools.

Mild-mannered, introverted, quiet, but not acquiescent—that is how Hameed saw himself. A mentally autonomous young man, he actively questioned his teachers and was never satisfied with the party line. If something didn't make sense to him, he persistently questioned it and would not take anyone else's answer as *the* answer. He often challenged biblical stories and images of God that were in the Qur'an. When presented with God as a being who punishes the bad and takes revenge for wrongs committed, he thought to himself, "God can't be that way—it doesn't fit with who God is supposed to be." His mind, already capable of operating in the spiritual sphere, took on the logical, scientific approach to the exploration of physical and metaphysical realms that he would apply all throughout his life.

❖ ❖ ❖

The ways in which Hameed and I were, and continue to be, different from each other are numerous. But it seems that our cultural backgrounds, personal characteristics, and even our gender difference have mutually enhanced our experience and capacities.

I would say that the similarities in our early development were the most significant for our ease of movement into uncharted territory later on. We were both very much wanted by our parents, and we felt loved. Especially noteworthy was our relationship to our mothers and the nurturing care we received from them when we were infants. The experiences of love and goodness that Hameed and I both had in infancy gave rise to a sense of being held in goodness, and we grew to acquire a basic trust in the benevolence of reality. This made us resilient rather than brittle in the face of life's assaults. We were able to get through painful circumstances later in life without closing our hearts and could move through each day with an innate sense of optimism, even amidst great torment.

Many other factors come into play, but the sense of assurance that Hameed and I both enjoyed in our childhood was seminal in our ability to relax into the inner landscape and allow the deepening into unknown territory. The importance of this outlook became more apparent as we came to know the inner terrain of the psyche and the fears that can arise when venturing inward.

3 ❖ Accidents and Opportunities

IN 1963, AT THE AGE of eighteen, Hameed traveled to the United States to pursue his education. Although oil had been discovered in the thirties, the development of industry in Kuwait wasn't full blown until around the time Hameed was leaving for college, after Kuwait gained its independence from the United Kingdom in 1961. Although some families immediately benefited from the boom, the affluence seeped into the culture slowly. The main visible impact was the expansion of health care and education, both of which had already been pretty good under British control. There was one university in Kuwait, but many students were sent to European or American universities, which offered a more thorough education in specific areas. Full scholarships were given, along with a stipend for living expenses. Hameed, along with several of his friends, took advantage of the opportunity.

His entry point was New York City. Hameed's father had taken him and his brother and sometimes the whole family on outings to Cairo, Beirut, Damascus, and London, so Hameed was not completely shocked by New York City. "Sometimes I was frightened," he says, "depending on where I was in the city, but mostly I found it exciting and interesting." His biggest surprise was how long the streets were.

It was a dramatic cultural shift in various ways nonetheless. Early in his stay, he and some friends went to Baskin-Robbins and he ordered all thirty-one flavors of ice cream. He thought it would come in tiny bites as it often did in Kuwait, but no . . . it was piled high, with a tower of whipped cream and a bright red cherry on top. He says he didn't completely betray his shock when the mountain arrived on the table in front of him. Playing it cool, he lifted the tiny pink spoon and began. He didn't gobble up the whole thing; he just scooped out tastes of each flavor and left the rest to melt into a swirled puddle.

A family in New Jersey had agreed to take him in as an exchange student, and he was now about to take up his studies in a prep school to ready him for the road ahead in the Ivy League. The school expected students to go to chapel every day, so when the headmaster noticed that Hameed was not in his assigned seat, he had Hameed called in and told him that daily attendance was required if he wanted to stay. Coupled with Hameed's bewilderment when he encountered the American obsession with football—especially the parades and parties for days at a time, which added more hoopla to a game he didn't understand in the first place—well, let's just say that he felt he did not belong there.

Within twenty-four hours, he fled back to New York City, where he had first tasted America and found he liked the flavor. He took up residence, met friends, dated. Public transportation was spotty and a car was out of the question, so he took taxis everywhere, and "tasted lipstick for the first time in the back seat of one of them." He shared this first, delicious kiss with a lovely secretary who worked at the Kuwaiti embassy; she became his girlfriend, and they were together until he left for California eight months later.

Berkeley was the optimal environment for exposing him to the spiritual richness that flourished there in the sixties. "I felt excited by all that was going on. I grew my hair to my shoulders," he giggles. As he describes this period to me, I see him enjoying the blend of memories from that time: the man of so little hair looking back with amusement at his younger long-haired self amid the festive aliveness within the maelstrom of a cultural revolution.

He found a place to live, enrolled at UC Berkeley, and sought out friends from Kuwait who had settled in California. Despite the urging of his art teacher back home, he chose to go into math and the sciences. The mental discipline required for scientific exploration refined his mind and became a support for the inner journey.

❖ ❖ ❖

It was 1967, and Hameed was in his junior year. He had spent the evening with a friend at the Steppenwolf Bar on San Pablo Avenue and started making his way home at midnight. About to cross the street, he hoisted himself off the curb with his crutch in his usual jaunty style. Just then, out of the darkness the light of a motorcycle appeared. Within moments, the bike slammed full speed into Hameed's small frame.

He writes in his journal:

> At the moment of impact, my body doesn't contract. There is a
> tremendous explosion of red energy in the pelvis and belly, and as
> the body is carried with the motorcycle, I glide out of the body,
> through the top of the head.
>
> The physical body is carried by the motorcycle for some distance.
> The motorcycle swerves with its shocked driver and slides aside, and
> the body (Hameed's) is lying on the street.
>
> I see the accident happening very slowly. I am above it, having an
> aerial view of it. I am aware of the quietness and peace of the night.
> It is a cool, clear, crisp night.
>
> I experience absolute peace. No disturbance, no emotions, no
> sensations can reach me. There's only peaceful black space. And
> I am aware of myself as a very subtle diamond-like presence. It
> is like a combination of black space pervaded by clear diamond
> awareness.

This is the presence of consciousness that coalesces into a dense, indestructible form similar to the precious gemstone we call a diamond.
Hameed continues to view the accident from the vantage point of this
divine geometry:

> I experience tremendous compassion, joy, and love for my body. I
> look at this battered body and I mostly see a pinkish light that felt
> like love. I also see green and yellow diamonds shining brightly.
> When I look at the earth as a whole and I see the suffering of
> people, the green diamond of compassion shines more. When I look
> toward the heavens I see this as a crystal diamond structure, of the
> same nature as the diamond presence.

How was he thinking, feeling, understanding, and perceiving all of
this? His body was not functioning or even conscious. He lay sprawled
on the ground with his crutch friend beside him, fractured, their bond
severed forcefully in an indiscriminate act of heedlessness. Yet, frozen
in time, he was able to peer into the world, and his own body, with
flawless vision. It was—he was—a form of consciousness that is clear,

aware, heartful, and precise. Not bound, as a physical form is, but not boundless either. What kind of creature was this?

He continues:

> People gathered around me as I was lying motionless on the
> pavement. I might have died at that time; I don't know. I saw
> luminous blackness on one side, which I felt I could easily go
> toward. And I also felt great joy and love as I thought about life. I
> felt that my life was not finished and I had a job to do. I descended
> back into my life with tremendous love and joy. The joy was what
> impelled me to get back in the body.

Hameed didn't feel he had a choice in the matter. He claims that he just saw how things were unfolding and yielded to the course. Love, and the lust to complete something he did not comprehend yet, seemed to compel him back into life.

This was Hameed's first experience of presence, which is the condition of consciousness that exists beyond physical sensation, emotional feeling, or mental constructs. This would reemerge later and become instrumental not only for guiding his own life but also, as the mind, heart, and body of guidance and revelation of the Diamond Approach. And it was this guiding presence that gave the Diamond Approach its name.

The complete understanding of the central function of this consciousness that was to unfold was not revealed until years later. Accident? Maybe. Was his polio an accident? Perhaps things simply happen, and it is how we use them that creates our opportunities. This event that set his direction was a treasure that never left him—in fact, it revealed that it *is* him. Later in his journal he writes:

> Now I can get back to this subtle space whenever I want to. And
> sometimes the diamond presence manifests in the physical body.
> Then there is no separation between the body and the diamondness,
> and I am that.

Throughout his entire hospital stay, Hameed experienced love as the atmosphere. He felt it in the air he breathed, saw it in the faces of the nurses and aides who served him for the many weeks he was there.

Sunlight sliced through the windowpane into his white room; the flowers at his bedside, flooded with the sun's bright warmth, exuded delight. Benevolence filled and pervaded everything and everyone.

The weeks passed, and he continued to feel great joy and love despite his painful internal injuries and broken leg. Everything was lit, he says, with a soft divine love, a sweet beatific glow imbuing all manifestation in total well-being. He knew he was okay. More than okay—he was safe, held by the arms of the universe, which generously responded to him with a holding and healing presence. Even so, he wanted to get out of the hospital as quickly as possible to resume his life.

The surgeries on his leg and abdomen had been extensive and initially there had been serious concern about how well he would recover. The doctors and staff were all surprised by how swiftly he was healing. Hameed was released earlier than planned and went back to school, grateful that he was well enough to go back to his studies.

Hameed always assumed he would one day marry and have a family. It was expected of him, and he had not questioned it. In March of 1968, he was wed to Wahid, a beautiful young Kuwaiti woman, on a trip home to Kuwait after his graduation from UC Berkeley. She returned to the States with him and soon became pregnant with the first of their two daughters. Hameed had just begun his postgraduate work, which included a teacher's assistant position in the Physics Department.

Hameed loved his wife and was generally happy in the marriage. During her second pregnancy, Wahid went back to Kuwait to be with her mother, and Hameed remained in California. He began to explore consciousness, delving into the opportunities available there during the sixties. This engagement with his new interest changed him in ways that did not become apparent until Wahid returned with their children after a yearlong hiatus. At some point, his feelings for her shifted, and he felt he could no longer stay married. He thought perhaps the change of heart was a result of his engagement with his new interests, or perhaps it was simply due to the length of time away from each other. More likely, a combination of the two. Their divorce became final in 1974.

The ending of the marriage, which his wife did not want, was only one example of how the changes in his life at that time went against the familial and cultural grain. Another challenge was brewing that would also have an effect on the course of his future. Hameed was close to getting his PhD, but when he went to his office on campus to continue his work on his dissertation, he would fall asleep within minutes of writing equations. This happened for several weeks in row.

In a journal entry made sometime in the spring of 1972, he recounts a lucid moment that was the deciding blow:

> I walked into the faculty lunch room at Lawrence Rad [*Radiation*] Lab and saw all these brilliant minds of our times who were at the forefront of physics. There was no personal embodiment, just big, smart heads. I saw right then that I didn't want to be like them. I didn't feel angry or upset. I just saw that that was not what I was after. I was not going to unlock the secrets of the universe in this way. Theirs was not the universe I was going to decode.

His teachers wanted him to stay and encouraged him to finish the program and continue on to professorship, but he remained resolute.

Hameed's family had always expected him to return home after he graduated, and he had assumed the same. His father was disappointed in him for "quitting." Although he had never pressured Hameed to achieve, he was proud of what his son had accomplished and was invested in his continuing on. Hameed felt such clarity and strength about the direction his life was taking that for the first time, he stood up to his father with firm conviction and said that he was doing what was right for himself. His father seemed to respect this and to accept the decision; he never brought it up again, and it did not have a lasting negative effect on their relationship.

Of course, pressure from other relatives back in Kuwait, especially his mother, weighed on him as well. She wanted him to come home. His mother made no secret of the fact that she missesd him and wanted him to return. He listened to her grievances, which arose occasionally in their frequent phone calls—one that recurred was "I gave you my love and brought you up and had to give you to America"—but they continued to have a strong bond.

Hameed says that at first he had conflicting feelings about the major changes he made in his life at that time. He felt remorse about the pain he was causing people he deeply cared about, but his attunement to an inner sense of direction, which was urging him toward a leap of faith, rendered him effectively choiceless.

This paradox of choice/choicelessness has woven itself through both of our lives, and we have had occasion more than once to discuss how a sense of certainty, coupled with faith, enables a person to make immense life changes beyond conventional reason. The decision, if we can call it that, is in the clarity.

Once Hameed saw what he needed to do, he was ready for the turn inward. And he discovered that what he had loved all along—and above all else—was the truth. His world started to right itself, creating the foundation for the real life that was burgeoning. Priorities were rearranged and the quest for inner experience became the driving force of this new life.

Hameed's capacity for focus, clarity, discrimination, precision, and synthesis had been well honed by his disciplined studies in physics and mathematics. These tools readied him for the next step into an unseen universe. He had engaged for years in the intellectual discovery of the truth of the external physical universe until that path had exhausted its potential. Now he would use the same discriminating capacity to refine his inner experience. The universe he would enter was the domain of the heart.

❖ ❖ ❖

Hameed took up his studies in consciousness deliberately, thoroughly, and with stalwart discipline. The engagement in all manner of spiritual disciplines, emotional therapies, and meditation practices served as his focal point and provided the necessary elements to further his personal maturation. With devoted attention, he began the long journey of working through his personal history and navigating the psychological layers of his psyche.

Therapists and bodyworkers of various kinds facilitated this process of entering a new world of embodied aliveness. Emotions and sensations of all sorts began to swell into his consciousness and move through him in ways he had not experienced before. He approached this work with trust and interest and learned to feel completely whatever he was experiencing. And his brilliant mind helped him to discern and comprehend the feelings that had lain buried within the windings of his spirit.

In the process of opening to the complex, lyrical beauty of the heart, Hameed began to express himself in the language of intimacy by writing poetry. From woeful depths to sublime delights, he traveled the exquisite terrain of the heart as an organ of sensitivity, portraying his first musings on the innate desire for the truth. He never expected these writings to be published, for the little pamphlet called *Heart Dweller* contains the most intimate secrets of his inner heart chamber at that time. The poem "Waking Up" has always been one of my favorites, perhaps because it illustrates how the truth was flowing through his heart long before it became conceptualized as being the essential qualities of his soul.

In a womb of luminous green
Vibrant, happy, and comforting.

The fresh white petals are so delicate
And so fine,
With clear drops of dew
Forming and sliding down.

The gentle petals do not protest the dew
Collecting in shimmering pearls
And sliding around,
Rather they welcome the refreshing presence
And relish the contact.

When the first rays of the golden sun
End their journey at its bosom,
The blossoming lotus
Stretching
Starts to unfold
Shaking off the dew and the long sleep of night.

Embracing the warm messengers of light
The young lotus sways gently
In a whirling dance
In a loving and teasing dialogue
With the gentle morning breeze.

The friendly breeze
Smiles happily

And caresses the petals
With infinite tenderness
And loving care.

The dance of the joyful petals
Titillates my awakening heart
Stirring expanding ripples
In its still and sweet waters.

The small ripples expand
In waves of release
Joy and delight,
Bubbling sweetness
Fresh fragrance
And a delicious tingle throughout.[1]

Sometime in 1972 or 1973, he wrote with lucid beauty about this experience:

How lovely to be myself, to be content with what is—wanting nothing more, desiring nothing else. It's like magic, even greater than magic. The moment I say "yes" to my experience, with all my heart, regardless of what it is, the waves start to subside, the clouds begin to dissipate. Calmness, peace, gentleness, an exquisite contentment. There is no more cause for discontent, no more reason for holding or protecting. My body relaxes, tensions let go. My heart is so peaceful, so light, like the surface of a quiet and still lake. My chest feels as if it does not exist, as if the flesh and bones have evaporated. I feel a gentle breeze going through my body, touching the very essence of my heart. There are no more barriers. Oh, it feels so good. So fresh, so new. Joy comes in gentle waves, just as the breeze touches the petals of flowers. It wells up from unseen depths. It involves the entirety of me. How sweet my heart feels; full, overflowing with its own nectar.

Hameed writes that he uses no analogies, no similes. "These are not images. I describe exactly what I experience, or whatever part of the experience I can put into words." Then he continues:

The breeze actually and literally blows within the cavity of my chest; the nectar is an actual soothing fluid that wells up, as if out of a spring right at the center of the chest. The experience is not physical, not emotional, not mental. It is all of these together and more. When the heart opens, when the real nectar of divine love flows within the body, all boundaries dissolve, all categories vanish. I am a flowing nectar. I am a budding rose. I am intrinsic joy.

His desire for others to understand that this type of experience is not exclusive to him moves him to end this journal entry with, "Such a unifying and vivifying experience of life is our rightful inheritance as human beings. And it is only a glimpse, a flavor of the potentiality of human experience."

A flame in his soul had been lit. Truth was showing up as his lover, showing him its many faces, drawing him into its engulfing arms and pulling him into its embrace, consuming him little by little. Loving the truth was the beacon he would follow, and it eventually became one of the central precepts of the Diamond Approach—*the love of truth for its own sake*. While mind is a necessary instrument for discerning and synthesis, the heart lights the way to uncharted territory and enables one to feel and know with intimate immediacy. The two work as one to charter the inner realms, much like the mariner's astrolabe. The heart provides the sense of direction toward the innermost reality; the mind contributes its gift through its capacity for discrimination and under-standing in the wake of experience.

The body is also an important instrument for living fully in this physical world. It allows us to sense, in refined and gross ways, the immediacy of experience, grounding mind and heart. The scrolls of hidden material accumulated throughout a lifetime are unearthed, un-derstood, and clarified by listening to and feeling the visceral story told by the physical body.

For a while, Hameed primarily studied this "body knowledge" on his own and with individual therapists. Then his bioenergetics therapist, Michael Conant, told him about a Gestalt and meditation workshop at Esalen Institute led by Claudio Naranjo, a pioneer of the conscious-ness movement and a key figure at Esalen. When Hameed attended the workshop, Claudio mentioned to him that he was starting what he called an inner work group in Berkeley and invited him to check it out. Hameed went to the first meeting and joined. The group's formal name was "Seekers After Truth"—how appropriate was that?—but everyone referred to it as SAT (pronounced "sot").

The group lasted about four years, and during this time Hameed's journaling became a more consistent and detailed discipline he continued after SAT ended. Journaling as a means of self-analysis and exploration chronicled his use of emotional, mental, and physical experience as portals to the world of spirit, leading to understandings that eventually developed into the Diamond Approach. Without these records, much that is of value concerning the exact connections and progression of experiences could have been forgotten or distorted over the years.

Hameed feels deeply indebted to Claudio for all he learned from him, as well as to the teachers Claudio invited to the group to teach various practices and traditions. The student population in the group was also a rich network of resources for all manner of growth work abundant in the seventies. A woman named Marie Bickford, one of Hameed's roommates in a house where a few of the SAT folks lived together, had trained in Reichian Therapy early in that decade. She is responsible for connecting Hameed with Phil Curcuruto, who was to play a central role in Hameed's continuing unfoldment. Phil had learned Reichian energy work from Wilhelm Reich's secretary.

Phil became Hameed's therapist and teacher of the craft for several years. In weekly sessions, Hameed continued to learn through his own experience how the impressions left by our personal history settle into the tissues, living in the body as tension patterns and influencing who we are and how we live. But he went further in recognizing that our physical tensions carry those historical patterns as an identity that must be deconstructed.

Eventually, Hameed turned his attention more completely to this aspect of his inner development and entered a graduate program in Reichian studies. And that is how, in 1978, the young man who had traveled almost eight thousand miles from Kuwait to Berkeley ten years earlier to get a doctorate in physics received a PhD in Reichian Therapy from the California Institute of Transpersonal Psychology.

4 ❖ Fledging

AFTER I HAD GRADUATED from high school in 1970, my father and my stepmother, Lyle, (my dad had remarried a few years earlier) wanted to further my education by opening my eyes to new cultures and points of view, so we spent three weeks of the summer in Europe. We made a whirlwind tour through several countries, but what was most important to my dad was that I check out my roots—most notably, at the family farm in Sweden—and come with him to the German concentration camp in Dachau where he had encountered the horrors that would mar him, and the world, for generations to come. He had been in Army Intelligence, and in his mid-twenties had been sent into the camps right after the war ended, prior to the tidying up of the worst of the evidence.

It seemed to me that by my being present with him to bear witness to the damage he had seen in such gruesome detail many years earlier, he was healing himself. After the tour, we sat and drank a big stein of beer together in a Bavarian garden. We talked and wept. Twenty-two years later, I would find myself teaching in Europe and listening to the stories of my Dutch and German students who had been through the war or whose parents had lived through that nightmare.

On the home front, Mother was scouting for a place for me to live. In the fall of 1969, she and my stepfather found a three-bedroom duplex on Terrace Street in Oakland. The ground floor of the reddish-stained old house had three bedrooms and would need two roommates to fill it. June set about crafting a colorful five-by-seven card advertising both rooms for rent and pinned it to the bulletin board at what was then called the California College of Arts and Crafts. She couldn't have known that this action would set in motion a series of events that would end with her standing in the driveway waving a teary goodbye to me four years later.

Within days of her posting the rental notice, the phone rang, and a voice identifying itself as Sandy Mandelbaum came on the line. "I called," she told me later, "because yours was the most interesting note on the board."

When Sandy (now Sandra Maitri) came to meet me, something about her delicateness touched me. Like me, she seemed somewhat timid—at that point, you could describe me as held-back and bashful, with occasional outbursts of exuberance once I felt comfortable. She appeared to me to be standing behind herself somehow, her eyes peering into the world from a distance. My mother left the room to give us a chance to get acquainted.

I felt increasingly at ease with Sandy as the time passed. A while later, Mother entered the room with her wide-eyed brightness. "So, girls," she said with chirpy optimism, "is it going to work?" Sandy and I glanced at each other, wanting the other to be the first to say yes. I can see the slight bow of her head, still characteristic of her today. She looked up from under her brow. "Yeah, I think it is," she said slowly, her words and smile blooming together into full assent. Our eyes met. I tried not to sound too excited when I said, "Okay!"

Our meeting galvanized my move into the world of higher education. Sandy and I became best friends for the next couple of years. We went through several roommates while trying to fill the third bedroom. The truth was that we didn't really want anyone in it; we were tightly bonded, and it was hard for a third to fit in.

One of Sandy's friends was a beautiful young woman named Hilda, who became a frequent visitor. She was soft and welcoming. She told Sandy about a group that had formed and that she was thinking of attending. And that is how, in 1972, Sandy discovered SAT and became part of the group. She was gone more often in the evenings, and sometimes for a day or two on weekends. Gradually her involvement became more of a priority and demanded more of her time. "Outsiders" were at times allowed to attend workshops or classes, especially when these were led by one of the many teachers Claudio invited to present, so sometimes Sandy would invite me to come along.

One evening, a member of her SAT group came by to pick her up for a meeting. Sandy answered the light but persistent knock at the door. A muffled mutual greeting was followed by the sound of a single footstep and a ker*plunk* immediately after. This odd syncopation gradually got louder as it proceeded down the narrow hallway into our living room, where I sat absorbed in an art project that was spread out on the carpeted floor. A very lean young man with thin, shoulder-length blue-black hair and shining, intelligent eyes appeared. He had a crutch neatly tucked under his right arm. Sandy introduced us, and a friendly grin spread wide across his thin face. "Hi" is all he said. I echoed the greeting.

That was all either one of us could do at this first meeting—smile and say hi. A meeting that still transports me out of the confines of time and which is as fresh now as it was then. Hameed's smile gleams much the same now. His eyes are still bright, but they brim with an additional richness. And the tone of kindheartedness has remained consistent between us throughout the forty years since that moment.

He took me by surprise that night. I was normally well hidden behind a curtain of hair that did not welcome complete entrance by others. It was usually taken as a cue to not turn the light on too brightly in my direction. Maybe he could see through the drapes. I took note of this unusual feeling of openness I felt from him. Then it left my awareness until a few years later, when we would meet again.

Another man who would become instrumental in the personal maturation of my heart and mind, Richard Gordon, entered my life through Sandy as well. About a year before she and I moved in together, she had met Richard while she was at Berkeley. He had just arrived from the East Coast and needed a place to stay, so she said he could crash at her apartment for a while.

He was an intelligent, sensitive, deeply thoughtful man four years older than I. Richard was long and lanky, with dark curly hair to his shoulders. Quiet, but when he spoke, he always seemed to have something pithy and meaningful to say. I was quite taken with him, and Sandy was interested in him as well. Our mutual interest in Richie, as he called himself then, became one of our first conflicts as friends. I talked with him about Sandy's attraction to him, and he assured me that it was not mutual. Richie and I became lovers. I knew Sandra had strong feelings for him, but the attraction he and I had to each other eclipsed my concern for her, and I did not handle the situation well. I later regretted that I had not talked it over with her first.

My friendship with Sandy had deep roots and endured nevertheless, but its character changed from the fused twinship it had been to embodying our own lives. In addition to my involvement with Richie, Sandy was becoming friendly with others in SAT, and the intense group work they were doing created a strong bond among them. A chasm was beginning to grow between us.

In 1972, she moved in with some of her SAT friends, where she came in contact with a number of individuals who would later be involved with the Diamond Approach, either directly or peripherally. Hameed also lived there, but I never seemed to run into him when I visited, which was becoming less and less frequent. The gap between Sandy and me had grown to such an extent that when we saw each other, it was friendly but somewhat cool. Our conversations lacked the depth and intimacy they once held. I felt alone. I missed her. She was my first friend after high school and my first "spiritual friend."

Within a couple of months of Sandy's moving out, I announced to my parents that I was leaving school, a half year away from getting my BA. I was not using the time at school well anymore and I felt I needed some time off to reevaluate my involvement. I went to live with Richie in Los Altos in a four-bedroom ranch-style house, which we shared with a succession of roommates, my younger sister and older brother among them.

My parents were disappointed and concerned. They thought I had lost my way. The truth is that losing my best friend had left me empty, and I realized that school would not fill the hole. Art had been important for me, but I felt my inner compass spinning. Art school was not my true north. I lived for a while searching for a direction. As difficult as it was for my parents to see me floundering, they did their best to leave me to my own devices.

Richie was kind and strong. He was forthright with his opinions but also welcomed mine—in fact, he demanded that I say what was on my mind. He wouldn't let me play dumb, as he called it. Richie loved all kinds of food, so he and I happily ate our way across multiple cultures over the years. We also nibbled at or swallowed whole many spiritual teachings together. A continual parade of teachers and gurus of all kinds would frequent the Stanford campus, holding audience on nights and weekends: J. Krishnamurti, Ram Dass, and others who were the big names on the spiritual smorgasbord in those days. I received *darshan, shaktipat,*[1] initiations of all sorts—you name it, I got it.

One such time was when we went to see Swami Muktananda. The auditorium was quietly awaiting His Eminence. As he approached the small throne atop an elevated platform on the stage, I noticed he was much smaller in stature than I had expected. But his dense, almost neutron-star presence captured my attention.

After some instruction, the audience joined him in meditation. My head began to feel light, as though it were being erased, leaving nothing but open space continuous with the air in the room. I slowly opened my eyes. The room looked like an oscillating image on a high-contrast black-and-white photograph negative. Startled, I looked around me. Was anyone else in this conundrum of sensation? Was anyone else even there? Had I lost my mind?

Odd question! Since I had no head, I guess it was obvious that yes, I had. But in what way?

I closed my eyes, centering myself once again. Drawing on what I knew from my own meditation practices, I remained quiet while attempting to ground myself. After the lights were turned up to signal the meditation's end, Muktananda spoke for a while in his heavy Indian accent. I do not remember what he said; I was still befuddled. Then it was time to get in line to receive shaktipat.

I watched quietly from my place in the queue as the parade of spiritual thrill-seekers and sincere students marched by him single file, some kneeling or bowing in front of him when it was their turn. The small man with the Big Presence extended a long peacock feather and brushed the top of each head or forehead. Occasionally—instead or in addition—he would switch the feather to his other hand and give the recipient's head a swat of his hand to deposit the Shakti.

My turn was coming. I was a little nervous. I faced him and bowed slightly to receive the blessing. The feather touched my brow. A gentle electric current tickled me. Was it my imagination? As I began to slowly stand upright, he gave the top of my head a sharp whack and sent me on my way. This put me off. I felt punished in some way. Had he seen me peeking? Maybe I was not being available enough. Or perhaps I had not meditated correctly.

In the following weeks, I had all sorts of Shakti experiences. I felt energy pouring through me and could see colors inside myself and other people and objects; it was as though they were lit up inside and I was looking at colored x-rays. At one point, my head cracked open and effervescent light poured in from the top and bubbled up from the base of my spine. Experiencing the vibrancy of Shakti was a significant opening, and it also affected more than my spiritual life; it made me more spunky and outgoing.

Richie became involved in Psychosynthesis and at some point started training to be a facilitator. I attended some of the classes on my own and learned how to enter my inner life in a new way, identifying and meeting my subpersonalities and befriending them. Using all of these methods, I was better able to see some of my inner dynamics as they presented themselves in behavior and actions.

Richie also brought Sufi stories into my life. He and a group of friends had been gathering every Thursday evening to eat dates and read stories about Mushkil Gusha. I was invited to join, and that is how I learned about this mysterious character who is called "the dissolver of all difficulties." Some say he is Khidr, known among some Sufi tribes as "the Green One," an important spiritual guide for illumination. Others say he was a real man who had the ability to guide people to the unseen universes. Years later, Hameed would use these teaching stories as a starting point for our group inquiries. They have many purposes and levels of meaning, and we continue to use them in the teaching today.

Richie also opened my eyes through peyote and psilocybin to other new spiritual dimensions. I had my first sampling of the texture and flavor of love during an intense and ecstatic trip while he sat with me as I ascended through wondrous heavens. I literally tasted love in my mouth, like a sweet elixir, and it spread throughout my whole body. I had occasionally used psychedelics in high school, and they had opened the way to various illuminated moments, but I was now using them more specifically as mediums for spiritual experience. Richie taught me about the responsible use of mind-altering substances; I took them rarely, but the impact was significant.

Richie was given a beautiful gift of a white Samoyed dog. He didn't want to take her in because he didn't know what was in store for him and felt the commitment was too big. I insisted that we keep her. "On one condition," he said sternly. "If ever I can't take care of her, for any reason, you have to take her." I agreed without hesitation. He named her Mushka—short for Mushkil Gusha.

In 1974, when I was twenty-three, Richie and I went our separate ways. He moved in with friends and took Mushka with him. I went to live with my parents while I figured out my next move. I didn't know what I would do or where I might go from there. I definitely had the feeling there was more to life than having a job and a relationship. I wanted more. I was determined to find more. For a few months, I looked in lots of wrong places. But I became clear about what was not working for me.

5 ❖ Out of the Blue

By the time I went to live with Russ and June again, they had moved to a small three-bedroom condominium. In keeping with the family custom of designating one room as an art studio, one of the bedrooms had ended up with that duty. I was installed in the loft, which opened up onto a catwalk overlooking the living room.

One lazy afternoon in the spring of 1974, when I was in my sun-drenched perch, absorbed in a book, the phone rang. "Hi, Karen. This is Sandy," said the voice on the other end.

My heart leapt. "Where are you?"

I felt really happy to hear her voice. How long had it been? I wasn't sure. Our contact had been sporadic over the past few years. I hadn't told her about my split with Richie, but it occurred to me that she had probably heard about it from my parents.

Sandy had gone back east to lead a Fischer-Hoffman Process[1] group in Boston and was living in New Hampshire. She had been invited by some friends to come to Boulder to lead a group there and was planning to travel back to California by car via Boulder to check it out before deciding whether to move to Colorado. She wanted to know if I was interested in meeting her on the East Coast and driving across country with her. I said yes without giving it a lot of thought.

We began to make plans to meet in Boston, since a friend of mine had just moved there. I had been musing about visiting him anyway. This would work out just right.

A couple of weeks later, I boarded the plane to Boston to spend some time with my friends there before hooking up with Sandy. Through them I met a bright and handsome young man named Perry Segal. He was attending Johns Hopkins Medical School in Baltimore and had driven up to Boston to visit his friend Peter. As fate would have it, I was staying with Peter that weekend as well. Sunday arrived all too soon, and it was time to bid Peter and Perry goodbye. Hugs and warm wishes swirled around. Perry gave me his address and phone number, and I promised I would let him know mine when I settled somewhere.

Sandy picked me up on a bright and sunny morning in her black-and-tan Toyota station wagon, and we headed north to New Hampshire. Along the way, she told me that she was now going by the name "Sandra." This was a bit awkward for me at first, but I soon got used to calling her that. The landscape became more rural as the road narrowed; the houses dotting the landscape were scattered farther and farther apart and the trees got denser. As we drove through little towns, we passed rickety old country stores with just-as-old guys talking on old country benches, cigars smoldering out of their slanted mouths. Finally, a gray slice in the thicket revealed a driveway leading to our destination.

After spending a few days packing up Sandra's belongings, we headed across country, chatting, joking, planning, and singing along with Leonard Cohen, Bob Dylan, and some honey-throated French lady. We had roots in the ground of friendship—but exactly what kind of fruit would it bear?

Sandra talked about her intention to gather people in Boulder for an initial evening presentation on the Fischer-Hoffman Process to see if there was sufficient interest to start a group. Fischer-Hoffman was, at that time, an intense three-month process of group work plus private sessions with a facilitator to examine the behavior patterns that remain from childhood conditioning. Its aim was to bring out the pain sourced in conflictual relationships, mostly with mother and father, so that it could be released and healed and a person could have happy, satisfying relationships. Homework assignments that required writing and making tape recordings had to be handed in weekly. The facilitators would record their feedback, which often made a point of challenging the members. Many participants had to redo an assignment repeatedly until the right note of authentic emotional discharge was achieved. It was a pretty thorough inner housecleaning.

Sandra explained in her lucid style how the Process (as it was called) worked, and told me about her initial meeting with the sponsors of the potential group, Jaison Kayn and Rachel Aspen, whom we arranged to visit as soon as we arrived in Boulder.

In 1974, Boulder was a small town with a slow and pleasant midwestern feeling, unlike today's tony downtown. Pearl Street was still asphalt. The walking mall that is now the heart of Boulder would not be built for a few years yet. We settled into a hotel and freshened up, then headed over to Jaison and Rachel's.

We stayed just long enough to determine that the plan was a go and pick up some information about rentals in the area and then started the long drive home to California. We went through Donner Pass, and I saw it through different eyes this time. Compared with the Colorado Rockies, the beauty of the foliage and the gentle mountain made me nostalgic. The moist, soft air, familiar to my lungs, felt good. But something was missing for me now.

As soon as we arrived back in the Bay Area, Sandra asked her friend Hameed to join her in the new venture. They had both gone through the Fischer-Hoffman Process when they were active in SAT and had been trained to facilitate it as well. They agreed that Hameed would come to Boulder and they would do a pilot group together.

Then she asked me if I wanted to come along. My yes was immediate, but I was reluctant to show my exuberance. I said I would let her know.

My mind was bright, and my heart was happy—but slightly hesitant. Going with them would mean leaving my home, leaving Russ and June, and leaving California (no one in the family had ever done that). But I didn't want to miss the opportunity if it turned out to be the step I had been waiting for.

That night I had a dream. I was swimming in the ocean. I could feel the cool water on my naked body and the strong pull of the tide drawing me into the aquamarine wave growing immense before me. "I should dive," I thought. Peering through a huge wave as it began to break over me, I saw the brilliant globe of the sun through the watery mountain. It became a whirling mandala of color and light. Time stretched, and I stared at the splendor of the spinning disk for some time, transfixed but unafraid.

I awoke with a decisive clarity. I said to myself in a whisper, "I am going."

I remembered meeting Hameed and feeling his friendly openness. The *yes* that bloomed in my belly was beyond the clarity of my mind. I felt pregnant with new possibilities.

I hadn't seen Hameed at all in the three years since I first met him at the house that Sandra and I had shared. She and I figured that since the three of us would all be living together in Boulder, we needed to find out if it seemed like it could work. The first step was to arrange a dinner with Hameed, which would be at Sandra's parents' home in Palo Alto.

The house was much the same as it had been the last time I was there, wall-to-wall exotic art and furniture from around the world. It was almost like a museum. The air was thick with spicy aromas from her mother's fabulous cooking. My mouth watered in preparation for the flavor orgy.

Greetings were exchanged among the five of us, and then Sandra led Hameed and me down the hallway to the bedroom that was always kept for her. The three of us sat on her queen-sized bed and, as Hameed and I talked, Sandra watched closely to make an initial assessment of whether we would be a fit. After a while, she politely excused herself and went to help her mother cook dinner, leaving Hameed and me alone to talk.

Without Sandra there, I didn't know how to continue the conversation, so I just said hi again, and then a few awkward phrases stumbled out of me. Hameed put me at ease with a question. "So how have things been going for you these days?" Coming from anyone else, this might have sounded superficial, but the way he spoke it turned my awkwardness into the same easy naturalness I had felt in those fleeting moments when we met years before. There was a remarkable familiarity in our connection, even though I didn't know him very well. It sealed the deal with a heartfelt ease. The rest of the evening was spent enjoying sumptuous food, good wine, and lively conversation.

Three weeks later, with all my affairs neatly tied up, the day came when my life in California would sign off with the flash of my mother's image in the rearview mirror. Hameed, Sandra, and I were off on the big adventure.

The weakness in Hameed's right leg caused by polio made it impossible for him to drive our stick-shift cars because he couldn't negotiate the accelerator, brakes, and clutch at the same time. So he would rotate riding shotgun, first in Sandra's Toyota and then in the VW. I had no idea what the two of them were discussing when they were together; I was just eager to get back to our conversations whenever it was my turn to drive with him.

We talked about everything. Our history, family, friends, relationships, interests, desires and dreams—a steady stream of excited stories with the pressure of years behind them, all waiting for the right time to roll out. The little blue Bug became a vehicle for seeding the miraculous. Two individuals—one usually bashful in social situations, the other intermittently shy (when she wasn't partying)—started talking and, as I often tell people, we haven't stopped since.

Hameed's openness allowed me to say what was on my mind and in my heart. But there was also something else. As we drove along, I searched for words for it, and then I got it—I felt trust. He was unpretentious and unassuming. There was no judgment, which freed me from my own watchful self-reflection. He didn't expect anything other than the honest truth from me. In response, my voice naturally formed the words that wanted to speak themselves into the space.

I felt easy with myself in his presence. His interest was boundless. He drew me out with his curiosity and stimulated mine. Amidst the many other details of my life, I confessed some intimate secrets. "I kissed a woman once," I said. I thought this might create a ripple in his evenness. "Do you think that means I am bisexual?" I strained my peripheral vision to catch any discernable change in his countenance. Nope—nothing.

Hameed answered with a calm "I don't know. It is hard for me to know since you still have the question for yourself." So I tried a few more prods of varying degrees of shock value—things I had felt, thought, or fantasized about. I was testing the limit of his tolerance to find out how much was safe to say.

I had never met anyone like him before. He was eight years older than I was, but that seemed irrelevant. I felt an ageless timelessness in our contact. What I came to see later is that it was not his culture that made him a unique being. He was, and is, unique because he is who he is and doesn't try to be like anyone else.

The openness of the road before us reflected the inner path that we started that day. Our dialogue became the inception of a method for opening up the universe of experience. Moving through the lush California mountains and through the states of Nevada, Utah, Wyoming, and then arriving in Colorado, was emblematic of the transport through the many states of Being that we would encounter in the ever-deepening explorations of inner reality. What we shared during that journey in my VW Bug remains the basis of our bond of friendship.

On that first day, we drove until it was very dark and then pulled into a rest stop on the side of the road somewhere in Nevada. The traveling trio slipped into sleeping bags that had been neatly laid out in a row. Our heads peeped out of the puffy cocoons into the cool desert night, peering at the vast sky with all its stars. I felt my heart grow to encompass it all. I was betwixt and between everything in my outer world, yet I was deeply at home inside.

We rose with the sun drenching our nests and steaming us out of them, then packed up our things and slid into our designated positions. We were about halfway there, and I felt some regret that our little caravan through the desert would soon be unhitched. The last couple of hours seemed like the longest of the trip, but as soon as we crossed the Colorado state line from Wyoming, I felt it. We were approaching home.

Hameed and I followed Sandra as she made her way through the small subdivision in Longmont, sixteen miles northwest of Boulder. Pulling up to Jaison and Rachel's home, where we would stay until we found a place of our own, the three tired but joyous wayfarers were met with quick hugs and hellos and ushered inside.

Colorado herself felt like a welcoming presence beckoning to be known. Which was how I felt about Hameed by the time we arrived.

6 ❖ In the Lap of Love

"LESS OXYGEN AT THIS altitude, but more sky makes up for it," I thought. Hiding behind my curtain of hair, I sat quietly, cross-legged on the floor in the hall, a bit out of the way.

It was a mild fall evening. The air was thin and still. The Rockies were a stately, craggy presence in the distance, framed by the picture window in Jaison and Rachel's house. I gazed for a while at the enormous blue sky, and then my attention turned to the people flowing in and slowly carpeting the living room floor. Chairs were few, and soon the space was crowded with young, healthy-looking folks sitting on cushions and angling their backs against the walls and furniture.

Hameed and Sandra sat side by side, facing the gathering, their forms backlit by the waning daylight filtering through the window. He, slouching back in the armchair, a mix of quiet confidence and slight discomfort at being center stage; she, a little nervous, her eyes flitting around the room.

They were already committed to doing the Process group and were confident that it was a go. Now it was simply a matter of seeing who was on board. I had not given much thought to what my involvement might be. So far, I was just along for the ride. I listened intently as Sandra began to speak, considerations and queries circling in my own mind.

The mix of voices receded to a background hum as I spotted a baby boy crawling purposefully toward me. A bubble of space opened and lit the moment. He stopped just in front of me, his goal achieved. Lifting his tiny hand and placing it firmly on my knee, he looked directly into my eyes with a glassy-eyed baby stare and croaked a gurgle of salutation. My heart warmed. I responded with a coo.

A gleeful babble burst forth from him. With a lively wobble on his tripod of chubby limbs, he tarried a while and then followed his mother's watchful gaze back to its source. The sweetness of our connection accompanied him as he approached his destination, made a partial pirouette, and planted his diapered butt in her lap. A wide, wet, two-toothed chortle expressed satisfaction with the completion of his task.

The introduction was nearly complete. Energetically his mother and I were already connected; only the formality was left. She was a pretty blond pixie of a woman with clear blue eyes and a welcoming smile. Her brightness embraced the young boy. "Hi," we said in unison as she rubbed his foot lovingly. We exchanged names in a whisper. Linne Krier and I had just entered each other's lives through the wordless wisdom of her eleven-month-old son, Shay.

At the evening's end, I briefly met Linne's husband, Walter, as the little family eased out of the crowded entryway into the spangled night to find their way home. The two would enter the first six-month-long Returning Process, which would begin on October 30, 1975.

Both Hameed and Sandra had facilitated groups before. Teaching the Fischer-Hoffman Process and going through it three times himself had given Hameed solid assurance about his knowledge of the subject matter. He also had experience designing a course of study. When asked to teach Claudio's fourth SAT group, he had not been given much direction, so he came up with his own curriculum.[1] Sandra had led several Fischer-Hoffman groups and had her own experience of it as a participant to draw on. I recognized her delicacy and also could see that she came across with a straightforward clarity that hit the nail on the head without much embellishment.

The moniker "Returning Process" had been adopted to differentiate the work from the Hoffman Institute's offering. The Fischer-Hoffman Process, or Quadrinity Process as it was also known, gave a respectful nod to spirit but was heavily weighted toward the psychological, without much spiritual practice involved. Hameed and Sandra made many adjustments to that protocol to make it more spiritually oriented, including guided meditations, chanting, and visualizations. Some of the practices incorporated physical postures and mudras that channeled the specific energies of the subject matter being taught. The new name implied the returning to one's original nature.

The group met one evening a week for three months. From the beginning, Hameed showed a calm intelligence, strong focus, and a sense of stately confidence. His no-bullshit approach revealed a side of him that had not been predominant in our interactions, and I saw him now as a force to be reckoned with when he was in the teacher seat. The strength he expressed was much needed to address the participants' issues, which were usually laden with heavy challenges. Yet he was sufficiently at home in himself to let his heart show.

Initially, I was invited to come along to witness the dynamics of the group. Sitting amidst the participants gave me an excellent vantage point for observing without being obtrusive. Sandra and Hameed found my insights useful when we discussed our observations after each session and discerned together what was needed for the group going forward. I gave up my hidden stance in the room and started to provide more overt support. I was asked to take on the role of assistant and got paid a small sum of money for that.

I began by being present for the group regressions into childhood memories. The participants would lie on the floor, close their eyes, and follow verbal instructions designed to move them through their defenses and resistances and into the feelings underneath. Taking cues from Hameed and Sandra, I would move around the room to offer a kind touch or word of encouragement, hold a hand, or just sit nearby. If someone was obviously in great pain, fear, or stress, I might talk with that person for a while. It surprised me how at ease I was with the strong emotions that could explode into the room; I felt natural and spontaneous in my responses.

As my involvement grew, Hameed suggested that I give individual healing sessions to help some of the participants get through particularly difficult barriers. When this turned out to be beneficial, some chose to see me regularly to aid them in unearthing tightly guarded antique concepts and emotions and bringing them to light. This felt like a natural progression in my skill development.

I've often been asked what it was like for us outside as well as inside the groups in those early days. Life with Sandra and Hameed for that year and a half definitely brought a variety of delights and on-the-ground challenges. My desire to live close to the mountains had been satisfied within a week of our arrival when the three of us spotted a small four-bedroom house on Grove Street and signed a rental agreement together. We didn't have a great view of the Flatiron mountain range, but the mere sensation of being more immediate to their magnificent presence felt supportive and grounding to me.

Money was scarce, but my physical needs were few. I took the tiny room off the hallway just past the kitchen. It was big enough for my futon and little carpenter's chest, and that was about it. I painted pictures of my eagle guide and other spirit friends, covering the little wall space I had.

We had the usual roommate issues about the division of labor and so on. For example, Hameed and Sandra became interested in stained glass and decided to take a class, thus transfiguring the kitchen into an art studio. Both of them were great cooks too, so the place became a creative potpourri of glittering cut glass and multinational cuisine. Though I was well acquainted with creative messes, I got grouchy when shards scattered on the counters had to be dodged when it was time to make my tea or lunch. Not to mention the debris on the floor. This sharply curtailed my barefoot habit, testing my forbearance.

A deal was struck: They tidied up after themselves more thoroughly and continued to cook marvelous tasty treats that we could enjoy—minus any sprinklings of colored sparkles—and I became a little more generous about doing more dishes and other chores since I was the recipient of their many kindnesses. It was a generous household. I was cleaning houses, since my assistant's pay didn't cover my expenses. I was twenty-four years old and determined to do whatever I needed in order to support myself. At the time, Sandra and Hameed had more financial resources than I and did a great deal to help me get on my feet. They bought me a down jacket for my birthday that year, since I was ill prepared for the cold winters. I (reluctantly) gave it to Goodwill only a few weeks ago.

The three of us sometimes enjoyed spacious days of walking downtown, lingering conversations, and evenings watching TV. Our weekly excursions to Taco Bell gave rise to nicknames inspired by our menu favorites. Mine stuck, and Hameed still refers to me on occasion as Kranjito Burrito, although I have picked up other, more suitable names over the years. We also went to bars, where we would down a whisky sour or Tequila Sunrise and dance like crazy.

Hameed says of these days: "We were free spirits. There was a lot of freedom and time and few responsibilities—no family or home-ownership obligations. It was a spacious time, and I look back on it with great fondness. Karen and I spent most every night talking very late by the light of the little cone-shaped fireplace in the corner."

In the evenings, Hameed and I would take our respective spots in the living room furnished with what I referred to as early American hodgepodge. He sat in his favorite chair by the bay window, and I lay sprawled over the faded gray cushions of the colonial couch.

Occasionally, Sandra would join in. Their relationship was friendly and collegial, but I wouldn't say they divulged preciously held secrets to each other. They shared a mutual respect and affection, but I believe I was closer to each of them than they were to each other. After we finished processing the day's group work, Sandra would usually wander off to her bedroom to do one of her many projects or go to sleep, leaving Hameed and I to engage in further discussion—often, as he described, deep into the night.

Although most of the processing Hameed and I did happened more casually, at times it could be focused and deliberate. But it never felt as though we were operating in student-teacher roles, in either direction. The way we shared our process was a natural expansion of our openness with each other, and it became a crucial part of our relationship.

For example, sometimes it was difficult for me to distinguish between what I saw others going through in the groups and the ways I personally felt impacted by the meetings. Strong emotions and reactions would blow through the group room, and my own undigested history would get swept into and become part of the current. One time after returning home from a tumultuous evening meeting, Hameed turned to me during a quiet moment after the TV had been turned off. "So how is it for you, Karen? The group was pretty intense tonight."

"Yeah . . . I felt I could be with all that was going on, but I *am* feeling a bit shaky at the moment."

"Scared?"

"No, not really. Quivery."

"Hmmm. Do you know when you started to feel that?"

Just then the memory came to mind of a large man in the meeting who had started to cry deeply, and I told Hameed about it. "When I went to him and spoke with him for a while, I felt inadequate. I felt sad for him and could feel his vulnerability."

As we continued to inquire into my feelings, the connection shot into consciousness—I had mixed this fellow up with my father. I had wanted to help my father and was not able to. Clarifying this led to more illumination about my difficulties after my mother left.

As we were getting to know each other in the early stages of our friendship, Hameed would talk about his childhood, including the emotional issues he had with his parents. Sharing our early histories was part of learning how we had each arrived at this point in our lives, and he was open and undefended as he spoke of these things. Those conversations expanded to include philosophical and epistemological views about where we now found ourselves.

Whatever the subject, he seemed so easy, so open and relaxed. His simple, earnest questions were utterly stimulating. And I felt I could be myself, whatever that happened to be. Even when challenging me on a sensitive issue, Hameed had the unique capacity to ask me about it without making me feel judged. His observations were crafted with just the right curve to make a landing in my waiting heart-ear. And he seemed to be similarly impacted by the shape of my delivery.

We fell into a feedback loop that parlayed the energy of exchange into a shared journey of discovery. Our mutual lack of self-consciousness spiced by an inquisitive interest formed the right conditions for our tête-à-têtes to evolve into multifold inner-life adventures.

Hameed saw potentials in me that I was not aware of and sensed my growing need to find direction and channel my energy into more meaningful work. I knew that cleaning houses was a means to an end, not my life's calling, so I was grateful when he encouraged me to lead workshops on healing and energy work and sat with me to craft flyers for it. He helped me to get involved in the Free University and the Rocky Mountain Healing Festival, where I met an assortment of interesting folks. I also met a healer through the Rolf Institute, Rosalind Bruyere, who taught inspiring workshops on the harmonization of mind and emotions with the body and spirit. At Hameed's urging, I continued to pursue my interests, and Rosalind confirmed my abilities, furthering me on the road to a more public expression.

The atmosphere in Boulder was abundant with fresh, burgeoning spiritual energy. Tibetan Buddhist teacher and Oxford University scholar Chögyam Trungpa had recently set up camp, establishing

Naropa Institute in 1974. Gurus and teachings were moving through town like wildfire, just like they had paraded through Palo Alto. Our little trio—sometimes together, sometimes separately—visited healers, teachers, and psychoanalysts to listen to their views. We were open windows, and experiences of all sorts were flying in and making their way into our discussions. What did we think of this one or that one—what she said, how he acted? How did they feel in their skin? How did we feel when we sat with them? We weren't there to make judgments or to align ourselves with a particular teacher or school; each opportunity was another contribution to the exploration we were already engaged in. I tucked each of these experiences safely into my growing being.

❖ ❖ ❖

Hameed had made a dainty glass window picturing the sun emerging from behind a green leaf—or maybe it was an apricot. It couldn't have been more than eight by twelve inches. It was now leaning against the old sash window in his room. I loved it.

"What does it mean?" I asked one day, watching the slanting afternoon rays shine through the pearlescent background.

"It is my heart," he said with a shy grin. The Hameed "that's private" look showed up in his eyes, and he turned away.

My trite notions about the heart were exposed and shattered in that moment. Through his eyes, I saw anew that the heart could have nuanced qualities and colors. I had never seen him vulnerable like that. I was touched, and leaned toward him to hear more.

"It is how I feel in my heart when I think about Marie," he added quietly, turning his gaze back in my direction. Marie Bickford, whom he had met in the SAT group a few years earlier, had made her way back into his life. I sensed a story there. Over the next days, it unfurled in brief entries of sadness and tenderness, delight and adoration, like so many love stories do. Hameed confided in me in a new and deeply personal way the true colors of his relationship with Marie. He had dated other women while in Boulder, but it seemed that his heart had been drawn back to Marie.

Hameed announced one afternoon that she would be coming to visit. Visitors were always welcome, and each of us had our share of them. As we prepared for Marie's arrival, it made my heart bubble to see Hameed so eager and vulnerable. A week later, when I walked in the door from my day job, I made my way down the white-walled hallway to the back of the house, following the sound of friendly female voices. One was Sandra's, and the other I had yet to put a face to. I reached the end of the hallway and peeked around the doorway.

A woman clothed in black from head to toe, a turtleneck and long skirt covering her petite frame, sat cross-legged on the floor, head bowed, deeply focused. She appeared to be mending something while talking with Sandra. What I didn't know then was that this is a quintessential Marie encounter. She became a world-class quilter, and you can find her in that same posture today whenever she is working on a quilt or another project and having a conversation.

Marie looked up when she sensed my presence. She smiled quickly to defray my shyness. Straight blond hair flowed over her shoulders from a middle part and halfway down her back. Her intelligent blue eyes were framed by small, round wire-rimmed spectacles. "Sweet, lovely face," I thought. "And bookish."

She and Hameed spent most of her visit engaged in important relational discussions and activities, with a few sightseeing outings sprinkled in. Over those few days, she and I had some short exchanges during meals made especially with her in mind. Marie had a friendly air about her that invited me to be open, but I realized as she was leaving that I didn't feel she had let me into *her* world yet. But I would grow quite fond of this woman who was about to become a major part of Hameed's life.

As for me, I was continuing my long-distance relationship with Perry, visiting him a couple of times while he was attending medical school at Johns Hopkins. We carried on in what would now be considered old-fashioned style, with handwritten letters—mine spritzed with cologne or herbal essences—relaying our latest news and heart pulsations. I was quite infatuated with him.

With our two budding romances, Hameed and I had similar territory to explore. Whenever we had visitors, our usual routine was interrupted until the house emptied again. I missed my playmate when he was less available. So I was always happy to jump back into both the serious questions and the celebrative joy whenever we returned to our topsy-turvy universe of discussion, discoveries, and new love.

My relational world was expanding on multiple fronts. In addition to my continuing friendship with Sandra, the growing connection with Hameed, and our respective love interests, more bonds were forming. Just around the corner from our house, on Spruce Street, lived the Krier family. My immediate attraction to Linne was growing over afternoon tea, brown rice and veggies, gurgling babies and piles of laundry, and thought-provoking discussions about her studies and training in body-work. Our bond would be a deep and lasting one galvanized by our shared love for inner exploration, like so many of the friendships I was being blessed with. The Krier family embraced me in their little circle, and I still consider them family. They had another child, Evan, who is my godson and occupies a special place in my heart. Although Shay is not formally my godson, our connection was obvious from the start. I have often thanked Linne and Walter for being the parents of "my children."

At the time, Linne was working with a bodywork pioneer named Judith Aston. She felt a deep resonance with Judith's groundbreaking orientation toward the body and trained to become a principal teacher of what came to be known as Aston-Patterning or Aston Kinetics.

Jaison, Rachel, and Walter were training as Rolfers and were among the first practitioners in the burgeoning bodywork modality created by Ida Rolf. I had the unique opportunity to be a model in one of Ida Rolf's classes, and when Jaison followed up with an offer to do a series of ten Rolfing sessions on me, I began to discover the woman's body that was rising like a phoenix from the lumpy clay of my uncertain teenage self. That crucial step enabled me to settle into my physical beingness and open to more subtle sensate experience. "To be in the world but not of it" began here for me.

I was beginning to feel into what it meant to be in my body in a new way, in much the same way that the heart and mind are honed through spiritual work to become portals to other domains. This opening led me into many years of Aston-Patterning work—as well as Reichian breathing, which I eventually trained in—and other modalities in order to integrate and mature into my body's potential.

My life there wasn't always easy. Amidst all this activity, thoughts of family and friends back in California would form like wispy clouds and grow opaque in my mind. I missed my people. For the whole time I was in Boulder, a floaty sensation of in-betweenness alternated with the elation of flying fearlessly into limitless opportunities, which could at any moment turn into an aimless, lost-in-space free fall. And the dry Colorado firmament still had me thirsty for the thick, moist ocean air of the West Coast. But in my bones, I felt the rightness of being in the high desert. Slowly, the mountains had become for me the manifestation of leaving the smooth and familiar to venture into the rugged and wild inner landscape.

As the rosy hue of the sun's last rays spilled onto the graying peaks one winter afternoon, the mountains appeared majestically above the earth's mantle. Their foundation remained embedded in a silence that held a different promise than the ocean depths.

"This stillness is not without heart," I said with a whisper of self-assurance.

A mystery was revealing itself slowly.

"Yes, I am finding my way."

7 ❖ The Golden Cog

"DO YOU REALLY have to go?"

Hameed pitched his jacket onto the back seat, the final act of loading his 1960–something, electric-blue Volvo automatic with his meager collection of clothes, books, and prized stained-glass projects.

My lip was quivering. I stared at a pitted hubcap.

"I will be back," he said in his matter-of-fact style, then paused as if to catch my attention. I looked up. "Often," he added softly.

He slipped into the driver's seat, tilting his crutch to ride shotgun, then pulled the heavy door closed. It submitted with a thump. The ignition squealed, then hesitated. My heart tripped. "Maybe he'll have to stay," I thought, but the cylinders fired up with a roar and then smoothed to a mild rumble. My pulse slowed, then evened out as I looked at Hameed in the bright April sunlight.

With the car window open to the breeze, his straggly black hair wafted across his thin, dark face as he turned to me with a brief glance and limp wave. His smile was friendly, but not the big and gleaming kind. He shifted his focus to the road ahead as he pulled away. The brake lights flashed a final goodbye as he turned the corner, leaving me staring blankly down at the ground in our barren yard, shoulders drooping and hands stuffed into the pockets of faded, baggy blue jeans. He would be back, but we both knew it wouldn't be the same.

My heart was swollen and empty at once. I knew he had to head back to Berkeley, where he had commitments and obligations. And I'd known from the start that he wouldn't be staying in Boulder for the long term. He had planned to be there only through the first Returning Process group, and Sandra was already putting together a second one—about fifteen people were waiting in the wings—which she would lead on her own, with my assistance. Still, I missed him already. He was the best friend I'd ever had.

Our house was sometimes haunted by the muffled plunk of Hameed's crutch on the living room carpet. The sweet/savory smell of apricot lamb stew and basmati rice was no more, though the yummy sweet-and-sour cabbage rolls Sandra would make for me on special occasions were a welcome replacement.

It was a girly household now, which had its benefits. Susan Rondeau, a gentle soul who had been Hameed's girlfriend for a while in Colorado, moved in. Sandra and I had befriended her when she came down from Denver to visit him. A lacy, lilting camaraderie filled the space. The discussions during this era were meaty in quite a different way than when Hameed was around—we shared stories and advice about men, makeup, sex, and the like, which I welcomed as I nurtured my long-distance relationship with Perry.

He and I had visited each other a number of times by then, and he was considering a move to Denver for his internship and residency in psychiatry. Denver General's fine reputation was a draw, in addition to its convenient location near me. Perry could have gone pretty much anywhere he wanted. Handsome, smart, and he wanted to be near me! Oh my! Perry's sister beat him to it, though. Several months before he was to make the move, Marilyn, just out of law school, moved to Boulder, took the bar exams, and stepped into our circle of friends.

We had a fourth roommate as well—Mushka had come to live with me. Richie had needed to take me up on my promise that I would take her if necessary. His commitments required leaving her alone for many hours during the day, and she had started jumping fences (though Sammies are normally not jumping dogs) and kept getting caught by the "doggie cops." We were not supposed to have dogs in our house, but I had given my word. So I hid her whenever I thought the landlords were coming.

I kept her on a chain in the front yard to make sure she wouldn't run away; that big fluff of fur liked being outside anyway. One night when I heard her clanking around and could stand it no longer, I got out of bed, switched on the front light, bent down to look straight into those big brown eyes, and said, "I know you hate being tied up like this, and I can't stand it anymore either. So I am letting you loose. Run away and find someone with a big yard and grass and everything you want who will take care of you. You can stay with me, but I can't keep worrying about you running away." I kissed her nose. "I love you, my sweet girl."

She looked down and then right back into my eyes. I unhooked the chain from her collar. She shook herself from head to toe, like spinning water off her fur. Then she lay down, rested her head on her paws, and went to sleep. I didn't sleep well that night. But when I walked out to the yard in the morning, Mushka was there to greet me. She never needed a fence again as long as she lived.

❖ ❖ ❖

Bam! Bam! "Take that, you fucking bitch!"

Whack! Fwap!

Gripping the bat and raising her arms high above her head, Donna swung down and smacked—full force—one of the metal poles that served as ceiling supports. Then she hit it again.

She swung a third time, even harder, with all her might.

"Yes," I yelled, "give it to her!"

"I want you out of me—out of my head—just *out*!"

Chestnut tresses flying anarchistically, body strong and flushed, sharp blue eyes glaring with wildness, Donna was ablaze. Her white top rose with each swing to expose the sweaty, rippling belly of an angry young woman-animal fighting for her freedom. The white sailor outfit and pale, delicate skin lent a sense of purity that belied the rageful deity now emerging.

In those days, padded bats were stocked in the arsenal of many healers and therapists. The Process group included several bitch sessions, as they were then called, to let out repressed feelings of anger and discontent that lay buried beneath a civilized façade. Many images of the past were burned up in the fury of this purgative ritual.

Spurred on by the upsurge of dynamism, I entered Donna's primitive war dance, jumping up and down and yelling. I was shocked at the depth and volume of my voice and the steamy heat that shot through my body.

Admiration poured out of my chest as I watched not only Donna go for it but all the other participants as well. Their trust and willingness to engage with such sincerity brought me to my knees. I felt a new desire budding inside me. I had already begun to be useful to others, but I wanted more knowledge, more skill, and more capacity. I wanted to match the students' fervor with everything I could muster.

The charge in the room built to an energetic cyclone. Then something in my chest gave way. Like a golden cog, my heart slipped into the open sprocket of the larger wheel that turns it. I was on track. And I felt that I had just taken a vow.

When the cacophony died down, the exhausted group slowly found their resting places in gradations of sitting and sprawling on the misty shag carpet. Loosened by the discharge, their breathing heaved like that of spent but victorious soldiers. Release shone in their relaxed faces.

"Cleansed by fire," I thought, "and not a trace of mother left to be found."

Sandra invited comments, and the responses confirmed what I had just witnessed in the room. As for Donna, she had beaten her history into ashes and risen up as the phoenix; a year later, she would take a new name, Alia, inspired by that evening and the character Alia Atreides in Frank Herbert's *Dune.*[1]

When the meeting was over, the group exited as one organism, flowing its way up the narrow staircase, then spilling out into the night silence and spreading through the streets of Boulder. As Sandra and I walked to her car, I felt sprightly and weightless, in the way that light has no mass. Kinda like Tinkerbell.

Back at home, I readied my room for sleep as Sandra went off to do her bedtime rituals. As I was unfolding the futon and retrieving my blankets from the closet, a soft glow caught my eye. I followed its source to the living room window and sat down in my spot on the couch. Alone in the dark room with only the light from the waning moon, I imagined Hameed in his chair. It was ten o'clock—our time to talk. I missed my buddy.

❖ ❖ ❖

Hameed did come back as promised, a few weeks later, and began a third Returning Process group with about twenty participants, held at the Boulder School of Massage Therapy. My supportive role in the work was expanding; in addition to sometimes assisting in the groups, I was more frequently supporting the students' inner unfoldment through private sessions. I felt fluid doing what was needed and what Hameed asked me to. I was well used and loving it.

He soon became aware of the growing need for continuing follow-up after the six-month bursts of intense work in the Returning Process. The Process groups had broken new ground, but only the surface layers of the archeological dig had been exposed; many layers would still need to be unearthed. In the meantime, Hameed had been busy discovering what waited underneath and how to skillfully probe into it.

Scott Layton, a roguish young man with a strong will and a nose for truth, had been in the Process group and felt deeply connected with Hameed from the outset. Others who had been through the group were eager to continue working with Hameed, so Scott took the initiative to make a call to encourage Hameed to come and finish what he started. Scott's honest and persistent request had an impact. Hameed took the opportunity to glide into the natural role for which he had been destined. Letters of invitation were sent to everyone who had participated in any of the three Returning Process groups held thus far, and the seed group in Colorado[2] was formed in which Hameed would introduce the method that would come to be known as Inquiry.

The format would be completely different from that of the Process groups. The new mission Hameed envisioned was about venturing further into uncharted territory but without a specific agenda or notion of where it was supposed to lead. Instead, the method of Inquiry fostered in his students a curiosity about their inner experience and a capacity to be present to whatever was arising for them moment to moment. He wanted to invite them to explore some new terrain that he had discovered, but he wouldn't try to direct them there. Where many facilitators would stop, he would just keep asking more questions with surgical precision. He was interested in whether this method of Inquiry would lead others to the same experience that he was having. In this new consciousness project, he was "the first subject for the experiment," as he puts it. "And no experiment is complete without reproducible results from many subjects."

About ten people sat in the circle at the first meeting of the seed group in July 1976. "For this group," he explained that evening, "just start with what you are experiencing now; or if you have a burning question that you want to inquire into, begin with that. A burning question is one that comes to mind that you just can't shake. It concerns your experience or something related to truth or reality that pertains to you personally.

We are not making intellectual inquiries into truth here; I am interested in what is *now*, whatever it might be. There is no plan or specific topic you must stick with. Nothing you have to do. And *no homework.*" Sighs and chortles of relief rippled through the little assembly.

Before I gave it any thought, my hand shot up. My move toward engagement was spontaneous, but I think I also wanted to be acknowledged in some way. And this was my first chance to be a formal recipient of Hameed's skillful means of examining experience in a group setting. It was bound to be different from the casual exchanges that took place between us as friends.

He turned to me. "Okay. So what is your question?"

My usual easygoing manner when we conversed was instantly replaced by a squirmy self-consciousness. I had put myself on the spot. Although his full-on attention was exactly what I wanted, I was not sure how this was supposed to go. I felt small and young and awkward, but I warded off those feelings with mild smugness sprinkled with rebelliousness. Then I tried to put my feelings into words.

"I feel like I am supposed to be a good girl. I might say the wrong thing."

"Oh, really? What would the wrong thing be?"

I could sense him also teetering on the edge of our friendly symmetry.

"Actually, I feel like I *wanna* be bad . . . say the wrong thing."

He grinned. "Okay."

I giggled—half nervousness, half smoke screen. "What if I swear?" I said with an adolescent sneer.

"Fine with me."

My friend receded and was magically displaced, in cellophane overlays, by various individuals from my past. Family mostly. Authority figures at first. Of course, Hameed was still there, but I was struck by how switching into teacher/student roles was altering our connection. Interesting. Useful. Also disquieting.

So I swore at him.

"And who are you seeing when you swear at me?"

"My father."

"And what are you feeling about him?"

Anger. I was angry. My body began to heat up. Then I heard my mother's stern voice: "Don't talk to him like that!"

I began to shut down, and my body cooled. I felt bad for feeling this. Hameed sensed the shift. "What happened?"

Curiosity filled the space formed by his words. I saw my friend again—simple, ordinary, and kind.

"I felt bad that I swore at you . . . and then I heard my mother admonish me."

"I thought you were swearing at your father."

"I was, but . . . you were him, kinda."

"Yes, I get it . . . but your mother . . . her voice—it stopped you. Shut you down. What did she do?"

I was doing my best to follow where Hameed was leading, waiting for each next step. "She said I shouldn't be like that."

"Maybe it's true—you can't go around acting like that anytime, anywhere—but she and your father aren't here. And it stopped you from feeling what you were feeling. But you can feel anything you want. If it is there, it is your right to feel it."

Then I got it. The inner critic was trashing my self-esteem. If I did as I was supposed to, I was a good girl. If not, well . . . I was worthless. I saw that nasty voice had made me so self-conscious that it had stifled my courage to expand into the world. So I made a stab at it: "I am *not* bad for feeling this!"

"Did that work? Do you feel some freedom from that attack?"

"No, not really," I said, feeling defeated. I was arguing with my superego, struggling to convince it of my value.

"Okay, try again. Try this: 'If I am so bad, why don't you find somebody else to bother.'"

"Yes!" Now I felt excited. I gave it a go.

"I *am* bad and I'm gonna stay that way!"

It was good to feel Hameed on my side again. I chuckled, already feeling more freedom after my attempts to skirt around my "badness." More convinced than before that I could say this and mean it, I gave it another shot.

"I—*am*—*bad!* Go bother somebody else!"

A cool sense of spaciousness opened up. My mind quieted. I no longer had that feeling of badness. Or wrongness. Or of not being loving enough. My heart perked up. I have a choice. I have some power here. I have some capacity to deal with this.

I thought I had pretty good parents—and compared with a lot of people, I did, for I was loved and cherished in many ways—but their well-meaning guidance inevitably placed limits not only on my external behaviors but also on my internal experience. Of course, I needed to learn appropriate boundaries and attitudes about living with others, but I had not escaped the tyrannical attacks of the superego, which are often harsher than negative parental influences. The superego had been using my fire to burn *me* instead of burn up the trash in my mind. I had some work to do to get beyond the limits of my usual experience and consciousness.

At one point, I felt my energy rising to my aid like a fluid fire, but this time as a protective force. I yelled a few times at the images of my mother and father. They disappeared, along with my feeling of being bound up. I hadn't heard such volume coming out of me since that bitch session months before. I liked it then, I remembered. But I couldn't have a bitch session every time I needed to be free of the coercive force inside me. This new technique was offering me something more: the tools to keep loosening the inner straightjacket. Nobody hurt, nobody upset . . . just more space for me!

This was my first taste of internal freedom from that critical voice. I started to come out more without worrying what others might think of me. At times, I felt deliciously irreverent.

Another of Hameed's teachers at the time, Henry, taught him about tough love and the art of defending against the superego. Henry was a hefty, strong presence. A no-bullshit kind of guy whom Hameed admired and modeled himself after.[3] I found the method of superego defense a powerful and effective stimulant of my assertiveness and confidence. I used it often over the next few years. All the appropriate cultural values and behaviors were still in place—I didn't act out terribly as I thought I might. I simply broke free of the confines of what I believed I was supposed to be feeling and thinking.

❖ ❖ ❖

We were back at my house after the meeting. Hameed was slow and quiet as he eased into the creaky chair at the kitchen table.

"I think you have to make a choice," he said, his voice heavy.

"'Bout what?" I looked at him, wide-eyed. I was feeling ebullient, even proud of how well I'd just worked in the group. My sense of triumph shrank to an anxious ball in my tummy.

He hesitated. "About being in the group."

I flinched. "Why?"

"Because it will change our relationship."

Dread punched my chest. Had I done something wrong?

He deftly addressed my confused space with an explanation. Our relationship had unfolded in a certain a way, he said, and my formally becoming his student in the group would change the course of that development. Not that it would be a bad thing, but I needed to consider the consequences—for each of us.

We talked for a couple of hours and waded through the feelings on both sides. Working through the issues helped us discern more specifically the nature of who we were together and as individuals, and as teachers, learners, and friends. I knew I still needed to learn from Hameed, but I also saw that joining the group and being his student would undermine the support I was providing for him personally. I was his confidant and sounding board; if I were part of the group, he wouldn't feel free to talk with me about his own inner struggles and difficulties.

Above all, we sensed that our friendship had an important purpose beyond what we could do for each other. Our primary concern needed to be what would be best for holding the group and for our work together. In the end, we agreed that continuing to learn together and from each other without being in a formal teacher/student relationship was the better choice. And we had logged enough miles side by side to feel some confidence that we could find our way in the maze of relational variations that would reveal the teaching—in its own time and its own way—through the many facets of our communion.

I was seeing a different side of him in the new group. The same confidence and clarity was present, but something else I was deeply attracted to had appeared. His strength had grown in breadth, his clarity was more searing, his confidence more rooted and sphinx-like. Maybe it was my vantage point, or maybe he was coming more into his own, but day after day, I saw him facilitating the students to open in fascinating ways I had not witnessed before. Whatever he had, I wanted to learn it, too. I sensed that this would require more discipline, and I was ready for that.

Until now, the Work hadn't seemed that different to me from therapeutic methods with a spiritual orientation; Hameed had brought a mix
of what he'd learned over the years from his various teachers, including
psychological methods such as Gestalt, psychoanalytical approaches,
techniques from the more confrontational Gurdjieffian model, and various meditation practices. As new types of experiences began to arise in
the groups, he would focus attention on them and point out that they
were not emotional, they were not physical, and they were not explain-
able in the usual terms. For example, the sensations I sometimes felt of
fluid, fiery heat or coolness or the open sense of freedom—hmmm . . .
what *were* those? This question brought us to the threshold of more
subtle realms of Being that Hameed was already aware of but was not
yet teaching and that we would begin to talk more about within the
next few months.

Hameed continued to investigate areas of experience that opened
us beyond our usual feelings and ideas and took us into the immediate
knowing of Being itself. In addition to holding space for feelings and
ideas of all kinds, any transference[4] that came up for the students in
relation to him became fruitful material for the work he did with them.
Regardless of which tools he chose, he always took a scientific investigative approach; he was clearly focused on why and how people were
experiencing what they were experiencing, no matter what it was.

During that period, I was making intermittent appearances at the
group meetings. I observed what was happening and learned how to
inquire into another's experience and my own simultaneously. Putting
myself in the participants' shoes, I would glide along, working silently
as they did their inner explorations, Hameed guiding them by inviting them to feel their inner terrain with more immediacy. Sometimes
I would take his seat in my imagination and wonder what I might ask
this or that student. I was just beginning to understand more precisely
what he had been experiencing, questioning, and pointing to in those
past few years.

On alternate weeks, Hameed would fly from his base in California to
lead the group in Colorado and do private sessions with students.[5] These
forums became the perfect laboratory of consciousness in which everyone who attended, including Hameed and me, were the guinea pigs. As
he had forecast, the Work expanded beyond emotional catharsis and

into other types of investigation that revealed deeper levels of consciousness. These experiences seemed to have a pattern of arising in relation to working through certain emotional issues, but they were not emotional in nature. Later on, as the Work became more refined, he would refer to these experiences as differentiated qualities of our nature. The working hypothesis was that they are accessible to everyone and that we only need to learn how to approach our experience with love, curiosity, and discrimination in order to avail ourselves of them.

While Hameed and I were planning the next steps in the group work he wanted to do, Sandra was busy considering her own options and making plans. She had signed on to stay in Boulder only until the second Process group was complete, and she was headed in another direction for the time being. She decided to move to England for a year and pursue her desire to study meditation by sitting with Dhiravamsa, a Theravada Buddhist monk trained in Thailand in Vipassana meditation. Claudio had introduced him to the SAT assembly in Berkeley where Sandra, along with Hameed and the rest of the group, learned Vipassana meditation practice, and she felt the call to go deeper into the practice.

My relationship with her had cooled a bit, as it often did just before we were to go our separate ways. It was hard to tell which came first—the cooling or the divergence of our lives. But I felt that our bond had been sealed through our time together in Boulder, so although we parted ways, she left behind a friend for life.

As soon as our lease was up, I rented a storage locker, stashed some of my stuff along with some of Sandra's, and made tracks to Denver in my little blue Bug, with Mushka smiling and panting in the back seat.

8 ❖ Cracking the Cosmic Head

IN THE FALL OF 1976, Perry and I began our life together in a small basement studio in a Victorian house turned apartment building. We were near Cheesman Park, which made Mushka and me very happy. With her big boa-like tail, she could sashay around the wide space like a twenties flapper, teasing and flirting with canines and humans alike. I took up swimming again and frequented the half-Olympic-size pool for a mile swim nearly every day. Susan Rondeau had rented an apartment a few miles away, and she, Marilyn Segal, and I remained friends and visited one another. Sandra and I wrote irregularly but managed to keep in touch.

Hameed stayed in Boulder every other weekend when he came to teach, so our time together had to be well orchestrated to accommodate his ballooning schedule and my new life in Denver. I would fetch him at the airport on Friday evenings, and our high-spirited greetings would propel us into an update chock-full of thoughts, experiences, and queries that had been awaiting retrieval since our last phone call, letter, or visit.

If anyone had noticed the occupants of the car, they would have seen four arms gesturing Italian style, and two heads turning this way and that as we chattered away down Highway 36 to the sputter of my trusty VW. Our destination was a lovely Arts and Crafts–style house owned by one of the group members in north Boulder, where Hameed would stay as well as lead the groups and do private sessions.

The group operated on a rigorous schedule by today's standards—two weekends a month, Friday through Sunday. Attendance was mandatory, but the students were eager, willing, and always on time unless something life-threatening interfered. As Hameed and I had agreed, I was attending as an adjunct to the group rather than a formal member. I didn't go to every meeting, but when I was there, Hameed and I would discuss what was happening in the group and other relevant topics while the students were engaged in tasks or exercises.

But I didn't have a specific function as I'd had during the Returning Process, so this left some students wondering what my role was in the group, especially those who had been at the initial meeting. I still found myself a little conflicted about the ambiguity of my position. Even though Hameed and I had worked through the issues and were comfortable with our decision, our clarity did not extend to people in the group whom I was beginning to know. I was neither fish nor fowl, an apt description of my experience—and of their experience of me as well, I am told by some who remember that time.

In the meantime, the dark underground studio Perry and I shared shrank as the activities and needs of our life expanded. Within a year, apartment living had become cumbersome. Unbidden, one Sunday morning my brother David called to declare his intention to invest in Denver real estate. He followed up swiftly with a five-thousand-dollar check made out in my name, which became the down payment on a well-maintained 1890s brick bungalow for Perry and me. The twenty-four-thousand-dollar, one-bedroom house was on a pleasant tree-lined street in an up-and-coming section of Denver, only half a mile or so from the apartment. In February 1977, we moved into our new home on Pearl Street and set up housekeeping.

Perry worked hard and often. Many days would go by when I wouldn't see him. I suppose it was a desensitization ritual. Whatever the case, it seemed strange to me that a man who was supposed to learn how to manage other people's feelings had to steel his own to get through the ridiculous boot camp of internship and residency in psychiatry.

Perry always welcomed Hameed into our home, and during the infrequent weekends when Perry was around they would engage in stimulating discussions that inspired Hameed to catch up on the new psychological theories of the day. The object relations theorists had become much more popular in the psychological and psychiatric communities, and this brought into the conversations a great deal more precision about how ego is formed and the nature of human relationships.

When he was not in Boulder or visiting me in Denver, Hameed and I continued our close friendship through the curly wire that tethered us to our landline phones. We wrote letters too, which I still have. They brimmed with appreciation for our friendship, our ponderings, our plans and insights. One letter revealed that he needed to find a way to remain in the States, so he had decided to go back to school to get his degree in Reichian Therapy, which would extend his student visa.

Hameed and Marie were not seeing each other at that time, and he was dating other women. He would tell me all about them, and I would offer insights and suggestions from the female perspective. If I felt a woman was leading him on or not interested, I would point out some cues he might not be aware of. I felt protective of him but tried not to butt in too much.

We didn't expect our friends and acquaintances and partners to be as interested as we were in the realms that were opening up to us, but it was becoming more obvious that what we could share with them was more limited than we had anticipated. When either of us ventured into social settings, we often got what-in-the-world-are-you-talking-about looks and other peculiar responses, discouraging us from discussing our experiences further.

This was especially the case with some of the residents and interns Perry was working with. At the parties I occasionally attended with him, mentioning the tiniest thing that smacked of spirituality flipped the eye-rolling switch, condescension rippling through the façade of proper etiquette. I guess I had the reputation of being a little kooky. I was an artist and a hippie, so from their point of view, I was caught up in the airy-fairy backwash of the fading Flower Power era. What Hameed and I had discovered was too precious to squander, and I learned how much to say to whom, and when. It felt good to leave certain experiences invisible, free of any inclination to offer explanations or court anyone's approval.

Hameed felt pretty much the same. One day while we were strolling down the Pearl Street Mall, I asked him what he told people when they asked him what he did for a living.

"I tell them I am a used car salesman." His signature toothpick danced about his lips as he chuckled.

"Really?" I squealed.

"Yes. It cuts the conversations down to a minimum. People lose interest pretty quick."

❖ ❖ ❖

After a long group meeting one night, Hameed and I entered the small foyer of my little house, hung up our coats, and eased into the living room. I sank into the sofa, and Hameed took his seat in the overstuffed chair. He seemed to be pondering something his chest could not bear the weight of. His eyelids matched the heaviness of his chest. Sadness molded his thin face into a younger shape.

"I am having trouble with something," he said, watching his index finger as he swirled it around on the plush velvet upholstery.

My chest filled with gentleness.

"What kind of trouble?"

"I keep having these experiences that Henry does not understand. He continually negates me. It's not only that he doesn't seem to get it— he tells me to forget them."

"You mean the presence we have been talking about?"

"Yes. I can't help it—it keeps happening to me no matter what I do. And now that it's beginning to happen to others and becoming more pronounced, I have a responsibility to stand for the truth—not just for myself but for them, too. How can I continue to learn from a teacher who is not seeing this or supporting it?"

"I see the dilemma. Maybe you can't," I said with a helpless shrug.

"That is what I think. I love him, respect him, and admire him. He has done so much for me. But I can't continue to work with him."

"Are you angry?" I asked.

His voice turned soft. "No, I'm hurt. I did get mad at the last meeting, though, when Henry said I was going off on a tangent, getting distracted. I challenged him, and it really pissed him off. But I stood my ground and didn't cave in. This sense of something that is so real and so palpable . . . almost physical—it's incessant." He paused to reflect on his state.

The presence he had discovered had become even more distilled and substantial in his experience. Now he was willing to protect it. He knew that Henry cared for him, but he also knew that Henry didn't know what this experience was—or if he did, he did not value it.

"I'm not mad or hurt at the moment. I'm just convinced of the truth of this and feeling determined to follow it. *That* is my teacher." His eyes came alive with light.

Hameed would continue to grapple with his relationship with Henry until he extracted all there was to learn from it. As for me, Hameed intuited that even though I had made forays into this invisible realm of presence, and we had discussed it, I was conflating presence with other experiences I was having. It was not crisp and discriminated for me yet.

Hameed fell silent for a while, then said, "Reach out your hand." I did. He cupped his hand and circled it in the air, as though extracting and gathering some mysterious nectar. Then he leaned over and stretched out his arm toward my waiting palm and poured the substance into it. I felt the viscous fluid pooling as it impregnated my hand with its immediacy.

The sensation continued to deepen and strengthen. Its slippery aliveness beckoned every cell awake as it moved up my right arm. It made its way throughout my torso to deliver its message into my heart and left arm, and then I felt it pooling in my belly.

My jaw fell open and took on a widening grin as the luminous elixir traveled its pathway, enlivening my whole body. My pelvic bowl brimmed with a lucid density that was spilling down through my genitals and into my thighs, legs, and feet. It quickened my spirit and lit me up with its weightless fullness.

At a loss for words to describe this magical medium, I let out a "Wow!" Eventually, some words stumbled out: "I mean . . . I am . . . *really here!*"

This substance was so real that it spoke for itself. I felt I was meeting the quintessence of hereness, the very substance of reality. I don't even know how I knew this. What I was feeling was presence—awakeness in its irreducible existence. Pure consciousness.

It had the features of sensate experience but was far more than that. I had experienced similar sensations as a perfume of this more palpable substance—the cloud-like wafting of compassion in my chest or the fluid fire that had risen through my body. However, it was the complete self-knowing within the substance itself that awakened me to its reality. The substance had neither color nor quality but was a fresh, scintillating, immediacy of consciousness. I submitted willingly.

Looking at my open hand, and still held rapt by what had just taken place, I took a breath, exhaled deeply, and followed my upturned fingers to Hameed's eyes. "I see what you mean" was all I could say.

I sensed that my reception of this elixir was a confirmation of Hameed's knowing. In some inexplicable way, he felt vindicated by my recognition of presence. I understood now the difficulty with Henry that

Hameed was facing. No one would be able to convince me that what I was experiencing was not true, any more than Hameed could let anyone deny him the truth of his very being. He didn't need his teacher to see him as special or unique; Hameed's discovery had value beyond any individual's claim to or negation of it. But he would have liked Henry's blessing to pursue this discovery.

This gift was far from anything I had been seeking. I felt as though it had found me. I felt initiated by this saturating intelligence. Gratitude flooded me. "Thank you."

He smiled with loving contentment.

This event revealed a profound level of my relationship with Hameed. He was my friend and dependable spiritual companion, but in that moment, he had been so much more. He was the living transmission of what I had been unknowingly waiting for all of my life. Hameed himself was not the origin of the experience—nor did he claim to be. He was a conduit for this fine gift that was beyond either of us.

One of the main ways that students receive or connect to a teaching, especially in many Eastern traditions, is via the direct transmission of spiritual energy. Depending on the particular spiritual discipline, a transmission of some kind is often considered mandatory for true initiation. It is often but not always done through touch; one example is the dose of Shakti energy I received from Muktananda years earlier. Many consider a transmission to be the event that makes one into a true disciple.

Transmission can bring about specific experiences characteristic of a spiritual teaching or, in rare cases, it can introduce the entirety of the teaching all at once. If nurtured through practices, what is experienced in only a few moments as a certain spiritual state can unfold its logos within the practitioner over time.

Although transmission can ignite a movement in consciousness that conveys the teaching of a particular path, it is the student's consciousness that must unfold the initial transmission by the teacher. Many levels are involved, and students embody a teaching in various ways and degrees. The extent to which the recipient's consciousness is open and already developed will determine how much and in what ways the teaching will take hold and begin to display itself, like a seed that has been planted under favorable circumstances.

The desire to be on a spiritual path will inspire one to take on its practices and apply oneself sincerely, but this does not ensure that the disciple will reach the full potential of the teaching. As most mystical paths teach, though practice is necessary, the rest happens through grace, or blessing—in any case, it is not the result of our efforts. "Enlightenment is an accident," one of my Zen-monk friends says, "and all we can do is make ourselves accident-prone."

Hameed himself received initiation, empowerment, and transmission from various teachers over the years. While many events have molded him into the teacher he is, two seminal experiences had a profound and lasting impact. The first was the motorcycle accident that propelled him into his initial experience of the diamond structure. This he would come to know as the guiding presence that is responsible for the method of the Diamond Approach.

In 1974, Hameed had a second experience that matched the first in its impact on him, especially in light of what unfolded in its wake. When seen in tandem, these two events provide a clue to the way the Diamond Approach has developed. Since he did not record the whole story at the time, he gave me a verbal recounting of the event.

When I was in grad school, I went with a few friends from SAT to see the sixteenth Karmapa, who was then the head of the Kagyu order of Tibetan Buddhism.[1] We were in a big auditorium in San Francisco, surrounded by thousands of people. There sat the Karmapa, in front of everyone, picking his nose. Really! In front of all those people, he just sat there picking his nose. He was very relaxed, obviously not the least bit self-conscious.

We knew that he was going to do the Black Hat ceremony—it's sometimes called the Black Crown ceremony—which is a transmission in that particular lineage. He put the hat on, and then everyone passed in front of him in a procession and got tapped on the head. That was how he gave transmission of his state of the Black Hat empowerment.

Many people reported immediate experiences of light and luminosity, *dharmakaya*,[2] and other types of expansive states. Me? I immediately got a headache, and it lasted for a year. I went to doctors of all sorts. One Hindu tantric guy told me it was gas. Finally, I had the opportunity to ask Tarthang Tulku[3] what he thought was going on. He told me that it was light in my head. I was not sure what that meant.

At some point, when I was meditating, I felt something open and begin to descend from my forehead. I recognized it as presence.

I think that because the diamond consciousness was activated when I had the accident with the motorcycle, I was open to presence, so the transmission from the Karmapa took hold. But the Black Hat ceremony was only the beginning of the knowledge of presence. It was so big that I just couldn't handle it. I was blocking the presence, so it had to work on the ego structures and unconscious material in my personality that were in the way. But it was this receiving of presence that eventually revealed and evolved everything.

In the tradition of the Kagyu lineage of Vajrayana Buddhism, the Black Hat empowerment is a transmission of the clear light. But Hameed's experience of this empowerment didn't occur in the way it usually does within that lineage. As the source of the Diamond Approach, he was not continuing any specific lineage. The Karmapa's transmission transformed and developed Hameed by stimulating all the barriers and blockages to experiencing presence. It was only at the end of that year of constant headaches that Hameed experienced a descent of light from his forehead, which he recognized as presence.

This was the moment that tipped the balance. It was the culmination of all the studies and practices he was engaged in at the time, including Gurdjieffian work, continuing bodywork and breathwork, superego work, Idries Shah's writings, Sufi stories, daily meditations of many kinds, and investigating the effects of early holding in his childhood.

It took some time before Hameed recognized the full significance of the presence he was experiencing. As it began to interact with the existing, albeit latent, diamond consciousness, the process of being taught through immersion began for Hameed. His desire to know the truth fueled the discernment of his direct, felt experience, making possible a more precise understanding of presence.

Hameed's astute approach to his experience would become the method he would teach others so that they, too, could perceive and know the invisible world—a universe of potential that could liberate them through the synthesis of many dimensions of experience. Inquiry would reveal itself as the main practice for students to open to the process of their own unfoldment within the teaching.

As for me, what happened to me that night in my living room was not merely an experience; it was the awakening of a force, a drive, that continued unbidden. Hameed's transmission initiated the unstoppable process of illumination for me; the presence opened my consciousness and has never left. It has remained steadfast since its first appearance, varying only in intensity and quality while doing its work of dismantling and renewal. It has its own intelligence that continues to flow into the nooks and crannies and bring into the light what has been unconscious. Whirling me inside out as it destroys cherished illusions. Sometimes it slaps me silly.

This initiation also marked the moment of the most immediate sense of meaning and purpose I had ever known. Presence showed me that something far more precious than I had ever thought possible could be offered to others. Helping people to lighten the constraints of the conventional world and awaken to another lucid and fulfilling reality that lies beautifully within all that exists seemed to be the most useful thing I could ever do. "I can," I thought to myself, "and I will." I felt determined and ready to serve.

In recognition of this living truth, I said yes in a whisper that shook my world.

9 ❖ When the Student Is Ready . . .
Essence Delivers

It was October 1977 on a bright day, as it often is in Colorado almost any time of year. I was gazing out the old rippled window at home, which rendered the world a dreamy reality. The baring trees cast long, spindly shadows in the golden light, like chilly fingers reaching for whatever warmth the sun could offer. I watched as the leaves, rich in red and orange muting to shades of brown, let go into their confettied flight to the leaf carpet below. The drama of changing seasons was another delight I had discovered in Colorado.

I was shaken from my reverie by the phone's ring cutting through the silence. An extra jingle in it this morning generated a tingling sensation in my chest. I leapt toward the antique telephone table in the kitchen and grabbed the receiver. Cloaking my zeal, I ventured a polite but inquisitive, "Hello?"

"Hi!" Hameed chirped from the other end. In my mind's eye, I could see him grinning.

"Hieee," I said, dropping the mannered reserve. "I thought it might be you!" We began with pleasantries and a discussion of the week's events. Our back-and-forth evolved into the investigation of our current experiences, and soon we were deep in conversation that felt more like communion. It was as easy for us as eating and breathing. We would talk about whatever was in our minds and hearts—even our prattle had significance for me—and it often evolved into creative exploration of all and everything.

It was as comfortable as being alone and talking to myself. In some ways, even more so. Hameed's continued unconditional acceptance and curiosity created an atmosphere in which I was far more likely to notice sensations, thoughts, or feelings that I might otherwise find unworthy of attention or value. I was more *there* simply because I could include more of me.

I was feeling particularly blessed that morning by the friendship Hameed and I had developed. While he spoke of his latest musings, his voice faded away as a panoramic vision ballooned in my mind. Our adventures together these past two years—the tremendous scope of all that had transpired, the friendship that had been nurtured—how could all that bigness have fit into such a tiny time frame? How to give thanks, and whom to thank, for the gifts of opening to this magical divine domain? How could I give back? What could I offer to show my appreciation and deep gratitude?

The deep sweetness in my heart melted me to an inward bow—humbled, grateful, loving—and then a searing clarity and thanksgiving shot through me.

"I would die for you," I exclaimed. Totally unromantic.

"Well, I hope it doesn't come to that." His soft chuckle felt like a gentle deflection that I knew was neither a dismissal nor a denial of my sincerity. It was more the Hameed brand of humility that I had come to know.

"I mean, really. I would stand in the Bay upside down in the mud if you said it was good for me!" Into my mind popped an image of myself in the San Francisco Bay with my head in the mud, surrounded by some whimsical sculptures that dotted the banks near Berkeley.

"You probably trust me so much because you know I would never ask you to do that." I could feel his warmth as though he were right next to me.

"You are probably right," I said.

I paused a moment, then heard these words spilling out of my mouth: "You are my teacher."

Silence . . . and then he voiced an "uh-huh" that contained just enough recognition to validate my statement. Nothing extra in it. He was not invested at all.

It was like an anointing with holy water.

We agreed to talk again in a few days' time. After our goodbyes, I laid the receiver gently down in its cradle, pausing to soak in the still-present connection. I floated through the day, yet felt more anchored in it.

"You are my teacher" were words that had waited in abeyance for the right time, the right teacher, and the right teaching. It is said that the one who points out the true essence of you when you are experiencing it is your teacher. I'd had many prior experiences that seemed profound. I had learned many things from various people and called them teachers of mine. What I was feeling about Hameed was different. It was the real known fact in my core of a sacred bond. It was much more than love, or valuing, or benefiting from his wisdom.

What I was proclaiming to Hameed was multifaceted. By my identifying this part of our relationship, something both settled and freed up in me. My words were a statement of commitment, devotion, and recognition, fueled by a deep wish to surrender. I didn't know completely what I was giving myself to, but I felt a deep love to serve the truth in whatever way it showed itself. Awakening to this crucial element in our relationship was a significant aspect of that service.

Hameed disclosed much later that, at the time, he had understood it was an important step in my development to have such feelings for him. I know this, now that I am a teacher myself. The surrender of a student to a teaching often occurs through surrender to the teacher. Teacher and student are always held within a sacred bond that is not for the teacher or the student alone but primarily for the teaching they hold between them.

When Hameed and I had discussed my participating in the group a while back, I had to make the choice of whether to take him as a teacher or whether he would be my friend. I seemed to have chosen both. Although he never attempted to elevate himself above me, our asymmetry was obvious. I needed his support to grow in proper relationship to the teaching.

Hameed didn't think of himself as my teacher in a formal sense; rather, he saw us as having a unique relationship that included this element. "A spiritual friend," he would say. He recognized that the value of what he was learning through our friendship was as important to him as his guidance was to me. So my declaration never changed our friendship. It only made it more realistic. He was invested only in my being real. This made me respect him even more. And I learned and grew as a result of this understanding between us.

Our dance would take many forms as we each developed together and individually. Each role had a function that would naturally arise when called for. As the rhythms of our relationship kept changing, we didn't always move in effortless unison. We bumped into one another and occasionally stepped on each other's toes.

Our connection as friends, colleagues, and fellow travelers is continually being reshaped by the needs at hand—his, mine, and those of the teaching. We couldn't mold our relationship into a static shape even if we tried—then or now . . . or ever.

❖ ❖ ❖

Throughout 1977 and 1978, the substance that had become ignited in our consciousness was catching on like wildfire in Hameed's work with students as the elixir continued its ceaseless flow into new states of consciousness. The reality of presence was beyond doubt and already established from our point of view. Now, through employing the particular investigative techniques that we were developing, other people were also experiencing presence in similar ways.

"I had come to know presence by the time I decided to invent a new group," he recalls. "I not only wanted to follow up on what people felt they needed, I also wanted to offer this finding to them." Now it was emerging through the Inquiry work he was doing with them. From this Hameed deduced that universal principles were at work. This was a significant step in understanding that a spiritual path was emerging.

The seed group was growing in number as the teaching gathered momentum. In 1977, Hameed shifted the meeting place from Boulder to Duncan Scribner's house in Denver, a few blocks away from mine. Duncan had been in the third Process group that Hameed had led, which became the first seed group for Hameed's new venture.

By now, many of the students who dotted the room had been steered toward Hameed's group through Lauren Armstrong. A lanky being with a forthright attitude, the power of astute observation, and talented hands, she was a principle teacher at the Boulder School of Massage Therapy in the seventies. One person she ushered into the group as it moved into this new chapter in Denver was Bob Ball. He is a kind and generous sort who started out as a background presence in a room while permeating the space with clarity. In contrast to his former shy, retiring style, he is now at the center of action as vice president of the Ridhwan Foundation. Both he and Lauren are teachers in the School.

It was obvious that the post–Returning Process group had evolved into a new entity. Hameed was now calling it a work group—in the style of the Fourth Way[1] and some Sufi groups—but it no longer resembled the work that had initiated the participants' first contact with Hameed. The hard, intense work on personal histories had already penetrated deeply enough for the next layers to show up. The participants were now bathed in the perspective that was subtly emerging. They began to venture more frequently into the realm of presence. Emotional experience was invited, but it was used to enter other, deeper dimensions of experience. The sense of release formerly offered by an intense cathartic experience could be achieved now by holding the feeling, feeling it as completely as possible, and letting it open to the new, the unknown, the subtle.

Hameed had started to catalog experiences of presence, not only his own and mine but those of his students as well. He asked them to write about their process, including experiences of engaging with him during group meetings. His own journals were already numerous, but the students' reports of their subjective experiences were particularly significant, for they confirmed and further illuminated the thread of the teaching that was revealing itself through all of us. From this, Hameed could see the common elements and synthesize his findings.

Hameed has always considered the groups an important part of the revelation of the teaching: "Consciousness within any gathering of people with like mind, heart, and intention," he once said, "will enable the teaching to express itself in new ways and, with presence, will enable it to develop." The deep level of required commitment paid off. As the participants probed their experience under the guidance of his skillful means, similar results occurred. "Repeatable results are important for scientific research," Hameed would sometimes say when reflecting on the Work. He saw what we were doing as a huge experiment; if his hypotheses were true, they would be borne out by other people's experiences. It was not enough that he and I became conscious of something; it had to be verified beyond the two of us. When the students' experiences began to duplicate what had been operating in Hameed and me for some time, it gave us further confirmation.

Presence flowed and revealed itself as varied colors and qualities. These were specific "answers" that corresponded to particular categories of questions and issues that individuals were grappling with. After the charge of an emotion had been released, further inquiry into the resulting relaxed state of a stilled mind and body revealed this restful homeostasis to be an opening to presence. Over and over again, students would show up with burning questions stimulated by their personal-life encounters, and Inquiry would lead them to experience the varied, differentiated qualities of presence.

During group weekends, much was done to instill discipline and increase the capacity to manage challenges, inner and outer. Many days and evenings were spent doing practical tasks such as housework, cooking, painting, and learning how to fix things while engaging in various forms of inner practice. The aim of such practices is to become devoted to the essential world while remaining in the physical, with all its obligations, in the manner of the Gurdjieffian model practiced in Fourth Way schools.

The discovery of presence differentiated this new work group not only from the Returning Process groups but also from many kinds of work happening at that time. In the '60s and '70s, the notion of being present usually referred to being in the here and now, mentally quiet and undistracted, and emotionally calm and unreactive. We were discovering that this was merely the entry point into a much more subtle and palpable universe of presence. The practices of being present that we use in the School even now grew from this early understanding. An example is Sensing, Looking, and Listening, which was our main practice for years and is still central among the many others that have been added. These practices led to the awakening of presence as a direct knowing of what it is to *be* the now, not just be *in* the now. That nowness, which is essence, began to show us its magnificent secrets.[2]

❖ ❖ ❖

Many students were now regularly experiencing presence. As it began to unveil its differentiated qualities with their particular colors, flavors, affects, and even sounds, Hameed began to refer to these as the essential qualities. "The true qualities of the real human being," he called them. He used the term "essence" to describe the fluid, substantial quality of presence, which seemed to be irreducible.

If you imagine the human consciousness to be like a translucent prism, it refracts light without distortion. The personality that develops through conditioning alters the prism. The light of Being has to move though the dross of our memories, reactions, and identifications. Through the occlusions, the light appears not only dimmed but distorted as well, and manifests as reactive emotions rather than palpable qualities of immaculateness.

Inquiring into my own personal issues created my access route to these qualities of presence. One after the other, essential qualities showed up— and I didn't have to go anywhere to find them. All I needed to do was sink into the moment, no matter its content, and understand what was arising. I learned to stand in the stream and let whatever was there wash through. Straining to get somewhere, I realized, was a product of my ideas and assumptions about where I should go. What I discovered was that the way to take that next step was to not try to take one at all.

The magical power of these elixirs was in how each one drew me in its own way, in its own time, and unraveled me with its intelligence. It exposed the rubble that was in the way—the mental and emotional content of the history that had formed my ideas about myself, others, and the world, layered messily over my awareness. All of this I offered up for holy, sacrificial inspection, assuming an inner posture of openness and inquisitiveness while feeling deeply into what was going on with me.

Sometimes a question for exploration would formulate itself conceptually. At other times, I felt as though I *were* a question—available and interested in finding out whatever was there while sensing and feeling my way into understanding. It was like reading my own inner braille . . . gently moving through the pages of my life and understanding the labyrinth of my mind and emotions.

Exposing the hold my past had on me freed up the "answers" from within. What I needed always showed up in unanticipated ways, through presence arising as a specific quality that seemed to be just the right solution to my query, similar to the particular herb in the wild that serves as an antidote to a poisonous plant nearby. I later understood that questions were the tiny bits of gold that led me back to the mother lode, to the source of Being. To presence.

I began to understand that my typical feelings, rich and important as they had been for me, had been ever so limited and unrefined compared with these upsurges that were now flowing forth. I came to see how my whole life had been lived within a rubber suit. The ideas I had of love, will, kindness, joy, strength, and so on were shrouds over the naked, beautiful truth of the light in me that was the immediate felt knowing of these essential properties. Kept at a distance by my usual way of experiencing, they now revealed themselves to be like pure waters of the heart's and mind's immediacy. Substances of different colors arose like liquescent rainbows from some heavenly palette—vibrant ruby red, liquid emerald green, flowing golden amber, swirls of sapphire blues and violet, fluid yellow sunshine.

Reports from our students, as well as Hameed's friends who were engaged in discussions with him about presence, matched our experience exactly. Without fail, those who experienced the red ruby-like light felt its heat to some degree and would declare they felt expansive, capable, assertive, or strong. So the red essence got named "the strength essence." Seemed appropriate! Also, without any prompting or having heard it described before—Hameed had not begun to teach the characteristics of the aspects explicitly—students would always feel the green essence as tender, gentle, kind, and compassionate. The liquid, delicate, yellow essence birthed a joyful, spontaneous feeling; the white essence, a feeling of grounded capacity and steadiness that brings a sense of confidence; and the black essence beckoned us into the unknown mysterious depth, erasing doubt and opening us to the luminous night. Each one seemed like a passage to a universe of its own.

Each quality exhibited itself as a refracted color inseparable from its specific sensate character and tone. But each was, and always is, part of the one pure presence of Being itself. It seems obvious now, but it took a while before Hameed arrived at the major insight that the states we were experiencing, and that he had known for some time, were all aspects of the same, pure presence. This is when he began to call the essential qualities aspects.

These aspects arose unbidden, in connection to inquiries into emotional content taken to their furthest end. Sometimes an aspect of presence might emerge within daily life or during a meditation and remain for minutes or hours—even for days or weeks. It would flush out unresolved, often painful, issues that would surface to be worked through. Blockages appeared after initial openings, but as these were understood, heavenly gifts followed, arriving one after the other—assistance, blessings, expanded capacity, surprising insight.

Sooner or later, the process would begin all over again from a different angle; another unconscious psychological issue would bring with it the pain of being separate from this blissful elixir. The power of presence lit up everything that needed to be seen, felt, and understood. As presence presented itself in various ways to be known, each individual's uniquely conditioned personality and beliefs would be exposed.

Presence emerged in our consciousness in various textures as well. One was a light and airy vaporous sensation. This was the perfume of the viscous, colorless presence that Hameed had gifted me. He referred to this light perfume as "the lataif dimension of presence."[3] Sufis differ from one another in their understanding and application of this phenomenon, but all share the view that the lataif are centers in specific areas in the body that become activated from a dormant state when true spiritual clarification starts to occur.

The Diamond Approach understanding of the lataif is similar to that of the Sufis in terms of the locations and colors of these subtle qualities, but our view diverges in significant other ways. We experience each latifa as an entrance into a particular quality of essence and do not know whether the Sufis would agree with this. For us, the lataif are not only the entrances into the realm of essence; as the spiritual purities, they also are the capacities that human beings need for worldly living—for example, strength, courage, sensitivity, peace, compassion, perseverance. And enjoyment of life, of course, for when the essential qualities are operating, an individual can function from Being, regardless of what type of task he or she is engaged in.

In addition, we discovered that specific emotional barriers must be understood and worked through for the lataif to open and operate. We have not encountered these understandings in the Sufi system either.

What we named "the theory of holes" began to develop as the patterns of each aspect of essence came into consciousness, revealing how essence had been lost in the universal process of developing a personality in early childhood.[4] We discovered that opening to and understanding a particular loss revealed an actual feeling of a hole in a specific area of the body.

I became very curious about that. If I looked at my body, it did not seem as though a piece were missing. But the way it felt from the inside was quite different. I could discern distinct holes in various sites in my torso and head. As I worked through the associated issues, one at a time, the "missing" aspects of essence related to the holes arose. I was flummoxed by the precise way in which the aspects answered questions I didn't even know I had.

The journey through the holes took me through the associated pain from the loss of each aspect of essence as I revisited my personal stories from childhood. Every pain was a wound bleeding with memories that had coagulated into what I thought myself to be. Each hole left a part of me open to the air. Defenseless and exposed. I felt so vulnerable and receptive, as I might have been as a child prior to the thickening of my skin. But this undoing left me open to new potentials. The process of wading through the emotional hurts and reactions as they lived in me now required earnest, kind attention, courage, and patience, but chiseling away at the ego, a little at a time, transformed me bit by bit and reunited me with the true, pure essential qualities.

It became obvious how a loss or hole is actually an opening to know another reality. It doesn't work to try to fill a hole by stuffing ourselves with achievements, with hopes and dreams of attaining this or that, with false self-images, or with someone else's love for us. In the end, the hole is still there and will continue to be a force behind those urges until we meet it face to face.

The defensive posture of ego attempts to compensate for the qualities it is missing by mimicking them. Hameed often said, "The ego is not original; it always borrows from the real and makes believe that it is the original owner." As ego appropriates the true qualities, it falsifies them, and they become limited or defensive. For example, our love is more self-centered, and kindness is a strategy to quell pain rather than embrace it. Fake strength or false will are hardened versions of essential qualities that always have openness but can be sturdy at the same time.

The poignant loss of a false quality is inevitable, but working through the associated distortions is the key to unlocking the truth. When we don't deny the emptiness, avoid it, or try to transcend it, understanding the emotional content associated with each hole eventually opens us to a more clarified sense of spacious emptiness. As false ideas and feelings become more transparent, the emptiness clarifies to a spacious emptiness, such that the hole can form a portal to the essential realm. An area in consciousness swept of history and assumptions about reality is like a window that is open to the arrival of the elixir, with its specific colored qualities of essence.

Many students of spirituality will be surprised to hear of this dimension of presence because other traditions are more focused on the emptiness or spaciousness of the spiritual realms. For many in the Eastern (mostly Vedanta) teachings who are familiar with presence, or pure consciousness, it is still radical to hear of these kinds of "smaller" openings to presence rather than the transcendent approaches usually taught. Even for students of the Diamond Approach, it will be news that we initially encountered the lataif as a subtle, perfume-like substance that became a more viscous experience of presence over time.

It seems more rare these days for Diamond Approach students to encounter the lataif in a gaseous state. Because these can be easily missed due to their subtlety, the more substantive sense of presence as a pooling, a flowing, or a fullness is more easily felt. There is no distinct line between these states, however; presence is more of a continuum. Thus, in the School today, the lataif and the qualities of presence are conflated and rarely discussed as different ways of experiencing the textures of the qualities.

The purity of the lataif was a striking contrast to the usual experience of physical existence. It was becoming more and more obvious how the body was being impacted by this conversion of consciousness from its dim existence to the awakened, transparent colorful elixirs of light. I was a grateful witness to the display of the first students in the School popping out of their gauzy webs, springing forth into the world in unsheathed glory with the characteristics of the Invisible One. People were becoming relaxed in their skin as liquid luminescence infused them.

We began to understand that tension patterns in the body are more than a matter of repression and negative emotional patterning. The Reichian model was a good start, and we continued to do healing and breathing sessions with one another, but the more subtle realms were opening to reveal new kinds of tension patterns related to our ego structure in general rather than specific defensive or compensatory holding patterns.

The way that the ego develops in each individual in connection with personal history and cultural context is unique, but the ego itself is universal: Everybody has one. So it was important that we first identify which ego patterns were expressions of a particular individual and which were common to all human beings regardless of differences in culture and personal history. This would help us better understand the various aspects of essence, including their associated psychological barriers and the way that essence manifests on multiple levels.

We discovered that the sites of the various lataif qualities were located in the same areas in the physical body in everybody, no matter the person's conditioning. The chest has three lataif: The green (compassion) is located at the sternum, in the center of the chest. The yellow (joy) is at the left nipple, near the physical heart. The red (strength) is at the right nipple, and it has an important relationship to the vital energy of the first chakra, which is also red. The white (will) is in the solar plexus. The black latifa, which opens to peace, power, and the mysterious unknown, is in the forehead. The blue latifa, related to relaxation, consciousness, and immediate knowing, is located in the middle of the head at the pineal gland. As we open to the essential tides rising in us, these areas in the body awaken and surge with light. The light puts pressure on the body's fleshy conviction, challenging the scaffolding that is trying to hold the body's defensive structure in place.

With the opening of these precious centers of light, the physical structure of my body was morphing. The filaments of the little girl that had molded my form began to loosen as the cocoon of my past dissolved. I felt more range of motion in every way, and the true colors of my present self began to permeate my stature. The subtle body was being developed and sculpting me from the inside out.

Even my physical appearance was changing—this was happening to others in the group too—in some ways, drastically. People noticed and exclaimed, "You got taller!" or "You lost your baby fat." Or they observed, "You look different," and then attempted to define the difference, inevitably ending with "but that's not exactly right—what *is* it?" I was enjoying my body, feeling more grounded and settled inside it. I started to wear clothes that showed my figure. I also stopped trying to hide behind my hair; I got it cut to shorten its drapey flow and began to show my open face in public. That curtain of hair had grown so long and heavy that my neck hurt for two weeks while I adjusted to the new length.

All of this discovery, change, and revelation was occurring with its creative intensity amidst life's difficulties and challenges. But that was the grace of it—I bathed in the beauty of this liquid light as it became more integrated into my body in the course of my regular, daily existence. It did not occur in a nunnery or monastery, cave, chapel, or temple—the venue was life itself, and the temple was me, us, everyone.

10 ❖ And Now We Are Three

THE FIRST RESIDENTIAL retreat was about to begin. It was summer, 1977, and Hameed had decided it was time for the work group to have its first intensive for practicing together. Thirty people would make their way to a YMCA camp in Evergreen, Colorado, and enter the inscrutable, invisible realms of the spirit. What would happen in those eight days? How would we be changed? What would we become? No one knew, including Hameed. But he was confident, as always, that what needed to happen would happen and that it was not in his hands. According to some accounts, many of the students were nervous, anxious, even resistant to going. Nevertheless, they all showed up, willing to explore.

I stayed behind in Denver because I had an important task to do. It was my job to fetch Faisal from the airport and transport him to the event. I would finally get to meet him! He and Hameed had been engaged in conversation throughout the year, but he was not a fleshed-out reality to me yet. I knew him only through Hameed's stories, but what I had heard about him was sufficient to arouse my curiosity.

Around the same time Hameed had transmitted the essential presence into my hand, he reignited a friendship with a fellow Kuwaiti named Faisal Muqaddam. Faisal and Hameed had been in the same class at school, "although not close," as Hameed reports it. Their names, and that of one other friend, would alternately show up at the top of their class. They were part of a small group of Kuwaitis who had migrated to California to attend university at Berkeley, and they occasionally gathered for dinner and entertainment, sharing spiritual interests as well.

Faisal had participated in the second SAT group led by Claudio Naranjo that began in 1972. According to Hameed, at some point Faisal went back to Kuwait for family reasons before he was able to graduate from UC Berkeley. In 1977 he returned to Berkeley and rejoined the cluster of Kuwaitis.

When Hameed began to share his discoveries of presence with his friends, Faisal responded with particular interest, so Hameed continued to discuss the specifics of what he had been discovering over the previous few years. As Hameed talked about the various states he was experiencing, Faisal's sensitivity enabled him to shift into the experience of presence himself.

I was glad that Hameed had found a friend in Berkeley to talk with about his discoveries; I knew he was missing that type of daily personal contact as his life was becoming more rooted in California. The relationship they began to forge at that time would soon solidify to a comradeship very similar to mine and Hameed's, although I do not know if Faisal ever considered Hameed a teacher in the same way that I did. But it was the beginning of an important chapter in their relationship, which would last through the initial years of establishing the Diamond Approach as a spiritual path.

The timing of Faisal's entrance onto the scene was just right. He came into the discussions just as Hameed and I were discovering the lataif, so when presence started to emerge as its specific aspects, we all became engaged in the process of unfurling the various textures, tones, and colors of presence as they arose. Even though I didn't initially have direct contact with Faisal, Hameed would occasionally share with me the pith of their conversations, and he would deliver to Faisal any news about what had been unfolding in our explorations. The additional collaboration was helpful for all of us right from the start.

As Hameed and Faisal talked with increasing frequency about the range of experiences that were arising, their friendship deepened. They made an excursion to Arizona, where their Kuwaiti friend Hameed Qabazard lived. "HQ" (a nickname that differentiated him from Hameed Ali) had chosen to attend university there instead of going with the crowd to Berkeley. During the visit, the three friends hung out and exchanged sessions.

Hameed, who was beginning to use Inquiry as a tool for the exploration of presence, facilitated a session for HQ that combined Inquiry with traditional Reichian breathwork. HQ later told me, "There was something very different about this session. Not your usual bodywork experience, for sure!" His body had deeply relaxed, as would normally happen in a breathwork session, but something more was present—a tangible taste of something refined, blissful, inexplicable. He became intrigued, and three years later moved to California to become involved in the School as a student and later as a teacher.[1]

Now that Faisal was part of our developing story of essence, I was looking forward to meeting him. But as I began to pack up a basket with food and drink for the ninety-minute ride up to the camp from the airport, I felt vulnerable and uncertain. What if he doesn't like me? What if he doesn't want to be my friend? What if . . . ?

I arrived at the airport with my mind still revved up and nervously surveyed the scene to find a match for the inexact description given by Hameed. Spotted him easily! He was the only Arab-looking fellow in sight. Small and lean but with a sturdy build and lots of dark, swirly curls. He was watching the cars go past and sucking a drag off his cigarette. The "what ifs" spun into "what's next?"

I jumped out of the car and introduced myself. He crushed his cigarette under his foot and shyly opened his arms for a hug. His eyes reflected the shimmering aura around him. I took him in with a deep welcome.

I felt a tender bud of friendship potential slowly opening as we drove up the mountain together. It was a hot, sunny Rocky Mountain–style day, the kind that reminds you that you are in the high desert. On the way, we stopped at the river to rest and refresh ourselves and to give Faisal a chance to catch his breath. Our initial contact had already eased into chuckles, sparky flirtations, and small talk, and it now deepened into areas we had each explored with Hameed.

We arrived at the retreat slightly out of sync with the quiet ambiance of the group room. It was midafternoon, and the participants had been engaged in work projects, deeply focused on the sensing practices that support the growing awareness of presence while performing various tasks. A serious gravity pervaded the space.

I felt proud to deliver Faisal to our circle. A cloud of activity and hushed hellos rippled through the thick silence in the room. Hameed and Faisal greeted each other with a hug, energetic pats, and a few Arabic words that sounded lyrically friendly. Hameed motioned us toward the door, and the three of us went outside so we wouldn't disturb the practice with our conversation. At first, I found myself awkward in their company. But when I stepped back to witness their relationship at a comfortable distance, I could see their connection. And I felt it in my heart. Between their mutual twinkle, and my anticipation of fresh eyes and new insights, I was exhilarated. A three-legged-stool sense of support settled in.

Faisal and I were woven into the fabric in short order when we went back into the room. I wanted to stay. I regretted that I couldn't. It would be one of two retreats that Hameed taught in thirty-five years that I did not attend from beginning to end. But I needed to return home because Perry and I had made plans to be together. With his terrible schedule, we had to arrange our lives around his time off, which happened rarely. In addition, I had a job! So I stayed through dinner and then made my way down the mountain to Denver, feeling happy and light all the way home. From my point of view, it had been a sweet beginning between Faisal and me. Friendly, playful, and meaningful.

❖ ❖ ❖

Perry had a stipend, but it wasn't much. In addition to giving healing-support sessions for some of the students in the group, I led some evening meetings between the weekend groups. Hameed paid me a small sum for that, but it wasn't enough to live on.

I'd had the good fortune to hone my healing skills with various curanderas in the area, had been giving workshops on healing, and had the opportunity to lead a workshop at the Rocky Mountain Healing Arts Festival and the Rocky Mountain Annual Conference of the Association of Humanistic Psychology in 1978. Gradually, I acquired a reputation as a healer. The intertwined mysteries of body and spirit drew me to this work, but healing in the manner I was becoming known for did not feel like my vocation. Plus, Hameed had cautioned me, as he had others, not to make teaching something I relied on for money; I might, he said, end up seeing the Work as a way for others to support me rather than the other way around. So I decided to scope out the area for something I would enjoy doing while bringing in some cash. And that is how the circumstances conspired to direct me toward acquiring a "real job."

I heard that Joseph Magnin's, a high-end clothing store in the Cherry Creek shopping area in Denver, was hiring salespeople. So I put on my best outfit, walked into the shop, asked for a job, and started work the following week. Some of my friends couldn't quite make sense of my new occupation. Only a few years before, I had been a blue-jeaned hippie with two pairs of shoes to my name. And now? Heavens! I had become a fashionable lady.

To top it off, I hooked up with a local dance studio and learned ballroom dancing, eventually performing and becoming an instructor. Dancing taught me the art and skill of intertwining mind, heart, and body from the stillpoint within as I twirled through the four dimensions. Essence became more embodied, expressing the dynamic fluidness of my being in a disciplined and organized way that actualized joy, precision, tenderness, strength, and excellence.

For the first time in my life, I wanted to show off—it was the first time I felt I had something to show! This new persona would present its own challenges down the road, but it was an important stage to go through. I was free from the need to be or look like anyone else. I had entered the world more confidently while I was learning about the deeper dimensions beyond it.

As profound a relationship as I had with Hameed, it didn't eclipse the life I was leading with Perry. My friendship with Hameed was of a different order, and Perry honored it with a naturalness that I deeply appreciated and admired. And they had their own friendship as well.

I had lived with Perry for about two years and then married him in April 1978. He was a good man. We loved each other and I was very happy with him. He was fun, smart, interesting. Our mutual enjoyment was enhanced by a shared love of hiking, biking, and jazz clubbing. When Hameed was in town, he joined us at some fabulous small venues featuring many of the greats up close and personal. Abbey Lincoln, with her intriguing, sweet velvety voice, was one of Hameed's favorites. In various combinations—Hameed, Perry, me, Marie, and other friends—we frequented the clubs. We saw Charles Mingus at the Blue Note on Pearl Street in Boulder and went regularly to a place called Clyde's Pub in Wheat Ridge.

Hameed's ventures into the dating world had settled down, and his relationship with Marie was becoming more stable. She accompanied him on one of his trips to Denver, and the four of us took up a social life that continued throughout my marriage to Perry. Marie and I connected more personally than before, our friendship initiated via trying out new hairstyles, sewing clothes, and shopping in vintage clothing shops.

As I continued to mature, my world of friends opened up and expanded through work, dance, and friendships with certain people in the group. Personal connections among group members were not discouraged, and there was no firm demarcation between students and teachers when it came to socializing outside of group meetings, but the rules of conduct for group evenings and weekends were quite strict—no social engagement and no commenting on other people's work in the group.

Since human relationships are usually built around getting needs met and filling our holes from the outside, Hameed wanted us to practice not acting those needs out. "You don't know the difference yet between acting on your needs and expressing a true connection," he would say. "That will come in time. It is necessary to become seated in what you truly are before you try to relate in a group." This perspective had been influenced by the Gurdjieffian model, which saw most social interactions as distractions from the deeper parts of ourselves. Thus, most of the Inquiry practice was done one-on-one with Hameed, with the group witnessing. Sometimes, however, he would also guide group discussions to bring out certain elements of the teachings.

Hameed and I disclosed less of ourselves to those we were working privately with, but we did not avoid social engagements with group members and felt free to befriend those we weren't working with one on one. This was a carryover from the consciousness groups of the '60s and '70s when certain barriers were broken down in a backlash against the rigidity of conservative psychiatry.

Faisal soon became part of the community and visited regularly. He began to work privately with some of the students toward the end of 1979, in much the same way I had done, and began his own relationships with the group members. The common bond all of us had in the Work provided a nourishing environment for friendships to flourish with a sense of depth and meaning. Over time, people became increasingly authentic with one another, and our social life, influenced by the group's engagement in truth-seeking, became more satisfying.

I felt particularly rich steeping in developing friendships. It was my good fortune that Linne, Walter, and their two young sons, Shay and Evan, had moved to Denver. They became more than friends—they were family for me. Linne was continuing in the group Hameed was teaching, and I often dropped in at their home, just to hang out and maybe get a bodywork session. By now, Linne was absorbed in studying essence and how the dimension of presence impacts the functioning of the body in motion and structure. She was keen to develop her comprehension further as she straddled the world of Aston-Patterning and the knowledge of essence that was opening for her. Her work has added dimension and balance to the Reichian perspective that continues to influence the embodiment of the Work in the School today. I am still her main guinea pig.

Alia and I had been close friends since I moved to Denver. She lived in the nearby suburb of Littleton. I introduced her to a friend of Perry's, a Reichian therapist who had to complete psychiatric training as a prerequisite to entering the Reichian Institute. The four of us would meet for dinner and socializing, which often included lively, interesting conversations about philosophy, psychiatry, Reich, and bad jokes, most often accompanied by a mediocre bottle or two of wine. Alia was outrageous and clever, and our time together was multidimensional and fun.

Another important relationship for me was with Deborah Davis, now Deborah Ussery Letofsky. At the second open house for people inquiring about the Returning Process that was held a couple of years earlier, it was announced at the end of the talk that Sandra—she was still going by "Sandy" then—and I would both be available for questions. Immediately I spotted a young woman making her way toward me in the church hall. She couldn't have been much older than twenty-five, but her dark brown hair was snowcapped with white, which lent her an otherworldly attractiveness. Her approach toward me was more a decisive slicing through the room than a walk. She looked directly into me with clear hazel eyes. "I really want to be in this group, but I can't do it right now. Will there be another one?" Her voice was soft yet crisp, with a hint of a Southern drawl. I assured her that there would be another opportunity to be part of a group, and her expression relaxed into a quick smile. I had little doubt that this would not be the last I saw of her. It wasn't.

Many of the connections created back then formed sacred bonds that continue to nourish and enrich my life today. Each one adds another dimension based on communion with a truth that is larger than any one individual, while holding us all.

11 ❖ Diamonds Are a Girl's Best Friend

THE FIRST THING THAT came into focus through my sleep-drenched eyes was the white plaster ceiling above me. Perry had been on duty at the hospital for a couple of days, and I had spent most of that time alone, enjoying painting and contemplating. As I lingered in our waterbed, I traced imaginary pictures in the tiny cracks in the plaster. One of them pointed in the direction of the long sash window and led my gaze to the snow outside. As I watched it swirl, I became aware of the lump in my stomach that had been plaguing me for the past few days.

The sight of new snow drew me out of bed and to the window overlooking the backyard, where I saw Mushka just disappearing into her snowy den, only her black and pink nose giving her away. My heart pulsed with love for her. I padded my way to the kitchen to concoct an herbal brew to melt this lump once and for all. No nausea, but I did have a thick feeling in my head that I recognized as a sign of some unconscious material rising. I thought it likely that new territory had been unearthed due to some recent essential experiences, but I didn't connect this with the discomfort in my midsection, which I was certain was physical.

I sat contemplating, drinking cup after cup of hot tea to try to melt this odd feeling. Sometimes it felt like tension and sometimes like a density. Just as I was verging on hopelessness, Hameed called. We had planned to be in contact about arrangements for his next trip, so hearing from him wasn't unexpected.

The strange sensation grew even more intense as we spoke. I told him how it had come and gone over the past few days. "I have done everything to try to make it go away, and it just stays there," I concluded in defeat.

"What if you just feel it without trying to make it go away?" he offered, with his usual interested neutrality.

"Oh, of *course*." My whining transformed to join his curiosity.

"So, what does it feel like?"

"It feels hard in there, like I swallowed a rock." I drew in a breath and let it out slowly while attending to the sensation, suspending my ideas about it for the time being. Hameed had reminded me of the main premise we had been working with lately: to simply be with anything that comes up; to be interested in what is there; to gather as much information as possible by letting things bubble up and feeling them; and to let go of any tendency to direct what might come next.

"I don't have anything emotional going on about it, Hameed."

I was puzzled by this. Then I realized I was looking for a feeling of some sort or even a recognizable quality, and this was creating a subtle resistance. I settled more into not-knowing, which led me into now-knowing.

"How does it affect you?" Hameed's tone remained neutral and open.

"I don't really feel the effect of it yet." I paused, noting that this was true, but not completely. I was feeling *something*—I was not numb—but couldn't quite land on the right words to describe it. It wasn't just presence, at least not in the way I had felt it before. It was distinct but unfamiliar. I slowed down and sat there for some time, breathing and attending to this lumpy phenomenon.

Then the clouds in my consciousness dissolved as though a brisk wind had been summoned to cleanse my mind. I became enthralled with a new sense that was beginning to pierce my consciousness. It wasn't merely the absence of emotion; it was the presence of clarity. Quite the opposite of the thickness I had woken up with. Only the week before, I had felt the presence like water, but it was viscous. Was this related? It felt similar in its lucidity but different in texture.

"I am very clear," I said aloud. I sounded emphatic to myself.

The pristine sense of presence continued. As Hameed continued to ask me about it, it became brighter. I felt as though I were seeing the world through eyes that had been washed with Rain-X. I was completely involved, yet detached at the same time.

"Wow, I feel as light and fresh as the air on the top of the Rocky Mountains!"

The "rock" became glossy, then a sharp sensation began to arise. It was not painful. As I paid close attention, things began to shift.

"I can actually feel the edges—they're like facets, Hameed."

"And how is the lumpy feeling?"

"Not there anymore," I said in astonishment. And then: "Oh my God . . . it's a diamond!"

I understood now. My assumptions that this lump had been a physical phenomenon, combined with the attitude that it was a problem, had led me to subtly reject it. My stance created the tension surrounding this presence, distorting the sensation of the lump so I couldn't see or feel what it was.

The sensate presence of clarity was definite, but it was neither a fluid elixir nor a fullness of presence. It was structured, faceted, translucent consciousness.

The line between the normal and the extremely unusual met in my mind. I was gobsmacked by the collision of these two separate universes. Even the ideas of presence as I had encountered it before were tossed into the void like so many wooden blocks. I sat in utter amazement at the improbable event of a gem displaying itself inside of me.

"This is absurd," I said. "I thought the liquid stuff was far out . . . and now this! Nobody is going to believe it."

"Do *you*?"

"Hmm . . . 'belief' is not the term I would use." I searched for the words. "It is its own statement, and it is quite certain of itself."

"You are right. It is real and indisputable. Not something your mind can grasp. At the same time, you know it by the felt experience of it."

"That is true. It really is mind-blowing, yet I can still talk about it."

"Yeah, I know. Interesting, eh? Just because your mind is more open doesn't mean it is not functioning. It might even work better this way. That is how pure consciousness works. As you become it, you know it." His voice receded back into silence.

Upon closer scrutiny, the rock revealed greater refinement and its exquisiteness became more apparent. As its image arose in my mind's eye, I could see it as a faceted glimmering radiance. And the visual matched the sensation exactly.

"It is so clean and light! I feel so . . . awake!"

Quiet now on his end . . . but I knew he was there, letting me find my way to articulate this precious gift that had befallen me. Hameed never said too much at these times. His hands-off approach gave space for my understanding to uncloak the truth of my experience in time with my own rhythm. Sometimes he knew the territory or state I was headed toward and sometimes he didn't, but I was always held in an atmosphere of trust and openness throughout the process, even if I struggled with not knowing where I was headed sometimes.

"And to think that I tried to purge it like some lumpy trash," I said to him, but truly more to myself. I wondered how many treasures I had missed by believing my assumptions and reactions.

"So, how ya doin'?"

"I am okay . . . a little sad to think I was on a mission to melt it out of my system."

"Yeah, you didn't know it was gonna dissolve *you* out of your own way."

"True, how true." The bright sharpness regained amplitude.

"Goodbye, my friend."

"Goodbye, Meedle¹ . . . next week, then?" I said in eager appeal.

"You bet."

While Hameed and I had been talking, a conversation came to mind that I'd had some months earlier with him, soon after his first experience of the clear essence during a conversation with Faisal. At that time, it showed up for him as the pooling substance. In his words: "The clarity was so crisp from the start. But as I felt into it, the flow of the substance was not the same sort of liquid in the way I felt it with the other essential qualities. It was an elixir of tiny diamonds."

Usually, I catch a state when he talks about it with me, but what he was describing struck me more as a metaphor, and I could only grasp it intellectually at the time. But it must have been working on me. I knew for myself now because I could see, feel, and be it. As usual, whenever I experienced a state he was describing, it bore little resemblance to the ideas I had about it; and with each experience, I bore less resemblance to the me I had known previously.

I walked into the bathroom to get ready for work and caught a glimpse of the person in the mirror. I *knew* it was me, but I felt like I was looking at a stranger. "How the heck am I going to tell my husband about *this* one?" I said aloud, hoping my reflected image might display a clue. It would sound so odd. How was I going to talk about this to someone who didn't have much interest in these matters in the first place?

Nevertheless, I decided to bring it up a week later after a Sunday afternoon bike ride. We secured the cycles in the shed and made our way through our little grassy backyard. Trying to sound casual, I asked, "What would you say if I told you I had an experience of becoming a diamond?"

Perry's eyes darted upward, searching the air for clues. "If I didn't know and respect Hameed and you, I would say you were delusional. But hey, new ideas have always been looked on as crazy at first."

"But this *isn't* just an idea."

"It is to me."

That stumped me. And then I recognized that I wanted my husband to experience that reality himself. But it couldn't happen. At least not through me. I was not his teacher. This was the first time I felt an urgent wish for him to understand what had been happening to me over those past few years. It was dawning on me that the experiences I was having were not simply nice additions to my life—they were a departure from the way I had known the world, which left me feeling disoriented and unmoored. I wanted to be anchored by Perry's understanding of them.

As usual after these kinds of openings, a dizzying process ensued as this clear diamond penetrated the opacity of my mind. It moved through me, revealing my hold on the known and stretching me to behold the newness of now. I cried as old wounds reopened. Ideas and beliefs unguarded themselves and evaporated as I understood my patterned thinking that held them in place.

For example, I had always seen myself as a loving person but not especially eloquent or smart, even though many friends reflected to me that I was intelligent and creative. Now I not only felt clarity of mind, I *was* that. Many such issues rose up as essence challenged my familiar self. I saw how my constructed identity was bent on maintaining itself, and how it automatically dismissed anything that didn't fit with my self-concept. Letting in even one new quality or characteristic was enough to create a temporary instability as my system reorganized to include the new element.

The presence of the diamond was a huge challenge to the sleepy bits of me. More and more distorted parts of my self began to stir from a long slumber. It's like when parts of your body fall asleep after being in one position for a long time. You are numb, and when you try to move, it hurts for a while because the body has been deprived of blood and oxygen—but the freedom of movement soon feels healthy. So even though the process of waking up can be painful, I learned to trust it more and more as I saw its innate intelligence acting on me in ways that were smart and good.

The process of clarifying the issues that impeded the embodiment of this essential clarity gradually eased, and the searing presence itself resumed its prominence and remained constant for weeks. The clarity was blissful. I loved that. My mind was unhinged and free. No longer was there a tangled web of ideas or associations to crawl through—just crisp awakeness. And I felt lucid not only in my mind—I was cleared out everywhere.

The diamond presence brought more understanding of my relationship to this new way of being, as well as knowledge of itself. It grew brighter, and I realized that it was not only an experience—it was an intrinsic aspect of me.

The presence of the faceted, compact light expanded, filling my torso. It was an inner diamond made of consciousness. I felt intoxicated with its limpid presence. I was diamondized.

Just as remarkable was the effect it had on my perception of the world. Everything appeared as though it had been polished. Each petal of a flower stood out; every cloud in the sky was distinct; each pebble came into high relief. Colors were so vivid that they were of another, otherworldly category. Everything appeared fresh, vibrant, and new.

All the essential qualities now began arising in diamond form for Hameed, Faisal, and me. Their self-luminescence verged on neon. There are no true color-correlates in this world, but try to imagine shimmering gems of green emeralds, crimson rubies, cerulean-blue sapphires, canary-yellow diamonds, and pinky-orange padparadschas.[2]

These diamonds began to act on us with more force, opening up and broadening the vista of Being that was unfolding before us and within us. Each one was a brilliant stepping-stone on the path toward greater illumination and more precise knowledge about the self and the various aspects of Being—and hence, a more precise understanding of the teaching. They were in very real terms the jewels of the teaching of the Diamond Approach.

We began to understand what objectivity means on the journey of inner realization. The vantage point of personality is inherently subjective, and each of us is deeply invested in keeping its point of view intact. Objectivity, on the other hand, means holding concepts about reality that are beyond the mind of the subject—that is, the mind of a given individual. For example, we might discover something about our past or our behavior that is objective—that happened or exists whether or not we like it or want to believe it.

There are degrees of subjectivity and objectivity, and it is possible to be somewhat objective about ourselves, other people, or reality in general while we are not in the diamond state. However, when that state is present, it can make our capacities and perceptions less driven by our subjective identity. Simply having the experience of a diamond state does not make our fallibility disappear, however, nor does it erase overnight the limitations of self. That is a long process. As long as there is a self, there are limits to objectivity.

To be outside of subjective mind is a well-known spiritual goal across many traditions. When people hear the word "objectivity" in that context, though, sometimes it brings up fear that presenting a truth as indisputable carries an agenda of fortifying a personal or institutional point of view. This, unfortunately, does occur. But the Diamond Approach works by enabling us to see and know the truth about who and what we are beyond subjectivity and without rigid assertions about what the truth is.

The concepts that the diamonds unveiled were inextricably linked to the basic qualia[3] of consciousness, very like the Platonic ideas—irreducible, precise, knowable qualities of being. They did feel impersonal, but their arising didn't move me into some distancing mental state. There was simply a recognition of truth beyond belief-based, associative knowledge. It was direct, immediate knowing, uninfluenced by history.

My subjective mind couldn't hold up against the diamond's bright discernment. It felt as though the top of my head had flown off, along with some very restricted views of "reality." But no matter what I did or thought, the diamond remained unaffected. It was an indestructible presence for weeks.

Many experiences of presence and transcendence had occurred for Hameed early on in his seeking. This was also true for Faisal and me.

However, the diamonds initiated a specific wisdom path that was revealing itself through us. It took us on a novel journey with its own logic, different from any we had known before. Diamonds were descending frequently, their presence continuing to flood our consciousness and show us the teaching as it was manifesting in our experience. But we needed to conceptualize these experiences in a way that would translate into an articulated teaching.

Even that was gifted to us. Without asking, we were being given a capacity to articulate the underlying truth without disturbing it. Bit by bit, we were taught how to walk the path and to decode its language. We were its instruments and its first students. But it was necessary to begin walking from square one—barefoot at each step and more naked than during the phase before. Each new insight tore a veil that had concealed me. In addition to becoming more transparent to essence, I was feeling less defended and increasingly open to others, more welcoming and generous. My desire to help, to heal, and to support people to be happy was amplified, but that came with an increased sensitivity to the suffering of others. Feeling their pain, unmuffled, was almost unbearable at times.

I felt the influence each of us had on the unfoldment of the teaching. Although Faisal and I did not spend a lot of time together at this point, I felt we remained linked through Hameed. Now that we were three—along with a committed group of students—and the diamonds were bringing in precise understanding, the teaching became even more crisp and defined. The theory of holes was completed with the knowledge of universal issues and their resolutions. These issues Hameed referred to—and we still do in the School—as diamond issues. This means that each aspect of essence is connected to a specific set of issues related to the separation from our essential nature. These issues are true for all egos, regardless of any other issues an individual might have.

For example, the disconnection from the red essence results in issues and conflicts related to strength and anger, the black essence will bring up doubt and distortions around power and peace, and the green essence will raise issues connected with tolerating hurt. Seeing through these issues will liberate essential aspects within our individual consciousness.

Another universal issue is reflected in my experience with the clear diamond, when I had no idea that the lump in my stomach was the presence of clarity. I had to see through my subjective stance about how I interpreted my own experiences. When we feel the clarity of the diamond presence, we begin to feel the meaning of "objective" as freedom from the individual subjective mind.

A series of discoveries enabled us to make specific connections between the qualities of essence, the psychological levels of experience, and the various kinds of emptiness that would result from the loss of each aspect as the ego develops. What we learned is that each aspect, in the form of a specific diamond, brings the understanding of and resolution to a particular way that the ego is separated from our essential nature. More than that, the diamond brings the immediate and experiential wisdom that opens the way back to our true nature through understanding the qualities of Being, or aspects of essence, and their associated barriers. It does that in part by showing us exactly how, having been separated, ego distorts the properties and qualities of essence.

For example, the false strength of tough defensiveness is an aberration covering the absence of the full-bodied heat of essential strength. Stubborn, resistant willfulness substitutes for the lack of confident inner support. Love with an agenda can limit the natural, generous flow of the heart that has no need for reciprocation.

When students would "fall into" a hole, we supported them to allow the accompanying feeling of emptiness and to understand what they had filled it with. If they were also willing to experience the pain of separation from the truth of Being, the specific true quality that had been lost would arise. That quality might be experienced, for example, as the direct and immediate sense of strength or of will or love or compassion or joy, rather than in the indirect, merely conceptual way of knowing these facets of our humanness as they come through the ego self.

Resplendent knowledge diamonds arrived more and more quickly, revealing a more objective and thorough meaning of each aspect from the point of view of essence itself—the presences just as they were with nothing added. Every new discovery of truth brought a feeling of greater freedom and a broadening of perception, stretching us three explorers in extraordinary ways.

We were beginning to feel like astronauts. With the arising of the faceted knowledge, we had lifted off from the gravitational field of the world as we had known it, our sights set on the diamond-studded universe beyond. We were now speeding along a bona fide spiritual path. The term "Diamond Approach" was created as the formal name for the teaching with its specific knowledge of essential nature and the method of Inquiry that opens human consciousness to our natural inner beauty.

12 ❖ In the Heart of Paradise

IN THE MONTHS FOLLOWING the August retreat, the concentrated presence in the seed group continued to build. The teaching was alive in the students. Their inner process had been accelerated by the intensive work together, and essence was bursting through like a lotus springing up out of the mud.

The group still met every other weekend at Duncan's house, and attendance was compulsory. Hameed became more ruthless about this, declaring it a priority over holidays and birthdays and all the other "unimportant" reasons to not show up that had begun to creep in. Many of the original teachers from this time miss this type of rigor, while others are relieved that it has relaxed. But it was an easy commitment for most members to make at that time, despite the busy lives most were engaged in. The unspoken recognition that what was happening in the group was a valuable and rare opportunity had become more evident since the retreat.

Not only was the group momentum growing, so was the force coming through Hameed. The blessings of essence had been pouring in ceaselessly for more than a year at that point, and others were on their way. These would mesh together to illuminate central understandings of the teaching, ripening the students toward a true and real personal existence.

We were now a few months down the road from the retreat; it was a fine afternoon in October 1979. I showed up at the airport a little late. Hameed had already picked up his bags and was standing at the curb, scanning the distance to catch my approach. His countenance lifted as soon as he spotted me.

He hopped into the Bug and slid his crutch into its resting place. We exchanged hugs and happy salutations and wasted no time getting to what had transpired with him since we had last spoken.

"I have been in an interesting process for the past few weeks. I feel like I am beginning to be more myself than ever. It has been wonderful and difficult. I am following lots of threads, but I am not understanding how it all fits together."

I felt drawn into the gravity field of his inquisitiveness. "Well," I said, "you do look different . . . plumped up somehow."

He chuckled with secretive amusement. "Yeah, I have been experiencing essence coming and going in all kinds of interesting ways. Without much obvious content. I feel so many states sort of undulating through me. Then a great deal of tension on my left side, intermittently. So it isn't clear what's happening yet, how all the tensions and all these states relate. Maybe we will have a chance to explore it more while I am here."[1]

"Oh, I'm sure we will," I said.

We continued our full-fledged *sohbat*.[2] Without a hiccup, we could shift between deciding what to buy for dinner and penetrating the newest features of an inner life that was in constant revelation. He continued the download of what he had been exploring while in California, both by himself and in conversations with Faisal.

"My heart seems central to what is happening," he said, as he maneuvered our cart toward the meat and poultry counter. "A transformation of sorts."

"Don't you think your marriage might have something to do with that?"

"Likely. But I think there is more to it."

Hameed and Marie had married in March of 1979. His dear longtime friend Ron Kayne presided over the event. Faisal, Luli Emmons—a friend of Marie's—and Dhiravamsa, the Buddhist monk Hameed had met in SAT and with whom Sandra studied—were present. Since it was a second marriage for both, they wanted it to be intimate and efficient, with only one witness for each of them and someone to officiate. Dhiravamsa happened to be in town, staying with Ron, so he was welcomed by Hameed and Marie. Hameed and I both felt that being there in my heart was the right thing, rather than my making the trip to California. The sweet little ceremony took all of ten minutes.

A few days after the wedding, Hameed had talked to me about the ways that their union had stimulated in him new territories in the heart that were opening for exploration. Their marriage felt like the outer statement of the love they shared, and the pleasure and love between them deepened after the ceremony. They had been living together with Ron in the house that Hameed co-owned with him, and after their marriage they moved into a place that Marie had found in the hills of Richmond.

As I listened to him speak about all the changes in his life, I realized that in spite of the new roundness I saw in Hameed, something was not yet settled in him. For one thing, his relationship with Henry was still not resolved. The external developments that had nudged him toward a more conventional life of marriage and householding had increased the compelling force inward, leaving him in a kind of limbo. The inner and outer threads would need to intertwine as weft and warp of the same fabric. But how?

As he adjusted to his new life circumstances, he struggled with how to reconcile his love for Marie and his growing desire "to be near God," as he expressed it in his journal. He sometimes referred to God as the truth of Being, in whatever way it showed itself—beyond his own individual being. Sometimes he experienced himself in relation to and moving toward Being, truth, or True Nature; at other times, he was within the divine matrix, inseparable from it. In addition, since the arrival of the diamond knowledge with its stark impersonalness, he had been pondering the question of how to integrate the impersonal with the personal.

"He is not going to be satisfied until he understands these things," I thought to myself. And neither would I. I had a tendency to enjoy various states without questioning them a lot, unless I was bothered by something. I had a big *aha!* once in a while when the dots seemed to connect effortlessly, but he questioned everything and probed all states with equal ardor. His line of questioning caught me like a fish on a hook. I couldn't help but get reeled in.

Hameed went on to thread together the occurrences of the past six months, which had been crammed with seemingly incongruent experiences and understandings. With his needle-like logic, he pierced each one at its center to pull a bead of insight into place on his thought necklace.

"For some reason, my mind has been thinking about the experiences that started in the spring. Remember the way the essential qualities arose for us in April?"

"Of course. I felt like a yummy puddle for weeks."

It would have been impossible to forget how the liquefied, heavenly qualities began to fill my heart, then my whole being, with rich, viscous nectars of apricot and pomegranate, honey, saffron, and liquid amber, and golden melting love. I was luscious and effulgent, relaxed and settled. It was paradise.

April had been a splurge of ripening with the sweet, juicy heart qualities of presence, settling into the state of completeness and contentment. This sense of fulfillment and ease lingered for several months.

The Arabic word Hameed chose to refer to this state is *ridhwan.* No word in English completely conveys the meaning, but the closest translation would be "contentment, contented, and contenting" all at the same time. Awakening through the joy of discovery and the love of truth opens one to ridhwan. It is the essential quality that expresses heart in a very particular way—a pink fluffy love, yellow joy, and rich apricot fulfillment as one fluid presence of deep, sweet, happy love. It is contentment that can't help but be contenting as our heart rests in its humble truth.

The pleasurable and fulfilled heart alters the feel of practice in a very important way on this journey of the Diamond Approach. It shows us how the practices can be expressions of the pleasurable love for Being. We were discovering that practice done in a state of contentment, abundance, and settledness—rather than from dissatisfaction and striving—made it natural to feel plentiful and find ways to share the bounty with others.

Hameed and I continued conversing as we passed through the checkout stand and wove our way through the crowded parking lot. We loaded up the car with our groceries and headed south. Time stretched beyond the ten minutes to my little bungalow as he continued his tale.

"I had been in this state of ridhwan before, for short times. I felt it like something descending over me. Then I felt it deep in my heart. The substance gained in density and viscosity; it became like thick syrup. That state became my station for a while."

"What does that mean?"

"A station is the state somebody finds themselves in when they relax. A consistent, recurring condition."

"Oh, like the time when I felt compassion for weeks?"

"Yes, that was probably a station for you for a while. As each of the lataif was."

"Oh yeah, I get it. It is like the resting heart rate of your consciousness."

"Yeah, kinda like that."

He continued to pull the thread of his experience through the year and into the present time. "The contentment seemed to be followed by some questions I had about my relationships with Henry and Marie and some other friends."

"That makes sense," I said, musing about the connections.

"Remember how I got very transparent in June, as though I had been released from the clutter of my mind and tensions in my body? I became very balanced in a fine, translucent state."

"Yeah, I remember that," I said, recalling our discussions about it.

"Well, the ridhwan state came around again, with that same sense of enjoyment and of feeling enough just being myself."

"Awww. That is great!" I felt supportive and happy about him appreciating himself.

"But listen to this . . ."

"Uh-huh . . ."

The excited momentum of his cadence slowed as if to draw attention to the point that he was about to make. "I started to feel a very specific tension, like a line that went all the way from the head, down the neck and over the heart, and down the left side. Sometimes into the perineum and down the leg, too. It's like a piano string being held taut along the full length of the left side." He and Faisal had been exploring the peculiar accompanying physical tensions that were showing up as part of this new mystery.

"What is also there is the strong feeling that I just want to be myself. And a sense that I am not living up to my potential. I am not being, acting, and working as I can. I feel some kind of dissatisfaction."

"So maybe the fulfillment and satisfaction you've been feeling since your marriage brought this up, eh?"

"Yes, that is what I am thinking. It is part of the equation."

"Say more," I prodded.

"The question is, *who* is satisfied or not? *Who* is living a life? I feel that I am comfortable in some way that is not real. Like I am not being impeccable in a way that I could be. Like a young boy who wants to be taken care of." We had just reached home. I turned my head to look at him, and he looked back at me with dark, moist eyes.

"Wow," I said, sitting between perplexity and a desire to do something to take care of him. I understood that this was only a feeling coming up for him, but what he had just told me rattled my image of him a little bit. I resisted my desire to rescue him from the feeling, realizing that he was just fine where he was. Instead I gave him a couple of gentle but confident pats on the knee and said, "I'll grab the bags."

As we walked into the house, Hameed was greeted straightaway by Mushka's "you are the most important person in the universe" yipping. He greeted her in return with his usual "you are the only dog I love" pat on the butt. Satisfied, she lay down on the floor, sphinx-like, panting in contentment. Hameed took his seat at the small wooden table near the window. I put the groceries away, then handed him an onion to chop.

"I feel so sad," he murmured.

I turned toward him. My eyes gestured an invitation.

"I feel conflicted," he went on. "I am concerned about being loved or not by others. Valued or not. But really, all I want is nearness to God. I don't want the conflict anymore. And this tension is painful." He rubbed his chest in a soothing motion as he described a green ember burning deep in its core. "I feel like a young boy. Kinda melancholy, shy, quiet. Innocent. Like I was as a kid sometimes. Sad that I am getting lost in the need for recognition and approval."

Looking up, he continued, "I feel this particularly in relation to Henry."

Something clicked into place for him just then. He saw not only how the relationship with Henry echoed the one with his father but also how he projected that onto others. He wanted the world to value and see him as he wanted his father to see him. He wanted Henry to know him as who he was.

I lifted the cover of the rice pot, and the steamy basmati clouded the kitchen with its aroma. Half an hour later, with the scent of exotic spices tempting our taste buds, we took our seats at the little table, grabbed our forks, and dug in.

"Yum." I bulged with pride. "I learned a new recipe!"

"Yeah, turned out pretty good," he said, alternately licking his fingers and chewing passionately on a chicken thigh.

After several minutes, Hameed noticed the tension on the left side beginning to soften. He stopped eating and just sat there, staring at the table but not really looking at it. His attention was drawn inward, and I could tell he was feeling his state with precision. He sank limply into the wooden chair. Then a shot of fire seemed to blaze though him. He straightened up and said, "I'm fed up with the feeling of needing others to validate me or what I am doing."

He had started the entire conversation on the edge of irritation, but a feeling of stalwartness had built to a peak of energy that was now coming out as anger. He was angry that the problem existed at all. Not mad at himself or someone else, just mad that it was there. He simply wanted to be free of his conflicts around growing up and needing others' approval. And he wanted to be free from the pain in his body that was the result of these psychological conflicts.

I was deeply interested in what he was going through, but at the moment I was in different emotional territory. I was happy we were together and felt much the way Mushka seemed to feel—"Yay! Our buddy is here! I am happy . . . what else would I care about?" By that point in our relationship, however, I had learned how to hold space for him, whatever he was going through, and still stay in my own lane.

After that night, Hameed took his insights to the next level and decided to watch his behavior and attitudes for signs of any need for approval. He took an aim[3] to not act out on a desire for acknowledgment. Instead, he investigated the issue further with Faisal and me.

❖ ❖ ❖

We finished our dinner and tidied up a bit, and then it was time to head off to the group. We arrived a few minutes early and went upstairs to the small room that Duncan had set aside for Hameed to rest in before the evening began. He looked strong, and I was wondering what was happening with him now. How would the meeting go?

It didn't take long to see that Hameed's teaching had matured over the past months. It was May of 1979, and the methods he had been developing were now reflecting with greater refinement and precision the objective knowledge of presence. It was like watching him handle a double-edged scalpel of sharp, brilliant clarity and exquisite gentleness to do exploratory surgery of the consciousness. Each piece of work delicately exposed a shell of falsehood to release the essence of truth and wisdom into the room for all to bathe in. Through their work, the students contributed to the field of growing consciousness, becoming openings for it to flood the space we all inhabited.

Hameed would often say, "Essence is the teacher." It was so apparent when he was working with people how the presence came through him to respond to their queries. Qualities of essence arose with intelligent attunement and influenced his questions and his answers, giving them elegant precision. Boldness arose to challenge limits and provide the expansion needed to go beyond them. Tenderness met any exposed wounds, allowing the pain to be tolerated and understood, rather than being soothed away and eliminating the opportunity for growth and insight. The sturdy presence delivered the endurance to stay the course into the unknown.

All the while, great curiosity, openness, and love would draw the truth that was within the students to the light of awareness. Hameed cleaved to the discovery of the truth for its own sake and demonstrated in every interaction how essence itself is the probe.

His words were exceptionally efficient that evening—packed with substance. He was not talking *about* presence but rather speaking *from* it. The inner process that had been so recently troubling him seemed to have no impact on his functioning at all. I was impressed. I listened and watched as he seemed to shape-shift from an unassuming thirty-something guy to a powerful conduit of wisdom, transporting the room and its inhabitants to some other realm.

After the weekend, Hameed wrote this in his journal:

I have been doing the scatter technique for some time now. The term is taken from Idries Shah, the Sufi teacher, who coined the phrase, meaning "to approach the teaching from many different angles." One of them is likely to hit the target.

I have been presenting and communicating and working on different aspects of essence: truth, love, peace, strength, value, etc. The point is to give the group different impacts and tastes that, if taken together, might produce a certain understanding of essence. My emphasis this weekend was on expansion and totality. I talked much about not fixating on any one area, experience, or center and showed how many systems are built to repeat a certain experience.

I saw how learning means constant change and expansion. Learning can't happen if a person wants to continue to be the same. This is to say, even if this sameness is a true and real experience, it is important to allow it to be held as one possibility, not the entirety of the truth.

Hameed did his best to convey how getting attached to wondrous states and subtly anticipating our next step based on what we have already experienced hinder our inquiry. He continued to encourage us in an ongoing process of discovery in which we let go of trying to achieve certain states or cultivate a particular experience. As we moved through the many awakenings that followed, we needed to hear that, because each time we became comfortable with some new state or a different experience of essence, we would be toppled off our posts.

On the short ride home, I asked him, "Where did the sad kid go . . . and the disgruntled guy with all those feelings?"

"Oh, the feelings didn't go anywhere. I noticed them once in a while, but that was not what was dominant for me. I felt strength by the time I arrived at Duncan's house, and I think this helped me to separate from the internal images of others and myself. When I teach, presence takes the front seat. I could still feel the line of tension, but it opened somewhat, and I was much more aware of how immense the dark, peaceful presence is."

"Yeah," I said, rolling my eyes, emphasizing the *wow* factor. "And powerful, too."

Onward down the few short blocks to home, the two intrepid explorers moved through the dark evening atmosphere with silent ease.

13 ❖ Labor and Delivery

THE GROUP THAT NIGHT had been one of the more potent ones. The black luminosity that created the backdrop for the entire evening appeared to have had an annihilating effect on everyone's individual boundaries, and the room had become one powerful energy field. Almost psychedelic. I think I was frightened by it but hadn't noticed yet. I was still in awe of the immense presence that engulfed the meeting.

Hameed and I got home around ten o'clock. Perry would be home in an hour or so, and Hameed and I agreed it was a good time to start the inquiry we had talked about before dinner. We went to the little back porch room that I'd made into a space for doing sessions and whatever artwork I had time for. Hameed slid onto the massage table and took a few deep breaths, crunching his brow ever so slightly, as he often does when focusing inward.

I assisted him to attend to and breathe into the places where his body was taut, in order to encourage receptivity from the guidance of my hands. Depending on what was needed, my hands would emit coolness, heat, energy, or some aspect of presence as I held various areas to support the unwinding of the messages inside Hameed. The particular essential quality or energy that was necessary to meet the hidden story and free it from unfelt realms would simply arise unbidden. Hameed reported in his journal:

June 30, 1979
Then she helped me to understand what's happening in the left side of my body. She saw a baby, really an embryo, contentedly asleep inside a womb. The embryo seemed to be spiritual, otherworldly, with silver and gold colors. Around it were colors of red and blue. The fluid seemed like blood that nourished it.

So it seems that my heart is pregnant with a new baby, and that is the reason for the continuing tensions. It seems that the full activation of the yellow latifa [*which relates to the joy center as the "left wing of the heart"*] will be the birth of this new baby. Also it seems there is a lot of psychological work required for this activation. It includes letting go of others' recognition, approval, and appreciation to reach the state of no concern with this issue. It includes letting go of the lataif. It includes letting go of any state or station.

Grappling with the questions of autonomy and love, pleasure and priorities, that had been circling in his psyche was sculpting him into a different type of maturity. Working the relational edge was melding his inner life and outer existence. This process would require more stalwart determination to drop any assumptions about what was to come. It demanded the willingness to let go even of essence, if this became necessary. That would be a step toward autonomy and a step away from ideas and beliefs about self and other, the world and reality, as he knew it. It would not be a single experience to integrate but rather a transformative process that would take time.

At one point in the session, the fear I had shelved earlier in the evening flew off its ledge and hit me smack in the belly. I felt as though I were watching Hameed wobbling on a cliff, deciding whether to jump off or not. I feared I might be caught in the draft and lose more than I had bargained for. My toes curled to try to grasp solid ground.

An alarming thought came to me just then—what if Hameed were sensing my apprehension? Would my hesitancy keep him from feeling what he needed to feel? I tried to manage the fear and hold it at bay while being as present as possible.

It didn't work all that well.

When we talked about the session the next day, he disclosed that he had felt my fear. His understanding had been supported by the session, he said, but the state of my consciousness had mildly affected him.

I sank into a sullen moment. I didn't want to hinder, but I simply hadn't been able to prevent or stop the feeling. Hameed understood, and what happened turned out not to be a serious impediment. Though he didn't feel like it was entirely his flavor, he knew that the fear he was feeling was also his own. He was able to acknowledge that and distinguish what was his from what was not.

It put me a little more at ease to know that I was not a deterrent to his process, but it became part of our ongoing dialogue to see how we were affecting each other. What we have discovered is that distinguishing his feelings from mine releases him from the enmeshment, which allows him to center in his own unfolding story.

In that same journal entry, he described how he saw his attachments to the gifts of essence and other pleasurable experiences as we stumbled into territory unknown either to us or to his friends and teachers. He felt invested in his desire to focus his study on this new kind of essence that was burgeoning.

> . . . partly because I wanted to establish my independence from teachers and partly because I wanted to understand the lataif more specifically. However, my need for recognition seeped in, and the desire for independence turned into wanting to be given the independence by recognition from outside, and my desire for understanding started to become attachment.

He goes on to describe the conflict between two impulses coming from different depths in him. One was his desire to know the truth of his experience and serve the truth in whatever way it guided him; the other was the desire to be validated, a need that every child wants a parent to meet in order to be himself and feel valued for who he is as he grows into being his own person.

The inner baby of the heart of paradise was growing and would gestate in his heart for a few more weeks as these issues came into greater clarity and understanding. As for me, I had issues to investigate in the aftermath of our session. What was *I* holding on to so dearly? What was I so afraid to let go of?

Not long after we wrapped up our session, Perry came through the front door as we were talking and having some tea in the living room. With a cheerful "Hi, Hameed," he gave him a hug, then kissed me on the cheek and sat down next to me on the couch to recount some of the offbeat characters he'd had to admit or treat at the hospital that day.

Talking when he got home was always part of the ritual. And there was always a lot to say.

Throughout the weekend, Perry and Hameed discussed the latest theories about the ego. Freud was now "old school," no longer regarded as the latest or greatest. Perry saw Sigmund Freud as a giant on whose shoulders many other theorists stood. Freud had laid the major groundwork regarding the unconscious and the tripartite theory of ego, id, and superego. This achievement was—and still is, in Hameed's and my opinion—not to be shrugged off merely because more refined theories now hold sway.

By the 1970s, object relations theories were all the rage in psychiatric circles. Margaret Mahler, in particular, added to our view. Object relations theory became a living reality for us, giving us a comprehensive, unparalleled understanding of the stages of development of the ego. We have yet to find another system that expresses this in such a specific and complete way. We now had a map to help us to understand the ego in its development, which gave us a language for our experience.

For example, the tension on his left side that Hameed had experienced in our session revealed what we call the ego line. The stiffness of this line is a tension pattern in the body that is the ego boundary in repose. It gets activated as boundary issues are stimulated. It is experienced by those who are dealing with the individuation process at the level of essence. As we understood the ego line more, it opened to become the boundary around the body that defines what each one of us is as a person distinct from other persons: "I am so-and-so, with such-and-such characteristics, who is distinguishable from you."

Mahler's theories about childhood separation and individuation matched our experience. We saw how each stage of the separation/individuation process is associated with a specific aspect of essence. It was a striking, elegant correlation. This filled out our understanding of the aspects that had shown up prior to our encounter with her work.

Most notable were the merging love essence, the red essence, and the will quality. The merging love is the bonding elixir in the shared orbit of mother and infant. The red brings in the perception of differentiation and the strength needed to fuel the process of separation; and the authentic expression of will emerges to support the child to begin to stand on her own, apart from mother and father. These aspects are the forces operating behind a child's outer expression as she moves through the stages of bonding, separating, and becoming her own person.

Hameed, Faisal, and I were each exploring issues related to the conflicts of separation and individuation. This gave us the chance to move through these issues again and regain contact with the essential underpinnings that had been lost in childhood. Now we could inquire from the perspective of essence into questions such as: Who are you? What am I in relation to what you are? Will love dissolve me? Can I love you and still be myself? If I am myself, will you still love me? Can I still remain myself if I am not willful? When I am in reaction to you, whom do you remind me of? What is real, and what is a veil from my past that I have made you wear for me?

Our inquiry wasn't conducted in the abstract, and we didn't have to venture far to engage it; we saw all relationships as venues for our investigation. The veils were hidden in plain sight like filmy substances over the world. I discovered that any situation could tell me what I needed to know about myself and how I saw reality. Old relics were tossed up from an ancient heap in me. Their stories needed to be remembered, told, sorted out, and clarified. I tried to look and listen to myself more judiciously, surrendering to the felt recall of unfinished childhood relationships and family situations. This was an ongoing process that became increasingly fluid, subtle, and refined, with cycles of intensity and cycles of freedom.

❖ ❖ ❖

The development of a human being begins within the family system, which incubates the child until she reaches adulthood. Each stage of the maturation process is necessary for the development of a well-rounded human being, and each displays a greater degree of individuation than the one before it. If the complex process of separation and development occurs without too much distortion, disruption, or distress, you get a kid with a heart, will, mind, and body of her very own—one relatively neat package ready for action in the business of navigating a worldly existence. On the other hand, the more the disruption, the more difficult it is to build a foundation for the subsequent stages of development, and compensatory ego strategies will be more defensive.

Navigating the physical world begins with an ego engaged in the process of learning how to live out its potential. Finding and creating rewarding work, building healthy family and social relationships, and learning what it means to be part of the larger society make adulthood itself a gestation period, a stage when the search for meaning and fulfillment can get stimulated.

The degree of estrangement from what we truly are, and how that occurs, varies from person to person, but we all end up growing apart from the essential nature we are born as and develop an ego. Hameed would often say, "There must be a reason for it. I don't believe that ego is an accident. Everything we know so far points to our usual experiences as limited versions or imitations of something real."

For many people, that feeling of alienation or purposelessness—or just getting downright tired of everything and wondering what else there is—becomes an existential crisis. It can arise as a yearning for something more—for God or truth or ultimate meaning. The dissatisfaction or sense of something missing expresses itself in myriad ways; you may be able to identify when and how this came about for you. But when this world will not provide what you long for, and you begin to recognize that and feel it in your guts, you take the step of becoming a spiritual seeker.

As we moved back in personal time through the developmental stages in order to understand them more, Hameed, Faisal, and I began to see that, indeed, the ego is not a mistake; it is merely the first stage of an individual's development. We realized it as a stage of learning about the world from within the world's milieu, which is a necessary step for functioning. It's like going to a new country where you will live for a while; you become immersed in the customs and the language so that you can function there. This view helped us to value the ego as a necessary step toward the completion of the design of the human being in the physical world.

What we take to be a person from the ego standpoint is only the beginning of the real person. Being *of* the world is ego. A being that is beyond the world but able to be within it, this is what a true person is—"in the world but not of it," as the Sufis say. The true human being is the transcendent formlessness entering the world and expressing itself through the access route of individual consciousness as a personal presence. In this understanding, the Diamond Approach appreciates both the Western value of the individual and the Eastern value of the transcendent: The real person of presence is one who is held in the loving arms of the universe, inseparable from it in its glory and purity, and who functions as an individual in the world, inseparable from essence.

If the ego is seen as the enemy, it will be regarded as something to bypass or transcend, and even to rid ourselves of. We are able to bypass or transcend the ego, but we can't get rid of it. We can, however, move beyond self-centeredness and ego concerns, and this is important for spiritual realization.

So instead of trying to transcend the ego or divest ourselves of it as though it were some demon, Hameed, Faisal, and I would do our best to understand it. As the ego became clarified, truth became distilled and remained as an authentic part of our being. Again and again, the three of us would pick up wherever we left off in our individuation process and let Inquiry take us further down the river of truth.

With the understandings we now had, the necessary properties of consciousness were released that allowed not only a healthy outer separation from mommy and daddy but also an inner separation that freed us from the heavy burden of introjection. The result of this radical kind of autonomy was illustrated one day when I was with my mother. I had just picked her up from a session she'd had with Hameed, and she asked me how I was doing. I started to tell her about the process I had been in about my mother, and my fear that I would lose my connection with her if she didn't approve of the things I did. As I talked, she nodded, and when I finished my tale she shrieked with delight, "I know exactly what you mean! I had the same thing happen with *my* mother!"

The thing is, I had been telling my mother the story as though she and I weren't even related. If someone had asked me who the woman sitting next to me in the car was, I would certainly have been able to answer, but at that moment we were simply Karen and June, two individuals who really liked each other as people. The freshness of personal presence had liberated us from our roles as mother and daughter. This was so much fun that we went out for a champagne brunch that Easter to celebrate the rebirth of our relationship in its new form.

Hameed, Faisal, and I saw how, as the personality became clarified through our understanding of its distortions, it gave way to the essential qualities that are the true unique characteristics of the individual. This was so liberating for me. I didn't have to reject my personality because I now recognized it as the doorway to my true individuality with its full-color spectrum of essential nature. After that, I felt even more kind and accepting toward myself. If defenses, resistances, or reactivity arose, I simply needed to attend to them, understand them, and listen to what the underlying message was.

Correlating the stages of development from infancy through childhood with the aspects of essence is one of the Diamond Approach's unique contributions. Of equal importance, this added to the understanding of the value and place of the individual on the spiritual journey. Comprehending ego from the object-relations standpoint was also a major stepping-stone to understanding personal presence.

Now it was easier to see how the action of essence can lead to a new and even more radical, but healthy, separation from family and the conventional world. This is a birth into a freshness that is unhindered by the overlays of our history upon ourselves or others. Not only are we freed into an immediacy of the now, but we also perceive and have real contact with others without their becoming walking stand-ins for mommy or daddy, brother or sister.

Recognizing the value of what is true and real is the amniotic fluid in which the divine person we each ultimately are manifests and grows. A mature heart is one that knows the true value of inner being and equally loves and values the individual who is an expression of it. This knowledge and attitude is necessary for the birth of a human being as a personal essence.

But we were also becoming more aware than ever that there's a big ocean of Being that we had only begun to touch. We wanted to be in the world, valuing human life and its everyday expression, and at the same time felt the draw inward to know the truth of what we were beyond that. If the truth we discovered revealed that individuality is illusory, fine. If it brought a completely different realization, that was also fine.

❖ ❖ ❖

Hameed was also pondering the question of how to integrate the impersonalness of the diamond knowledge with the personal. The impersonal states of the diamond presences rolled onto the margins of the personal, and the lataif had shown us how the qualities are necessary to live a human life. But what does it mean to be personal in a real way? And how do the essential qualities play a part in this process?

A journal entry in the fall of 1979 gives us a window into Hameed's gestating process around this question.

> A couple of weeks ago, I was interested in integrating the impersonal with the personal. Feeling some hardness in the heart, I experienced as if a hot rod went through the chest, burning front and back. After a while all I was aware of was a burning inside the chest.

The center of the chest, at the sternum, is the area of the green latifa. If one can tolerate the burning sensation, the green latifa can open up and deepen, sometimes becoming a pillar of bright, mentholated green or a soothing, deep balm that helps the burning subside. In this case, the burning was crucial to what happened next in an active phase of spiritual labor and birth.

> . . . and then an intuitive image of a pearl appeared. The pearl felt like a presence—as a coalescence of presence almost like personality, but not at all emotional—filling the body. Then there was a descent of precious fluids into the room. The pearl was bathed in the amber liquid of value and contentment and fulfillment.

The personal essence, "the pearl beyond price"—which we simply named "the Pearl"—had arrived, born of the love and value of the personal expression of truth as a human being.

The fullness that began in the left side of Hameed's chest (at the yellow latifa site) was the first stage of the pregnancy. The fullness then migrated to his belly, where the presence coalesced to roundness. His belly became physically distended, and then Hameed felt it extend beyond his body by several inches, as though he were eight or nine months pregnant.

What followed as the last stage of gestation and birth was the movement of the plump presence to the heart center in the middle of the chest, the site of the green latifa, where the "birth canal" burned with a searing, intense, yet deeply tender compassion as the offspring of the formless truth took form as a human being. The presence filled the whole of Hameed's chest and extended beyond the body boundary, then spread to encompass the whole body like a pearlescent living orb.

The birth was completed as it became embodied. It felt like a real body of presence in complete union with the physical. Each cell seemed to be plumped up with health and vigor, like so many tiny pearls.

We now understood how the nectars of paradise that we experienced during the prior spring were the waters that sufficiently matured the heart to develop the personal essence. The ripening of the heart is needed to set the right conditions for the Pearl to grow. Valuing ourselves as individuals was the step that inseminated the process.

If we had not recognized the primacy of the value of the individual, I doubt that the Pearl would have shown up in the very specific way that it did in our teaching. The personal element is a major contribution of the Diamond Approach to spiritual discourse. The pearl beyond price is described as "the Princess Precious Pearl" by the Sufis, and a pearl is sometimes referenced in Buddhism, but the distinct knowledge of this way of being was beginning to come forward in ways we had not heard about before. For example, the Pearl showed us how the separation and individuation process continues on even past the establishment of a healthy ego.

The Pearl's preciousness carries the inherent sense of "I am what I am," so after his experience of the Pearl, Hameed no longer felt the need to distinguish himself from other teachers or to compare himself with them. He settled into the presence of who he was and what his role actually was, without using anything else—whether it was other people's ideas or his own ideas of what he should be—as a guide. This is the true autonomy of the Pearl: living undefined by others' views and free of one's own mental definitions of oneself.

Hameed's autonomy also brought in the answer to his haunting question about Henry. It became evident that it was time for him to separate and venture out on his own to follow his destiny.

14 ❖ Westward . . . Whoa!

HAMEED HAD NOT ONLY discovered presence, he was intensely interested in understanding it. He knew that this presence of consciousness is a deep and fundamental truth. He knew in his bones that it was authentic. But he needed to know what it was—completely. He had experienced many aspects of presence and had even embodied diamonds, but he sensed that there was more to the story.

He also felt an urgency to find out *how* he could know unequivocally that what he felt without a doubt to be true was actually the truth. No one can dispute this felt sense of certainty in the heart—the heart that is in every human being and that *knows* the naked truth and resonates when truth is expressed, discovered, or revealed. But where does that level of certainty come from? Inference? Intuition? Logic? All of these . . . but that was not a satisfactory explanation for Hameed. He had to be certain. What is the irreducible feeling of truth that we feel in our being? Many people are familiar with the basic sense in the heart of knowing that something is true or false. But what is the source of that capacity?

Hameed had followed his truth sense for years, but now the understanding arrived. In the midst of his exploration into the question of truth, a golden diamond made itself known to him. It was very similar to the clear diamond but had the added feel of solid gold. It had a sharp crispness with a golden glow—a diamond made of solid gold and light as one presence, which invoked the felt sense of truth itself as an objective presence. Hameed already had experienced presence as strength, love, compassion, clarity, and so on. And he knew that presence was the source of all these affects that we feel innately or that are obvious to us as part of our usual knowledge. Now the golden diamond made it evident that presence was not an idea of the truth but rather the truth itself—the truth of existence. The unmistakable ringing in the heart— "Yes, this is true!"—has its roots in the ground of Being itself.

Truth is an intuition for many people, and it is usually relative to the accuracy of an idea or assertion about something. But as it rose up in Hameed's experience, he discovered the sense and feeling of truth itself apart from any specific content—simply as an unmistakable quality of consciousness. In the Diamond Approach, love for the truth is the central feature that guides the method along the way. "Truth for its own sake" means that truth is not for any end other than for each of us to uncover what is next to be discerned, revealed, and understood. This makes truth a dynamic revelation of knowledge and understanding.

Thus the solid gold of the heart truth leads to greater freedom. The perfect blend of warmth of heart and crispness of mind guides us beyond both the heart and mind from the subjective, conventional realm and into new vistas. Here it is understood that discovering the truth is not a single, static, or final experience but rather the action of love and discernment in a continuous expedition of rending the veils.

By pursuing this question in his usual unrelenting fashion, Hameed had arrived at a realization that highlighted his ongoing conflict with Henry. When he first felt this particular presence of truth in his heart, telling Henry about it was a turning point. When Henry refuted Hameed's experience, Hameed felt personally slighted, despite his clarity about what was true. Faisal and I became his allies in helping him through the maze to recognize and feel what remnants of ages past he might have conflated with his experiences with Henry. Writing in his journal about an inquiry made with Faisal, Hameed says, "Faisal helped me to see that Henry was castrating me, which makes me feel what it was like in childhood when my father would overpower me."

With this understanding, a new kind of will opened for Hameed, and the will latifa revealed a silvery, substantial quality that added to the white we had known before. It was more mature and solid, rising from his perineum and settling at home in his belly and solar plexus like liquid metal. In response to the need to stand up for himself, it provided the sturdy inner support for what was true in him—exactly what was needed for the essence of his manhood to emerge in a real way.

Henry's not supporting or seeing Hameed's truth was perpetuating falsehood. Although this was not Henry's intention, Hameed felt that the lack of support and encouragement from his teacher was in effect cutting him off from his power and strength—and thus from the inner reality he had realized. But the ongoing process of more fully embodying the personal essence gave Hameed the strength and true autonomy to see Henry from a centered place of contactful presence and truth, without overlays of the past on himself or Henry. He didn't have to fight for either recognition or autonomy.

Paradoxically, Henry had taught Hameed how to be strong and stand up for himself; now Hameed had to stand up to him. He felt gratitude for all the ways he had grown under Henry's strong, guiding hand, and he loved and valued Henry, but it was undeniable that the relationship was complete. It had fulfilled its potential for him. He would attend another couple of meetings and see what it was like to be with his peers and his teacher from an unreactive, balanced place of personal presence. Man to man.

During the week of December 25, 1979, Hameed left Henry's group. Not pushing against or shying away but taking the correct action that expressed what he had become.

As usual, Hameed and I were flowing down the river side by side in our own boats. The theme of separating and individuating was playing out in its own way for me. The pearly presence was beginning to challenge my sense of self in my work and relationships, even with Hameed. He and I had our own relational hurdles, though of a very different nature. So much of our time together was effortless and simple, but conflict is inevitable in any relationship that progresses in an authentic way. The love in our friendship was its indisputable trusted ground, but things were not always rosy between us. The closer we became, the more we rubbed against the other's edges.

I had led one of the evening groups for him as I sometimes did in between his trips to Colorado. At the end of each meeting, the cash that was collected would be placed in an envelope, which I would hand to Hameed when I picked him up at the airport. He'd look inside, see how much was in there, and hand me some or sometimes would buy me gifts for the work I had done.

This time I helped myself to some of the booty. The forty dollars I had taken would fill in the gap between what I had and what I needed in order to buy myself an item I had been eyeing. "He wouldn't mind," I thought. And I was expecting him to give me some, even felt that I deserved it.

When I picked him up at the airport and handed him the envelope, he noticed that it was thinner than usual. He peeked in, and his face twisted with puzzlement. "What happened?"

I shrank, then quickly puffed up with defensive confidence. "I used some of it," I said, feigning innocence.

"You mean you took it!" He sounded stern and displeased.

"Yeah, I suppose so," I said in a small voice.

"That is not okay. It is my money!"

The rest of the car ride home was thick with silence. I realized I had taken advantage of him, and now he was pissed. The cool distance between us was still there the next day when I tried to apologize. He would have none of it.

"Fuck you. You are just apologizing so I won't be mad at you."

Henry had taught him that an apology is usually an attack, in the sense of being a way to deflect attention away from an action without being accountable for it. I knew that Hameed was feeling attacked, but I also knew that my apology was sincere.

"I really mean it!" I looked at him with glaring eyes.

"It would be more honest if you understood why you did it!"

This was our first argument of any substance, and we were both staunchly dug in.

"Well, I will," I said, jamming my hands onto my hips, "but first you need to know it hurt me to see that I did something that made you doubt and mistrust me."

Hameed softened. "Okay. You got the point. Let's talk more later."

Hameed and I had disagreed on occasion and had lively debates about one concept or another, but we had just landed in our first head-on, bona fide fight. It happened during a time when I was learning new capacities, one of which was to assert myself. At the dance studio, my retail job, and interpersonally, I had become more confident and straightforward, though sometimes I resorted to my more timid side simply because I didn't know what to say or do. I could be real and quiet or else real and outspoken, but either way, I could also act out my unconscious. In asserting my place and value by taking money that was not mine to take, I was asserting myself, but I wasn't being straightforward. The feeling was, "I deserve it! And you should give it to me. And you love me, so it should be fine." So I just did it. This was acting out in a passive-aggressive way.

Very childish, I know. But not asking for what I needed or wanted or felt was fair was part of a pattern. The feeling inside was, "I shouldn't want anything"—when in fact I did. The truth is that I felt that if I asked for something, I would surely not get what I wanted, so I should just take what I could get now and deal with the consequences later. It was a setup for rejection; I brought in the very response I had been afraid of.

This incident was a deep teaching for me. I knew Hameed loved me. How had I invited the opposite? On the other hand, I had taken a bold action. I would often lose my ability to speak up when in a conflict. But this time, I had asserted myself by saying, "Hey, wait a minute! I do feel sorry!" in a way that was optimizing instead of recapitulating similar past events when I felt I shouldn't or couldn't say what I wanted to say once I was in touch with my true feelings.

I was also pushing against his authority, in the sense that he was in control over the group and the money. However, as we discussed it further, I saw that in acting out of my own need, I had disregarded his. We both had a point and a part in it. I had assumed complete acceptance from him no matter what I did, so I saw that I needed to raise the question of coming to another arrangement if I felt the one we had was unfair. And he saw that he needed to be clearer about what he was paying me.

Even though it was a difficult experience for both of us, I knew even as it was happening that our underlying connection would not be severed; I had a basic trust in the relationship, and the openness we always expected and enjoyed was merely temporarily out of order. But I still had a way to go to learn how to assert myself in a relationship with another person without acting out my unfelt needs, wants, and desires. How could I find a way to welcome these and understand them myself, first of all, and then find ways to communicate and dialogue about them?

Each relationship offers new opportunities to grow. What was different for me with Hameed was that the added element of essence brought in more intensity than in a usual friendship. I would see the import of this much later. But new energies were afoot now, and I was taking all kinds of risks, emerging more out of my shell, seeing new parts of myself being revealed. The essential realm was pushing my—and our—

limits further, upping the ante and challenging my personal sense of self both inwardly and outwardly. And developments on other fronts were contributing to the creation of the perfect storm.

❖ ❖ ❖

In June of 1980, Perry would finish his internship and residency, and he had to make a career decision that would determine our next course of action. We knew we didn't want to live in Denver forever, so we needed to make a choice and go with it. We decided to move to California, where he could find a job and slowly transition into a private practice as a psychiatrist.

I began to try on what it would be like to leave. I had been nourished in Colorado in profound ways. I had come to know so many fine people—to say nothing of all my new experiences of the inner world. These blessings had set my life on its true course.

I was confident that it was the right choice overall, so at first I didn't have much feeling about it. Little by little, a sense of emptiness seeped in with a mash of old and new textures. Then the tears came, with musty historical associations. Separation from the sweet, merge-y love nest with my mother had not happened at my preferred pace, and neither would this move. I always knew it was inevitable that Perry and I would eventually leave Colorado, but our plan to move had zoomed into action before I truly settled with the idea.

As the time to leave got closer, anxiety would hit me like a sucker punch as I went about my daily routines. Leave? What had I been thinking?

"Nothing to do but power through it," I thought. But then I began to regress back to a defensive insecurity, becoming grouchy at the slightest provocation and then whimpering like a child. Undigested feelings of my early years were activated.

According to my mother, as an infant I was content and easily satisfied, to the point where she would have to wake me up to feed me. She would sometimes leave me propped up in a corner of my crib or playpen where I could observe the household activities, and I was so undemanding that I would stay in that position until I was moved into another one.

My brother Erik was born when I was fifteen months old, just as I was making my first steps away from my mother. I could walk away from her with some confidence, but when I needed to walk back into her arms, they were occupied. I always had a giving nature, and she said I was happy to help and provide comfort and love to my younger siblings, and even to her. Nevertheless, this predisposition would be exploited in our relationship. Connection with her meant "helping her with the baby." I actually enjoyed that, changing my dolly diapers when she changed my brother's. But then, when I was three years old, my sister was born. Mustering my very sweetest tone of voice, one day I asked my mother, "Can we flush one of them down the toilet?" I'd had enough of the interlopers.

She picked me up in her arms and hugged me. "No, honey. They are here to stay." She got my dad to hang out with them for a while and took me into the kitchen, where we whipped up a batch of cookies together. My momentary disappointment was quickly replaced by the delicious, hot smell of oatmeal raisin cookies baking. They are still my favorite. As for my sibs, I got used to having them around and even began to see their presence as an asset. They became willing playmates in my lonely times.

Dealing with these feelings from childhood on top of everything else made the separation from Colorado a very bumpy process. My initial go-with-the-flow attitude had shifted to a scratchy frustration. And there was no one to throw down the toilet this time.

As soon as Perry was through with his training, we emptied the house of its extraneous contents and had a sale. Knickknacks, books, and miscellaneous kitchen items dotted the white sheets that were spread out on the lawn. Clothes on wire hangers hooked over a rope that was strung across the porch swayed in the breeze. I surveyed the bits and pieces of the last five years of my life and readied myself to let them go.

I glanced over at my sister, Kristin, who had come to help us with the moving sale. After visiting me on a holiday and falling in love with Boulder, she had made the trek in the spring of 1979 with her husband to settle there and start a family and, eventually, a career in law as a public defender. Now, less than a year later, we were leaving.

She sat quietly on the grass, her six-foot-tall frame slightly hunched, protecting her innocent heart. My big-sister affection made me want to go near. Touch her hand. Or say something. A shot of guilt stifled the impulse. I felt I was abandoning her. I was awkward and sad. I wish I could have just said, "I don't want to leave you."

In addition to leaving her behind, I was exiting a circle of friends—the kind who become part of you. I needed more time to get used to the idea of leaving. That time was not available.

I arrived early at Duncan's house for the meeting on the evening when I would announce my departure. Hameed had a dinner engagement and hadn't arrived yet. The front door was ajar and I slipped in, unannounced. I headed down the hallway leading to the living room, toward the sound of playful banter.

As I turned the corner, to my right were some heavy mahogany pocket doors common in early 1900s architecture. To get through the opening and into the group room, we had to step over one of the hard, backless wooden benches that lined all sides of the room.

My jaw dropped.

Four or five of the students were cheering on Carol Kircher, now Carol Carbon, who was gaily jumping over the bench. Using an upside-down broom as a substitute for a crutch, each person was taking a turn trying to hoist themselves over the bench with the grace Hameed always displayed when he floated over it so effortlessly.

I softened when I realized it was a way to show their admiration of him, like the times when they would show up at group with wooden toothpicks dangling from their mouths or fondling mala beads—Hameed's signature props. They barely noticed me as they continued their attempts to perfect flinging themselves over the barrier.

When it was time for me to speak about my plans, I was brief and matter-of-fact. As I explained the situation, I was surprised by my dry, emotionless tone. Following a short statement of the reasons why Perry and I were leaving, I said goodbye, ending with "I will miss you all."

I cloaked my emptiness by promising them I would be back to visit as soon as I could. I scanned the room for a plea, even a command—I wanted someone to tell me not to leave. Not now, anyway. I snuck a look around the room, avoiding eye contact. Some people looked sad. A tear appeared and made a pathway down my cheek.

The day to move arrived, and my big brother, Dave, who was always eager to help me whenever I needed it, loaded up the U-Haul. The trip across Utah and Nevada seemed to take an eternity, but Perry, Dave, and I finally made it across the state line and into California. The smell of pine and thick air shifted my homecoming into a sensed reality. My heart lifted, and I began to feel some optimism, even a little happiness, as we drew near my parents' condo in Mountain View.

The possibilities of what awaited me here started to brew in my mind. Hameed was spending more time in California now and had started a group there in 1979. I would have the opportunity to participate in some way I wasn't sure of yet, but I was open to whatever might happen. In my heart, that one thing felt right to me. My upbeat mood quickened even more as I anticipated new possibilities for this developing work that would become more widely known and appreciated. Faisal and I might have more opportunities to get to know each other as well, a welcome thought that shifted my sights even more into the bright zone.

Still, my excitement wasn't exactly mushrooming, muffled as it was by the not-fully-felt loss of all I had just left behind. Autonomy is an exciting proposition when it emerges in an internal exploration of truth, but out on the road heading away from so much that has been loved and treasured, it can be downright tough.

15 ❖ Diamond Buddies

OUR STAY IN RUSS AND June's small condo in Mountain View disrupted their routine, but they could not have been more welcoming. Even Mushka was received with love, and she adjusted well to this proxy for apartment living. Perry quickly landed a job at Valley Medical Center, and I spent the days scoping out the area and looking for houses. Whenever I was dissatisfied with this as a full-time occupation, I would take a drive up to the East Bay to see Hameed, generally for a day or two every couple of weeks.

One day, with no houses to see and nothing that had to be done, I was lounging around and decided to take the drive up to see my buddy. When I rang him up, he cheerfully acceded to my request to come on short notice. He would meet me after he finished work at one o'clock—and Faisal would be there, too.

My energy surged. I made my way there in record time. Marie was on her way out when I popped in the door. We had a quick hug. Catching up would have to wait.

Waiting on the slick leather couch in the den for my inner-travel companions, I melted in a half twist toward its ample back, my chin cradled in my folded arms. One foot hung off the edge and the other rested on the soft rust-and-cream Persian carpet. Soon I was lost in the tree-dense view through the picture window . . . carried to a dreamy land, riding the waves of the backlit fog as it billowed through the valley. The mid-July sun struggled through the fog to make her brilliant entrance, only to be swallowed up repeatedly.

My attention was reeled back to reality by the energetic voices of two men coming up the front stairs. When the front door opened, I heard Faisal saying something to Hameed about going up to Odiyan, Tarthang Tulku Rinpoche's center in Cazadero.[1] I untwisted myself to greet them as they walked into the den. "Hey, Kran!" Hameed said with his award-winning grin. His uncrutched arm extended out to hug me. I got up, responding to the overture.

"Hey, guys."

"Hi, there," Faisal said shyly. We exchanged a friendly hug in the middle of the room, and he turned to address Hameed, who had taken his seat behind his big oak desk.

"They've just completed a beautiful stupa up at Odiyan," Faisal said, "so there's going to be some kind of celebration. It's a closed event, but Farouq has been invited, and Rinpoche told him he was welcome to bring a couple of friends along. Want to go?"

"I wish I could," Hameed replied, "but I have a group to lead this weekend."

I looked at Faisal coyly, hoping he might consider me as a companion for the trip. He returned my look with a knowing shimmer and said with a giggle, "Do *you* want to go?"

"I'd love to," I chirped. I had never been to Odiyan, but was keen to see it.

Faisal looked pleased. I couldn't quite tell if he was happy I was coming or happy he had made me glad. Either way, I was tickled and saw it as an indication that we were finding our way into a friendship beyond our mutual connection with Hameed.

"Why don't we head down to the café and get a bite to eat?" Hameed suggested. I could almost see the image of a steaming-hot latte in his eyes. It was refreshing to change venues for our discussions, carrying the inner world around with us to various spots. I preferred our car rides, where the shifting scenery complemented our spirited discussions. But cafés were a favorite of the guys, and our time was limited today, so we hopped into Hameed's '68 white Mercedes—a surprise gift from Marie for his birthday the previous year—and off we went to discuss the rising tides of consciousness over a cappuccino for Faisal, a latte for Hameed, and multiple cups of herbal tea for me.

As I drove up to the appointed spot to meet Faisal for the drive up to Cazadero a few days later, I felt tingly all over, like a ten-year-old about to be taken to Cirque du Soleil for the first time. Farouq Aqeel, who had been part of the Kuwaiti group of friends attending UC Berkeley with

Hameed and Faisal, shared their spiritual interests, and they had been discussing with him over the past couple of years some of what we had been discovering.

Farouq was kind and easygoing. A smattering of jokes, idle chatter, and some interesting tidbits about our personal lives filled the two-hour trip north, and we pulled up just in time for the main event at sundown. As the gong sounded, we unfolded ourselves from the car and joined the crowd as it spilled into the clearing near the 113-foot stupa and organized itself into a linear stream to begin the procession. I noticed the Rinpoche easing into his seat near the entrance and positioned myself between Farouq and Faisal to become part of the slow-moving, oversized centipede—comprising about 150 segments and twice as many arms—which circumambulated the stupa once and then entered inside.

The immense presence of the ten-ton prayer wheel at the center saturated the atmosphere inside the turret-shaped building, which felt spacious. Arms and hands rose and fell in silent waves to palm the enormous whirring cylinder that spun compassionate blessings out to the universe for the betterment of all humankind. The deep drone-chanting of many voices blended to become one unified sound.

Inside and out, through and around the stupa, the procession moved along the circular pathways surrounding the prayer wheel and the space just outside. The pace slowed to a halt whenever the people segments dominoed into one another, starting up again as the space stretched between them.

I had been trying not to stare whenever I passed in front of the Rinpoche, but on one of my entries into the stupa, I couldn't help fixating on him. Slightly reclining on one arm, he sat like a stout, relaxed garden Buddha in his aluminum-and-woven-plastic lawn chair. He was motionless except for his eyes, which smoothly scanned the crowd. The last time I had seen Tarthang Tulku was during a meditation day with him in 1971, while I was still in art school. He was shorter now than I remembered him, but his cocoa-colored skin, round face, and lidless almond eyes matched my memory of him. No fancy robes, no throne— just a regular guy in jeans and a T-shirt. His presence, considerably larger than his appearance, exuded gravity and depth.

Each time I passed by, I wanted him to notice me. I wondered why.

It seemed to me that the attention was misplaced—I should try to see where *he* was . . . I was on a mission to learn!

As my focus shifted away from myself, a larger view opened. I had been identifying with something that kept me tucked in the envelope of my smaller self. Now that my awareness had allowed me to slip out, my curiosity was kindled. I wanted to feel into the Tulku's presence. Getting a sense of who he was would go hand in hand with letting myself be molded by the whole environment for the few hours that I would be there.

We continued to walk as dusk transformed almost imperceptibly into night. Quiet, black spaciousness calmed my mind into profound peacefulness. Sensation, feeling, and thought were absorbed into its depth, and I lost track of time and space. The next thing I was aware of was of approaching the Tulku again. I knew my body had been walking, but for some unknown span of time *I* had disappeared.

The night grew deeper as we continued to snake through and around the building. As I walked, I peered into the Tulku's state with fresh intention. During the past few years, my subtle vision had become more acute, so I could see beyond the energetic dimension and into deeper levels of presence itself. I was not completely confident about this but had come to appreciate the fact that I was still learning. My bodily sensing capacity was becoming more developed too and provided a good balance. I had been learning the importance of trusting what I get in the moment, leaving room for my perceptions to build and change over time, and remaining open to other people's takes on a person or situation.

Rinpoche's inner peacefulness was visible on the surface of his skin, like an inky emanation blurring his body edges into the night. The quietude he exuded invited me to drop into its great belly of silence, erasing the remaining wrappings of myself with a dark, pristine spaciousness.

It was close to midnight by the time my companions and I found our way to our rustic accommodations. I had a dreamless sleep and in the morning felt deeply rested and awake. Discussing our experiences on the ride home, the three of us discovered that we had all felt an utterly quiet innerness; but the experience seemed to have been slightly different for each of us. Faisal agreed that the blackness had been dominant in some way, and that its stillness prevailed throughout the night and into the morning, with various permutations.

I melted into my private space in the back seat and watched the world go by as Faisal and Farouq's words mingled with the hum of the engine. Continuing to marinate in the experience, I noticed the presence of clarity beginning to dominate, yet remaining intermingled with the darkness.

This was only one experience of many we had of spiritual teachers in the '80s. Faisal, Hameed, and I often went to lectures, workshops, and seminars in Berkeley and beyond. We had an intellectual interest in learning about other teachings but were also curious about how these interfaced with the specific experiences we were having, and how they might contrast with or add support to the knowledge we were acquiring. We assumed that these teachers would be able to offer some insight into the realms that were showing up for us.

Our learning process was like collecting pollen. We would get the soft, fragrant grains all over ourselves and inhale them into our consciousness, then carry the pollen back to our hive for investigation. The way our inquiries unfolded helped us understand from within our own perspective our experiences of other teachings and transmissions. This wasn't our intention; it happened organically.

The honey made in our hive was permeated with the aromas and flavors of the various flowers we encountered, but we were growing our own blooms too. We discovered that our garden was not a collection of imports that had made their home in our soil; our plants were indigenous to this new world we had discovered and were species unlike any others. Through our investigative tending, they were blooming in glorious colors and scents. It was becoming more obvious that our work was a uniquely unfolding spiritual path. The experiences that followed would verify this. Through its main messenger, Hameed, our approach was about to make itself distinct from other teachings.

Some of the pollen from the Odiyan experience got spread the following Monday when Faisal met with Hameed. According to Hameed, while Faisal was telling him about the event—not yet mentioning any particular state of consciousness—Hameed spontaneously began to have certain experiences. Faisal was unaware of what was happening at first. Through their colloquy, however, the honey from the encounter with the Rinpoche started to be produced. The groundbreaking knowledge that was awakened would lead to one of the central means for teaching the Diamond Approach. From Hameed's journal entry on July 28, 1980:

> In talking with Faisal about his time with Tarthang Tulku Rinpoche over the weekend, I started getting some of Rinpoche's influences. First there was an intense activity in the forehead. The substance was clear. Then it became obvious that the diamond in the head was operating. It felt as though the diamond moves in a channel across the head, backward and forward. The more it moves forward, the more there is focusing in the mind.

He goes on to describe how mental functioning and visual perception and focus are rendered more precise and vivid by this presence. Hameed detected the sensation as very focused intensity. His journal reports that as they explored the diamond more thoroughly, Faisal saw a blue/green presence in the diamond as well as the clear aspect.

The emergence of the blue/green gem was the spearhead of a larger and more elaborate structure of diamonds. Imagine a diamond sparkling as it rotates; some facets might appear green and others blue, while in others the colors overlap. At least, this is the way I saw it, though others may have perceived it differently. In any case, these colors are significant because the total opening of the green latifa, centered in the middle of the chest, leads to the capacity for selfless compassion, and the blue is the relaxed mind and the presence of knowledge as consciousness. The blending of the heart and the mind as one unified, functioning center became a conduit for the first vehicle of the teachings that would carry the wisdom of revelation of our path, our method, and the specific knowledge of Being from the vantage point of presence itself.

While working with students the next day, Hameed began to feel some activity in his head, which continued throughout the day and into the evening. Then the sensation increased and became painful. It continued to mount and then subsided slowly over the next few hours. He thought it might be a reaction to a presence emerging.

> When the headache left, there was a tremendous force pressing on my forehead. I was dizzy and couldn't focus. I saw that I should not

try to focus on anything and instead should let go of directing the experience in any way.

Hameed went to bed without understanding what was happening. The next morning he continued his inquiry alone.

When I woke up in the morning, I felt a tremendous presence filling my whole body. It felt like clear substance, but not exactly.

He remained aware of the clarity through the day, and then he and Faisal reconvened and continued the inquiry. Faisal was witness to it and assisted Hameed in the unveiling.

I saw, with Faisal's help, a huge column going through me as if descending from above the head, down through to the perineum, and then getting wider to encircle the whole body. It was the substance of the Void, of nothing, of space itself.[2]

Hameed's process reflects the fact that when this particular diamond vehicle emerges, it arises most often within an atmosphere of clear space. This is a powerful opening of electrifying clarity that enables the diamond consciousness to settle and, if conditions are favorable, to begin to function.

In the experience of boundless space that is characteristic of certain states achieved through various Eastern meditative disciplines, the practitioner transcends the confines of ego identity. The three of us were familiar with this experience, but the clear space that now arose was a channel within our individual consciousness, without the sense of vastness. By putting pressure on the ego's bounded state, this space, rather than producing an experience of transcendence, would now begin to expose the layering of concepts and self-images that amalgamate to form the ego identity.

Now that this column of space had opened the way for this diamond vehicle to descend, the exploration of inner space kicked into higher gear. The diamond vehicle had already been functioning at warp factor one—but behind the scenes. Now, at warp two, its operation was becoming obvious as the action of the multicolored conglomerate of diamondized presences.

About five days after Hameed and Faisal had their pivotal explorations of the diamond consciousness, I was sitting in the living room of my parents' condo, biding my time as I waited for the real estate agent to call. My mind was wandering, curious about what was going on with the guys. Just then the phone rang, and I had the feeling it was Hameed. It was.

As he filled me in on the latest news from beyond, the description of the experience he had with Faisal registered immediately as being of quite a different order than I had known before. I was picking up on his excitement, but it was more than that. I was glued to the phone as Hameed's voice came through the receiver and reverberated through my body. A suspended sense of the world took me back to those days as a kid when I would lie spread-eagled on the grass, feeling the soft, verdant freshness all around . . . my gaze unfocused . . . absorbed into a cloudless blue expanse. Nothing demanding my attention. No emotional churning.

My head felt like someone had unscrewed the top and let the sky in. The love of discovery and freedom sang in my heart. Just then, a blue/green jewel emerged as a dense, lucid presence in my torso. A natural ease filled my body as a presence of precision and kindness unified and set my heart free.

"My God . . . we can use the mind to *free* us from the mind—and the mind can be part of freedom too! This makes so much sense, Hameed."

My first entry into this new mind realm was only a taste of the possibilities to come. It would be a while before this diamond presence actualized itself more completely. A lot of mucky self-images and identifications still coated its shining surface. I would have to deal with the bugs on the windshield before I could see reality from the diamond perspective. I had my work to do.

As our investigations unfolded, it became apparent that this vehicle of wisdom had been implicitly guiding our process all along; it was the wizard behind the curtain, revealing the understanding and knowledge that was arising. We had used the mind's capacity for discrimination, clarity, and synthesis in our search for truth but didn't recognize that there was a presence that was the source of it all. The diamond-structured consciousness made its debut to teach us how this vehicle, which uses the capacities of the mind for inner investigation and knowing, effectively expands our usual mental operations to include more dimensions of the human psyche.

We also found that remaining open is fundamental to the operation of this new kind of intellect, which can traverse and function within any level of experience, information, or knowledge. Unless one has an open mind and a love for knowing the truth, this diamond consciousness will not operate. It will remain only an experience of presence. On the usual level of thinking, if we take the position that we know with certainty that something is true, then we won't let in any new or conflicting information that might shift or deepen our understanding. This doesn't mean that what we know is wrong, but it might be incomplete, and we won't find out either way unless we are willing to consider new or different data.

Love for the truth liberates our natural curiosity and leads the way into deeper levels of discovery. And the more open and available our mind is to novel connections and other ways to comprehend, the more the process of understanding can become experimental and playful. When we are no longer locked into a rigid adherence to position and point of view, learning can be fun and lighthearted. Then every new vista becomes a playing field of opportunity.[3]

The diamond vehicle sometimes appeared as an inner spaceship that moved around and inside our physical bodies, unimpeded by the usual material obstructions because it flew through another kind of space. We had donned spacesuits of light a while ago and were venturing beyond the world we had known. Now we had a vessel to show us the way.

For this inner spaceship to find its proper landing spot, the three of us each had to look into our ideas and beliefs about the capacities and limitations of our intellect and mental processes, so that the presence could become functional and integrated. The diamond structure would vanish and reemerge, revealing new tidbits of insight each time it reappeared. My curiosity and love of learning bought me a good seat on this vehicle. I had the right orientation, but it would take some time before I would develop enough to enter the cockpit.

❖ ❖ ❖

One day, about four months after his July journal entries, Hameed understood for the first time the central importance of the experience he'd had during the motorcycle accident thirteen years earlier. As the memory of the accident was crisply recalled in his mind, he saw that he had become a body of light-filled, faceted gems of consciousness. The experience guided him to turn his life around and move toward a single purpose: to become an instrument for the teaching. Now his capacity was so expanded that he was having full-blown experiences of this body of wisdom, which filled his physical form and expanded beyond it.

Hameed had already experienced many essential aspects in their purity as glittering jewels. Now he was experiencing an entire structure in the incandescent colors of all the aspects of essence, in cut shapes of stunning clarity. They appeared together as a unit, supported by a base of solid gold topped by a brilliant point. The gleaming, faceted light—exquisite and refined—was unmistakably otherworldly but indisputably real. Hameed was no longer just feeling the *effects* of this activity in the functioning of his heart and mind; he now knew the *source* of the capacities it was infusing into him.

In his journal, Hameed initially referred to this structure as the diamond entity because at first it felt like a visitation of some kind that entered into him. Soon this new structure of presence came to be called "the Diamond Body," largely due to its body of diamonds but also because it held the body of knowledge that was developing into a distinct teaching.

Because the arising of the new blue/green diamond had occurred right after the Odiyan visit, Hameed often attributed it to the transmission from Tarthang Tulku. I got curious about that while writing this book and asked him what the relationship was between the Rinpoche's transmission and the revelation of the Diamond Body. This was his reply:

"It is not certain. When I last saw him in 2013 and talked to him about the Diamond Body we thought had come from him, he responded as if he had no idea what I was talking about. But even if I didn't catch the state of diamond consciousness from the Rinpoche through Faisal and you, whatever permeated us at that time functioned as a catalyst. Perhaps in their tradition, there is something like it but they experience it in a different way. His writings show a discernment that speaks to his keen intellectual faculty."

"And what about your experience with the Karmapa?"

"Well, a transmission from him surely happened. But it had the effect on me of the descending of presence, which is not the pure, clear light of emptiness that the Karmapa supposedly transmitted. Instead, the intense experience with the Karmapa seemed to stimulate the descent of pure presence, which is the focused consciousness of our path. Years later, I went through all the barriers that stood in the way of the states of clear light and emptiness. Many states of consciousness also arose that are typically not taught or emphasized as part of the Kagyu tradition but became the levels and dimensions of the Diamond Approach Work."

As I learned more about the Diamond Body, with its graceful, economical, yet sublime mental operation, I could feel my mind pulsing with the vibrancy of lucid focus and extreme precision. The freedom of cognition sent me soaring to new heights. Concepts looked to me like light beams with space all around them. Greater clarity arose in my capacity for subtle seeing. Even Hameed, whose primary modality has always been to *sense* Being, began to have greater capacity for inner seeing. And I became more attuned to the subtleties of sensing presence. Our expertise was beginning to even out.

The Diamond Body opened the way for all the other vehicles that would follow.[4] This first of the diamond vehicles to appear is the flagship for the journey through the jeweled portal and into the center of the cosmic vortex of the teaching. It allows essential knowledge and conventional mental processes to function simultaneously, making possible a type of insight that is inaccessible when we are functioning in only one or the other. Such a capacity brings about the direct recognition that the spiritual and the conventional are one continuum—that consciousness is unified, even at the individual level.

No unaided mind or heart could have come up with what we were discovering; something not of this world was teaching us. Being itself is the source of all teachings, and the teaching of the Diamond Body was no exception. This kind emissary from the invisible universe worked through us to its own end, slowly showing us who we are and where we really came from.

Sometimes I teased the guys because their Kuwaiti accent made it sound like they were saying "diamond buddy." And that's what the Diamond Body felt like—the perfect, true spiritual friend who is kind and responsive to our true desire for freedom and learning. It is the guiding light of revelation and joyous discovery, fueled by a pure love for truth. However, this vehicle has no interest in the spiritual dabbler. The necessary attitude to draw this guiding presence to yourself is a passionate love for the truth, a longing to know what is real.

You yearn to get to the other side of the ocean, but you see no boat to take you across. The helpless feeling of not knowing how you will get there creeps in. At first you feel that you *can't* know. It's humbling. But it is possible to accept that helplessness, and if your love to know is strong enough, it pulls you beyond anything your mind already knows. You are left with a deep hunger for the other shore and a thirst for what only the intimate knowing of Being can provide. But the love of the truth for its own sake must eclipse the desire for selfish goals and attainments if the Diamond Guide is to show up. Then, and only then, can the energy of that love vibrate an opening through the fog, welcoming the guiding vehicle of knowledge to enter.

This attitude is described precisely and eloquently in the Sufi story known as "The Land of Truth." Khidr is the secret guide of the Sufis— the inner guidance—who remains hidden until the correct atmosphere of heart allows his approach. Listen as he responds to the call of the seeker:

"I will grant you one desire," said Khidr.

"I wish to know why I have failed in my search and how I can succeed in it," said the man.

"You have all but wasted your life," said Khidr, "because you have been a liar. Your lie has been in seeking personal gratification when you could have been seeking Truth."

"And yet I came to the point where I found you," said the man, "and that is something which happens to hardly anyone at all."

"And you met me," said Khidr, "because you had sufficient sincerity to desire Truth for its own sake, just for an instant. It was that sincerity, in that single instant, which made me answer your call."

Now the man felt an overwhelming desire to find Truth, even if he lost himself.[5]

After these latest adventures with my diamond buddies, I was flying high with excitement. But as I was patting myself on the back, a question slipped through my hubris and pushed the pause button. How sincere *was* I? What was I actually willing to give—or give up—for truth?

16 ❖ Unsettled in California

As HAMEED CONTINUED to discern the purpose and results of various meditations and other practices, important supports for Inquiry were refined and incorporated into the Work. Of the three of us, Hameed was the most stalwart in his meditation practices, as far as I could tell. He was already spending several hours daily in meditation and deep contemplation, in addition to exploratory conversations with Faisal and me.

Compared with him, I was lazy—more like inertia in motion. I was whirling with energy most of the time and it was difficult for me to sit still, so I avoided meditation. Since I've always been curious by nature and in touch with my emotions and sensations, Inquiry came naturally to me; I could do it as I engaged in many of my daily tasks. And I was stepping into exalted states just walking down the street. So why bother to meditate? The answer landed hard as I bumped into the limitations dished up by my slothfulness.

At some point, Hameed found that he needed even more solitude than before, away from the influence of anything or anyone else. Although he frequently made himself available for Faisal and me, he guarded his time alone ferociously. One evening, Perry and I were invited to a dinner party at Hameed and Marie's. In the spacious, sparsely furnished living room, Marie had spread a large tablecloth on the carpet and set out her best dishes, wine glasses, and silverware. Sitting on the floor to eat was like being back home for the Kuwaitis, who comprised the majority on the guest list of about ten friends.

Marie had spent the entire day, plus a chunk of the day before, cooking. Food was a big part of Hameed's social lexicon, and Marie had learned how to make some of Hameed's favorite Middle Eastern dishes. She prided herself in doing it just right, and I admired her ability as both a skill and an act of love for him. The meal was beautifully displayed on the flowered cloth—huge round platters heaped with crunchy, crusted rice called *hakuka,* tureens of *dakkus* tomato sauce to top it, and wide, shallow bowls brimming with savory stews and vegetables.

As the discussion meandered between news from Kuwait, politics, and the latest movies, Hameed sat cross-legged, quietly munching his chicken stew and offering the occasional nod or comment. He seemed to be engaged in the conversation, but his mind must have been chewing on something else. Slowly, he withdrew from the crowd. While others were eagerly scooping up second helpings, he rose from the "table" without a word and disappeared into the other room for the rest of the evening.

Hameed has never been wed to social convention; it is easily forfeited if it interferes with the task at hand. He was on a mission, and it was driving his actions. Not only was he working to open to his own inner world, he was tapping into a universe that was displaying itself as a teaching. But his lack of decorum was driving Marie nuts. After a few more incidents, she asked him to at least excuse himself when he needed alone time; he understood that this was important to her and made an attempt to be polite.

As it become increasingly apparent that inner, solitary abiding is the hallmark of essential autonomy, I came to understand that I, too, needed time apart from anyone or anything else—including the expectations embedded in any teaching or social conventions. Hameed was simply braver in acting on the impulse to be by himself when it arose, and it was prudent at times to follow his example.

Sometimes Hameed even needed a stretch away from Faisal and me. His sensate capacity was well developed by then; he could feel the states of everyone around him and detect how in touch with themselves they were. He perceived people in their totality—both in their states of illuminated consciousness and in the occluded personality. So when my unconscious, or Faisal's, became too activated around him—manifesting as tensions before we were aware of the content that had stirred them up—Hameed felt that as a physical contraction inside himself.

This sensitivity is one way we are able to understand our students from the inside out. It is like wearing another person's consciousness for a time and feeling what it's like to be inside their perspective, from their hats down to their underwear. All three of us had this capacity in varying degrees—it was part of how we "read" the states of the teachers we received transmissions from.

Another area of sensitivity concerned giving and receiving feedback, which turned out to be a growing edge. Working things out between us was quite different from helping one another to recognize the inner truth of what we were. All three of us were beginners in the art of communication, especially about interpersonal difficulties, so it was not always easy to bring up disagreements and upsets with one another. It was obvious, however, that none of us could see ourselves completely. For the work to flourish, we had to rely on one another for checks and balances.

I think it's fair to say that we each got caught up in defensive or resistant patterns from time to time. Hameed made his fair share of mistakes and unskilled moves along the way, with us and with students, but accepted himself as someone who, like anyone else, could get reactive or be unaware of the implications of his actions. But he saw his limitations as opportunities to learn.

When we called each other on our issues, blockages to various states, or emotional reactions, sometimes our feedback was offered skillfully, with clarity and kindness, and at other times, one or another of us was too blunt. Even so, we were better off being not so nice than saying nothing at all. Interpersonal conflicts seemed important mainly when they interfered with our inner realization, so they were not in themselves our focus. Our emphasis would eventually shift more toward using the skills of communication and human relationships as part of the practice of being effective in the world, functionally and interpersonally.

We were excitedly budding into ourselves, feeling the satisfaction of the deeper autonomy and self-confidence that comes with the discovery of our authentic personhood. The sense of liberation was wonderful, but we had a ways to go before we could say that our relational intelligence was spiritually integrated and mature. Life kept dishing out perfectly crafted situations that forced us to reevaluate ourselves and balance our priorities. Sometimes I felt like I was on a seesaw.

Hameed, Faisal, and I were like silk threads weaving through the experiences that brought into relief the rich textured fabric of the teachings. We would stand back and watch the beauty of the patterns emerge as living knowledge articulated itself. This shared focus naturally brought us to a deeper intimacy and gave me the opportunity I had been looking for to get to know Faisal better. When he was in Colorado, which was about half the time, our dynamic triangle was missing a side—but not in spirit. Developing my relationship with Faisal did become more intermittent as he spent more time there, but the momentum of our friendly affiliation continued.

❖ ❖ ❖

Hameed did not get his PhD in Reichian work until 1978, but he had been offering private sessions as a Reichian therapist in San Francisco since 1976. Some people went to him specifically for that, and others to "work on themselves," which was the order of the day back then. Explorations using the same techniques that had been so successful in Colorado were woven into the sessions. Hameed's special approach had gained a reputation among bodywork and spiritual practitioners; they— as well as friends of his who knew he had begun to work with people in a unique way—sent people to him.

As I understand it from some of the first California students in the School in the '70s, they had no idea what he was doing. When I first met Jessica Britt, who is now a principal teacher in the Diamond Approach, she was a quiet, inward being with a mystique that would develop into a dauntless power. She once told me: "I went to him thinking he was a Reichian therapist. I had been in training with Curcuruto myself and wanted to pursue work with a good Reichian practitioner. Hameed never said a word about being a spiritual teacher. But I realized he was asking me questions no one had ever asked me before, such as 'What does the emptiness feel like?' or 'What is the texture of the feeling?' So I started to pay closer attention to what he was directing me to." Many of his other clients also became intrigued by the effects of Hameed's skillful guidance and began to see that it was of a different order than what they expected or had experienced before.

Because the issues of daily life were used to enter into the deeper experiences of self, it was easy for those who didn't have the whole picture to frame what he was doing as therapy when describing it to others. Soon Hameed's work had the reputation of being the best therapy in town.

In January 1979, while I was still in Denver, Hameed invited some of his private clients to participate in a group he was starting. Word got around, and some folks who had been in the SAT groups in the early '70s joined as well. Marie began to refer clients of hers whom she felt might benefit from attending the group Hameed was starting. Jessica Britt was among those who accepted Hameed's invitation to join the group to supplement her private work with him. Years later, when I asked her about the experience of the first meeting, she described it as "the oddest group I had ever been to . . . it was just too strange," she said, gesturing sideways with her big brown eyes and shaking her head slightly to emphasize the point. It seemed that nothing of any substance happened, so she didn't go back until it was required as a prerequisite for the teacher training.[1]

Janet Green, who is now a teacher in the School, tells the story of what the first meeting was like for her:

A few months after I started to do sessions with Marie, she had to go to England to help her sister with a new baby. The whole reason I was in California was to work on myself, so I asked her what she thought I could do while she was gone. She told me her husband was starting a group, so I went.

The first meeting was over-the-top odd. A small group of people sat in a circle in dead silence for forty-five minutes . . . or more! No explanation, no introduction—nothing. After that long silence, Hameed said, "Well, I guess we should hear from everyone about why they are here, what each of you is wanting."

I remember telling him that the summer before, for a two-week period, I'd had an experience of quiet, calm serenity and the experience had gone away. And that nothing I could do could make it come back, and I wanted it again. I thought I saw Hameed nod slightly. I felt like he understood me. Nobody had ever asked me what I wanted, what I was looking for. I had never been around other people who felt anything like me—looking for something, dissatisfied, hungry.

The impact? In the subsequent meetings, when people started having essential experiences, I realized we were having experiences that most people I knew didn't have; but it took me a couple of years before I really got that I was doing spiritual work. I only knew I was in the presence of something true, real—and I had to be around that.

Hameed says he was explicit at that time about what he was teaching, calling it inner exploration, or essential work, or "learning to be in the world but not of it." It seemed obvious to him, but it was vague to most everyone else. It was important to Hameed that the participants got on board experientially and valued presence as a felt knowledge, so he began to talk more about presence and provided the students with meditations, chanting, and various practices to supplement the understandings that were arising in them.

Because "spiritual" had become a buzzword carrying a weighty sum of connotations and trappings, Hameed refrained from using it to describe the Work. But what was explicit for him remained an enigma for others for quite a while. The people who were benefiting from the group and spreading the word about it didn't know what else to call it except spiritual. Eventually he would have to use the term to differentiate what we were doing from purely psychological work.

During its first year, the small East Bay group met in a room atop a garage that had a glass dome over it, so the meeting place was aptly named "the observatory" by the group. Hameed also started to see students there for private sessions as he slowly made the transition from his office in San Francisco to the East Bay as his center of operation.

Word of mouth generated the interest of just the right students. For many years, there was no formal advertising for the group, and very few workshops were open to the public. The group fluctuated in numbers for about a year, then settled into a solid fifteen members and slowly grew from there, many of whom would become teachers in the School.[2]

It would be a couple of months before I made an appearance in the group. I was busy living the middle-class dream. In August 1980, two months after our arrival, Perry and I bought a house in the Santa Cruz mountains above Los Gatos. The serene rural setting invited a slow and quiet life. Our neighbors were the Douglas firs, the redwoods, the bay trees, and all sorts of oak. This was how I had often imagined living— near my big brother, not far from my parents, and only a twenty-minute drive from the ocean I had been sorely missing in Colorado. Perry was now setting his sights on starting a private practice before long. This was heaven. Or so I thought.

As an old (at twenty-nine) hippie turned fashionista, I still had conventional ideas about the right kind of life for me. I loved Perry and liked being married and thought I would be happy with a life of ease. I had time on my hands and felt spacious and simple. I could read, swim, paint, and hike for hours. I was free to contemplate and investigate. I had no ambition to be much more than a dancer, artist, and housewife. Our sexual life was very satisfying for us both, which was an important part of relating for me. What more could I want?

I might have saved a great deal of heartache had I taken the time to think things out more completely. As it was, my inner compass was spinning. Pulled in different directions, I kept losing track of true north. My experience with the Rinpoche seemed light-years away. Although I would recall it intermittently, it was like watching a movie trailer of some other me in another universe. The opening to depth with the Tulku had jostled me so thoroughly that I rebounded and clung to the known world more strongly to stabilize myself.

I loved creating beautiful, contemplative home environments, but soon it became evident that homemaking wasn't sufficient. My need for intimate relationship, security, and comfort were demanding drives guiding the flow of my choices away from the inner life that was burgeoning in me.

I also hadn't considered the distance from Berkeley. After all, I had just moved two thousand miles closer to Hameed! How close did I need to be? The phone seemed a fine mode of communication at first. I knew I could drive up to see Hameed as often as I wanted, and he knew he was welcome to visit our new home anytime. But I soon realized that when I was with Hameed, or with both him and Faisal, the focus on our inner states would return with more amplitude, then fade into the background until the next phone call or visit, when it would amp up again.

I was talking with Hameed on the phone every day or two and driving up to Berkeley every other week or so, but Hameed was feeling that he couldn't always confide in me. I would learn much later that he was not consistently able to connect in a satisfying way, especially when he could sense the emptiness in me and some of the inner conflicts about my life that were starting to show up.

Hameed's closeness to other people is directly proportional to how aligned they are to the truth in themselves and how committed they are to living an inner authenticity in their outer life. Other factors such as proximity and availability are part of the mix, but one's central purpose is paramount. This is not a choice on his part; it's how his heart naturally functions. His feelings simply adjust to the truth sense in his own and others' orientations.

A force stronger than casual friendships was implacable in its demand, and it had Hameed by the scruff of the neck. For him there was simply a job to be done. Hameed had obviously noticed that I was fading in and out of our focus on the Work as I took on the role of a doctor's wife. He wanted me to find the life I wanted and even felt I was doing exactly what I needed to do at that time. But the message had always been, "I am headed this way. If you want to come, please join in; if not, we might meet (infrequently) for tea and some small talk, and I'll be happy to look at the photos from your vacation." No judgment.

As a person in his life, you are either with his priorities or not. So, I had to ask myself, where *were* my priorities? I was still teetering back and forth, unable to get both feet on the ground. I realized I had returned to the Bay Area as if I were the same person with the same desires and life goals as when I had departed six years earlier clothed in a more contemporary package. Geographical location, proximity to my family, and a life of ease had gradually eclipsed the adventure of exploring the interior world, which I had come to value so highly during my time in Colorado.

Our heartfelt connection did not change. Hameed still loved me—I knew that—and there was always the sense of ease and friendship. But our contact was noticeably more superficial at times. So it wasn't surprising that, on and off, Hameed would feel closer to Faisal. At any given time, Hameed felt more drawn to one of us for reasons unknown. Sometimes, specific areas in the teaching would emerge that he felt he could explore more easily with one of us. This is similar to dynamics I have seen in many threesome friendships. But beginning around January 1979, Hameed's journals had begun to reflect that Faisal and he had become closer. During the period when I was spiritually stuttering, Hameed and I were having tea, talking smallish, and sharing photos, while he and Faisal were more often hanging out in Essential Land.

The months passed, and the lighthearted ease I had felt shifted to a gray ennui. It was now autumn of 1980, and I was completely moved into the house, with nothing more to organize. How much rearranging of the furniture could I do? How many drawings or paintings could I create? How many walks on the beach could I take? It was all turning pale.

One morning as I was loafing in bed, a sense of determination dispersed my morning torpor. I just knew I was going to the group that evening. My attentiveness had grown undisciplined and sporadic, but the teaching was still alive in me. A silent, invisible current marshaled me northward in spite of my sluggishness.

As I wound my way up Highway 280 and over the Bay Bridge, sputtering along in the slow lane in the Bug, I felt unsure how I would fit in. After waffling back and forth between excitement and anxiety, I realized they were two sides of the same energy. Wilhelm Reich used to say, "Fear is excitement without breath." So I drew in a deep one, grasped the wheel, and punched the gas pedal. Mushka smiled big, and the wind from the open window tousled her furry ruff.

By this time, Hameed was holding group meetings in the house he and Marie had bought on Park Avenue in Wildcat Canyon. Mushka sounded the yipping alert of arrival after I headed up the short, curvy road to their house. Hameed, Marie, and I sat down for a quick meal, then Hameed attended to his preparations for the evening. The den had been arranged with a half circle of chairs, with Hameed's seat in the center of the open crescent. I chose my place before many of the students arrived, reverting to my old tendency to position myself as inconspicuously as possible, since I didn't know anyone there. As dusk drew near, I watched as the participants placed their shoes neatly along the wall outside the room and entered the open glass double doors in silence, scanning the room for the right spot. By seven o'clock, the chairs were filled and we were all ready and waiting.

The group began with a meditation, as it always did. After about thirty minutes, Hameed's voice broke the silence. "Begin sensing your arms and legs. Open your eyes, and slowly add looking and listening." He guided our attention back into the room without breaking contact with the presence that had been generated.

As the meeting continued, an obvious question hung in the air, along with some oblique glances in my direction. Hameed addressed the unexpressed curiosity. "This is my friend Karen, and she is here to be with us in our work together." There were some questions about what I would do there. All he would say was, "You will find out."

Nothing was ever spelled out beforehand regarding changes in the group. Students were encouraged to deal with their reactions to whatever was happening, regardless of how justified or not those reactions might be, positive or negative. The group field was a holding for working through reactivity. Responses to other students or their work in the groups, to Hameed, to shifts in the group structures—everything that happened was a lesson in how to look into any experience to see what was real within it.

These were basic precepts for functioning in life, and life in the group was no exception. We were expected to manage our feelings, understand them, and resolve them to a level of presence, making it more possible to respond with the freshness of the moment rather than being caught in knee-jerk patterns. There was to be no acting out of negative emotions. We had to own all our feelings responsibly, be with them, and inquire into them, neither suppressing nor discharging the energy of the emotion. Then, if we still had something to say about a matter, we would be able to speak directly about it without the charge of personal history attached.

Sometimes, when there were reactions or questions about his choices, Hameed would concede and talk about a given decision or even explain why he had made it. And sometimes he wouldn't. So he was being as straightforward about my participation as he could be. The truth was that it was mostly an unknown, so we would all need to wait and see what would happen. What we did know was that I was not their peer, but I was not their teacher either. I was just me, and even that was a work in progress.

As awkward as I had felt when being introduced, I became more at ease as the evening progressed. My body sent the message: *Ahhh, this is right.* I had landed somewhere solid, as though I had been floating around without feet. I could feel the value of being in this room with these people, with essence and presence as our shared focus. "I *want* to be here," I thought to myself. "I will be coming often."

As I was getting my bearings and finding my place in the California group, Faisal was doing the same in Boulder. Since he was going back and forth, we each began to work privately with some of the California group participants. In addition, Faisal started seeing students in the Colorado group, incorporating the Reichian breathing work that he, too, had learned from Phil Curcuruto. He also facilitated some of the evening small groups held there between the weekend meetings led by Hameed.

Hameed, Faisal, and I would discuss the work the students were doing, which helped Hameed to stay on the pulse of the group field. Faisal and I offered suggestions about what Hameed might emphasize in the teachings and how they could be structured. The three of us would also talk about how the private sessions were going for each of our students and come up with ideas to hone the teaching to their specific needs. But neither Faisal nor I taught alongside Hameed at that time; he was *the* teacher, and everyone viewed him as such.

It was now understood that a necessary part of the teaching was to help students settle into their sense of presence in an embodied way. The breathwork that Hameed had learned was incorporated into the private teaching to support the embodiment of Being. Regardless of how people found their way into the group, from this point on it would be mandatory to also do individual sessions combining breathwork and Inquiry, a requirement that was set for the Colorado group as well. This is still part of the Work today.

There was an interesting difference in how the Work originated and developed in California and in Colorado. In California, the group evolved mostly out of individuals discovering the teaching as it began to impact them in private breathwork sessions with Hameed. When he felt there were enough possible candidates for a group, he started one. In Colorado, it was just the opposite: Those who did the Returning Process and saw the value of Hameed's approach initiated the group, and Hameed added private Reichian breathwork sessions to assist the students' process. But the purpose, orientation, and basic content of both groups were the same from Hameed's point of view.

As I continued to attend the group, and my embodiment of presence moved more into the foreground, it scared me that I had veered so far from what was most vividly satisfying for me. I was saddened to see that this most important part of my life had taken a back seat to the external pulls of comfort and familiarity. A sense of betrayal pierced my heart, and remorseful disbelief rushed in. Presence had never left me, but somehow the volume of its message had been muffled. That felt more tragic than if I had been severed from the connection altogether. To have the capacity to know the magic of the divine and not attend to it felt like a self-inflicted wound.

The more time I spent in the group, the more I realized that it wasn't enough to simply be capable of experiencing deep states. Recalling the value I had always felt in supporting others to discover their inner treasures made my eyes blurry with tears. The real question was no longer "What else is going to fulfill me?" but "How am I choosing to function and serve with the gifts that I have?" My selfishness had concealed my true purpose.

Every cell now seemed to be magnetized to the pull of that quest. It was time to get going down the road again, this time with a renewed perspective. As I regained my balance, my love for the truth and the work it takes to live it reignited. And I was determined to share it with others. My heart turned over with a rumble in my chest like a rusty old engine starting up after a long period of disuse.

I became more reliable and enthusiastic in my attendance than I had ever been in Boulder and Denver. The group meetings were being held one evening a week and every other weekend, and I rarely missed one. Hameed said at the time that he was surprised; he didn't expect me to become so involved. But I was honoring the visceral desire not only to know more fully who I was but also to support the unveiling of hidden riches in all who sought them.

I was back on track, headed to my true home.

17 ❖ My Guardian Angel Flies Away

IN OCTOBER 1980, my stepfather was diagnosed with cancer. It had already metastasized from his lungs, and he was told that he had less than a year to live. Russ traveled to Mexico for laetrile treatments and tried other alternative remedies; nevertheless, he declined rapidly. The man who had fathered me in the most supportive way I could have hoped for was leaving this world.

Russ and I denied, raged, bargained, cried, and grieved together. But the time arrived to accept the inevitable, and he responded by asking me to be his guide. As I watched his body gradually thinning into the atmosphere, I knew that helping him to know himself as honestly and as deeply as possible was the best I had to offer.

By pointing my stepfather inward, I could show him the universe he had encouraged me to go toward. He deserved to reap the fruits of seeds he had sown in me that he never fully actualized in his own life. He had fathered a lonely, shy, insecure girl into becoming a woman of substance. He had given me the courage to pursue what my heart drew me toward. In sum, he had given me a new chance at life—I wanted to return the offering in kind.

Faisal and Hameed, who both knew Russ a bit, stood by me like two pillars of friendship throughout the process of his transition. With his dexterity in directing people toward essential states, Faisal taught me how to shift Russ's consciousness to help him enter into the world of essence and living spirit as we knew it. Hameed lovingly helped me to differentiate between the psychological material holding my stepfather hostage and thus needing to be challenged and what was best left alone.

Whenever I was with my stepfather as he moved through deep emotional and physical suffering, I felt a remarkable equanimity. When I left his side, grief sometimes overtook me. But although I was dreadfully sad, I wasn't afraid of his death. During this time, Hameed, Faisal, and I learned a great deal about conscious dying, which would serve us in guiding students and other important people in our lives in the future as they faced the mysterious passage from this world.

In March of 1981, Russ was released from the hospital. Family and friends filed through his room at home to offer love and farewells. My sister arrived from Colorado to say her goodbyes and support Mom. One afternoon she, Mom, and I were sitting together at Russ's side. His hospital bed was positioned so that he could view the sky and the miniature jungle of thriving potted plants lovingly kept by June on the small balcony beyond the sliding glass doors. Russ browsed the room, his eyes dancing through the atmosphere as if visions of many worlds were mingling. A crooked-toothed smile spread across his translucent face. In a voice thin but reminiscent of his deep, authoritative tone, he said, simply, "I am surrounded by angels."

A couple of weeks later, as April bloomed with the beauty of new life, the final vigil began. For days, a lustrous atmosphere was palpable in the living room. One particularly bright morning, I walked over to where Russ lay. I was hit with a mix of medicinal smells and the acrid odor of his body shutting down. My body recoiled instinctively, but my chest billowed with a wish to draw near.

I kissed him on the forehead and took a seat near my mother. We sat quietly as the black, hollow space of death opened its mysterious portal into the room. Russ's breathing became increasingly shallow and . . . then . . . just . . . stopped. He unwound from the mortal coil, leaving his bright presence as a blessing whilst he faded from the physical world.

I reached out to June and held her hand as she witnessed his departure. Sadness grayed her eyes, but the stress in her face relaxed. Her beloved husband's suffering was over, and a measure of hers was released as well.

Like sunlight through a diamond, glittering refracted rays poured into the room. I perceived an iridescent chariot of light descend and embrace Russ's consciousness. My heart burst out of my chest and took flight, expanding into the space of liberation with him.

Russ's aura permeated the room for many days. Gradually, it faded to a void, which then filled with my tears. No more heart-to-hearts by the fire and walks in the park, no more drinking tea or wine and listening to my stepfather lovingly pontificate about his latest theories or ply me with pragmatic advice. The man who had launched me into the mystery of existence was now subsumed into its invisible depth.

A few days after Russ's departure, I sat in Hameed's living room with my diamond buddies, inquiring into the experience of my stepfather's passing. I felt the big, aching hole in my chest that had been left when part of my heart flew off with him. I felt how much I missed Russ, and then the hole filled with deep love and gratitude. My chest expanded with a breath of ease, and my mind was emptied by a cool, breezy sensation. I felt my stepfather's presence in the room and our connection of undying love.

I had already told Hameed and Faisal that something extraordinary had descended and embraced Russ's consciousness at the time of his death, but I had not told the whole story. Now it felt important to describe what I had seen. "The chariot bore a resemblance to the horse-drawn carriages of the 1800s, but without the horses," I began. "It had a metallic silver base instead of wheels. And it was studded with glistening diamonds—emerald green, ruby red, sapphire blue, canary yellow, padparadscha orange, and other colors. Some of them I've seen before. I felt that I was in the presence of a holy being, though it was not a human form."

The very act of describing the diamond structure became a sacred invocation. It filled the room and engulfed the three of us into its body of glinted light. But this time, it was elongated slightly into a teardrop shape, with a star at the top like a blazing beacon. Its presence was a palpable statement: "I am here. Deal with me head-on."

A delicate pulsation in my forehead and a tickling at the top of my head built up and combined into a pressure that called for my focused attention. Then came a sense of delicate sharpness on my forehead—not painful, but definite and crisp like the facets of tiny diamonds.

The diamonds were gorgeous, but it was like peering into mirrors reflecting the intensity of the sun. I closed my eyes in reaction. Then my resistance thickened into a sensation of a rubber blindfold wrapping itself around my head. I tried to resist the resistance, but that only made matters worse. Hameed suggested that I relax into what was happening and try to understand it. I knew well enough that this was good advice, but I wanted to push him away.

And then it clicked. I had come to believe that the illuminating lantern of intellect was not for me; it was for other people, and I was supposed to follow whoever had it. Usually, for me, that meant a man.

I began to feel another kind of loss. An associated memory arose of empty-headedness, a sense of lack of intelligence, accompanied by the image of a little girl. Tattered vintage memories of my father surfaced. At first, they were disjointed—choppy images like in the magazine collages I used to make in art class. But then a more complete picture of my father and myself came into focus. As I put words to what I was seeing, Faisal and Hameed pointed out that the sense of emptiness I was feeling was not only the loss of Russ but the loss of my real inner father as well. I realized why I'd had such a strong *no* to Hameed's help.

It's not that I had felt a lack of love. My father and I had a sweet connection. His big physical presence often felt comforting to me, and I felt protected by him. I could climb up onto his lap and melt his brash exterior to expose his marshmallow heart. But his own childhood was so lacking in supportive direction that he had no real guiding hand to offer me.

When it was time to do my homework, for example, I would go to my room that I shared with my little sister and sit at my desk, determined to get things right. I tried hard to make the letters and numbers remain fixed on the page, but they kept shifting and floating around. When my father came in to check on how I was doing, I tried to follow his instructions, but he couldn't understand that I was struggling just to focus on the darn symbols. At other times, I didn't know how to translate my picture-thinking into words. More often than not, I would end up crying, and he would walk off in a frustrated huff. I discovered later that I had tested high in IQ, but nobody had told me that. All I could think was, "I must be stupid."

Other memories of times when I tried my hardest to please my father and gain his admiration erupted into consciousness, bringing a heart-wrenching hollowness again, and the pain of his dismissal. Then I felt my body blaze with rage at his lack of ability to understand what I needed. After a few minutes that seemed like eons, I cooled and slumped back into the emptiness.

Then the wish to know the truth, whatever it might be, lit up my chest. Sincerity activated the lion heart that now had the courage to walk me through the jungle of my history toward the understanding I was seeking. Because she did not believe she was smart enough to take his directions, that little girl had decided that she was not worth his time. In defeat, she had handed over to her father the diamond chalice with the brilliant elixir of intelligence that was her own.

"I feel sad for her," I said, each word landing in the soft silence that had been created for me in the room.

Hameed's and Faisal's kindness was a palpable, attuned, wordless response. My head cracked open, and I felt a specific sense of lack. My deficit had been exposed to the world.

"I feel stupid, and I can't talk right," I blurted out.

"Just feel the emptiness without calling yourself names," Hameed said with tender firmness.

"I am scared."

"It will be okay."

I felt the eight-year-old-Karen shape of my body and wanted to hide. I shrank into a lump on Hameed's couch. I could hear the *click click* of his mala beads as he reclined casually on his left side, supported by pillows on the rug, completely relaxed and right there with me. I was positioned higher than he was, physically speaking, but I felt so much smaller than him.

"Is it really okay? What if you see how stupid I am?" My cheeks were soaked with tears that had waited years to let loose.

"Well then, we will know the truth, won't we? Remember, we don't know what we will find. Let's see."

I cast a furtive glance at Faisal, who nodded with a friendly gesture of encouragement.

The musty image of the deficient young girl vanished as spacious freshness took over the emptiness. My body felt as though it were lengthening. I was growing up—literally. My breath became huge, and I began to shake all over.

"What's happening, Karen?" Hameed asked quietly.

"An intense brilliance is exploding from my diaphragm . . . and it's rippling into my head!"

"How does that make you feel?"

"Bright . . . and relieved." I was giggling and crying, uplifted and puzzled at once. "I thought I was going to be in that hole forever. I believed that was some kind of ultimate truth about me."

"You have been believing that for a long time. Stay with this," he said gently.

The whole room took on a soft sheen.

"What do you see in your forehead?" This time the question came from Faisal.

"I don't see anything yet. I feel something, though." The tingling pulsation that had emerged earlier was returning, and it was stronger now.

"Yeah," he said, with a whisper of recognition, "it is a diamond."

"I see it now. It is a bunch of them all lit up and tinkling. Hey, you guys! I can hear them!"

"What do they sound like?" Hameed asked.

The gems penetrated my frontal lobe as the lid of my fontanel slid open like one of those astronomical observatories atop a mountain. "Like a celesta," I replied, charmed by the sound.[1]

The more interested I became in what I was experiencing, the more my experience opened up. "I feel very clear," I said with a twinkle of delight, "like my mind is clean and well lubricated . . . and now I can *see* the diamonds."

Just as each essential aspect reveals the ways that we have been disconnected from its true presence, this diamond-studded vehicle exposes issues and particular ways that the functioning of mind is cut off from presence. Now I could see that the emptiness I was experiencing in my head was a disconnection from my real potential. My distorted self-image as a child had kept me from knowing that this potential was actually mine.

Connections began to knit together: the self-image I had formed as a child . . . the loss of Russ . . . the qualities I needed from my biological father . . . the emptiness I felt because he couldn't be there for me in the way I needed. For too long, my heart and mind had been weighed down by the cramping image of that desperate little girl. I now felt airy, free, and intelligent.

"I feel really smart!"

"And brilliant," Hameed said. "I've always seen you as bright."

Faisal nodded in friendly agreement.

I understood that the chariot I had seen when Russ died was the grace-filled presence of the Diamond Body. It had wobbled for a while on the landing pad of my mind, its thrusters disbursing clouds of particulate matter from the past for me to see. Now I felt the diamond structure land in its docking station right at the center of my forehead. My mind began to function with greater precision and elegance as the presence of essential qualities blended with the conceptualizing mind like a multidimensional, well-oiled machine.

As bits and pieces of my history, feelings, and ideas about myself drifted into consciousness, the Diamond Body threaded them together and lit up each insight. The presence in my head intermingled with my heart in the dance of the cosmos. I felt at one with the primordial intelligence inherent in biological processes and universal rhythms. I was riding on the pulse of evolution.

It popped into my mind that the brightness is not the same as the Diamond Body itself—I had been conflating the two. The Diamond Body has an intimate relationship with the aspect of essence called brilliancy, but they function differently. Intellect is related to but is not the same as intelligence; intellect *uses* intelligence to operate. The Diamond Body is the discriminating wisdom, and intelligence is the light that makes it work more effectively and efficiently. With the diamond discrimination available to me now, I could analyze with more exactness and pull the bits together, see the connections and meaning of experiences. But the quickness and elegance was the action of the brilliancy. This intelligence can manifest through thought, but that is only one way that it appears. And it is far more graceful than our mental processes: It is the intelligence inherent in revelation and transformation.

Dealing with one's father history turned out to be a central issue for virtually all our students, one that needs to be resolved before the guidance of the Diamond Body can emerge, for it opens up the questions concerning true intellect and intelligence. When a child feels properly guided by her father, she senses that he is right beside her, taking her by the hand and helping her into the world. When he is protecting and fathering her well, and she is embraced by his intelligent larger view, she is better able to find her place in life. As he attends to and supports her in ways that foster her development, he also embodies the archetype that sets a foundation for integrating intellect and intelligence on the spiritual level. Without this integration, these faculties are projected onto others, and it requires working through the sense of deficit and loss in order to retrieve them.

I found it interesting that even though my mother was smart and capable, I had projected the intellect and intelligence onto my father. As head of all the fine arts departments in a school district of almost all male teachers, June was their boss as well as their role model. They respected and admired her. But perhaps my father ended up carrying the projection because he idealized the intellect, while as an artist, my mother was more connected in my experience to the creative process.

Our culture is in flux regarding these stereotypes, so it might shift to an altogether different kind of understanding of and relationship to the archetype of intelligence. In any case, the Diamond Body not only turned out to be the perfect guide for dealing with father issues and re-owning the faculties of intelligence, it also became the master key for unlocking the teachings as they unfolded in every aspect of the Work. The operation of this kind of "presence of mind" is all about the synthesis of presence and knowledge at every level. It enables us to decode whatever is arising in the moment and penetrate it more deeply so that it can reveal itself.

The term "Diamond Body" was puzzling to many of our students because they connected it with the physical body rather than with a grouping of diamonds. So we began to call it "the Diamond Guidance." A fitting name because clarifying precisely where we were and understanding what we were experiencing opened the way for the next step to reveal itself. And it did so without telling us what to do or what not to do because its job is simply to provide the correct orientation for understanding. But, as we discovered, the Diamond Body can only arise and stay fueled for the ongoing journey if we have a devoted commitment to love of the truth for its own sake, not in order to arrive at a certain destination. It was not our goal to deepen into Being, but that's what happened because of our love to know the truth and understand the real.

By the end of May 1981, Hameed, Faisal, and I were engaged in varying degrees of integrating the Diamond Guidance and working through the issues impeding its full arrival. The blending of heart and mind into one operative center continued to lead us into deeper places. As with all spiritual knowledge and teachings, such comprehension could only come from a source beyond the human realm.

18 ❖ The Proof Is in the Pleasure

IT WAS A FEW MINUTES before ten, and *The Tonight Show* was about to start. After *Star Trek*, top rated in Hameed's book, Johnny Carson came in a strong second. Hameed, Marie, and I enjoyed watching the shows together whenever we could; Faisal would join in when he was in town.

The four of us sauntered into the den, and Faisal settled himself comfortably on a pile of pillows on the floor while I stretched out on the couch. Hameed swept by the television, flicked it on, and took a seat on the couch. Forsaking his typical casual slouch, he perched like a rocket poised to take off. He then launched into an animated recap of that evening's meeting, just adjourned.

"The Guidance was so active!" he began.

Catching the contagious spirit of our friend's zeal, Faisal and I exchanged a nod of enjoyment and turned our attention back to Hameed to hear more.

"It was there in such a strong way. Amazing! The brilliancy was there for sure." As he hunted for the right words, his cadence slowed. "I felt natural, efficient, and effective . . . I was also feeling very personal. The pearly presence was strong all night. But I also felt the sharp clarity of Diamond Guidance."

I felt my body straighten with attention to match Hameed's commanding posture. His eyes were like two glittering orbs. The light of the TV flickered on his skin as Johnny gesticulated in the background.

"I felt that the work with each person was easeful and spot-on. I felt really precise but simple . . . and ordinary in some way too."

"Yeah," Faisal inserted, then continued thoughtfully. "You know, Hameed, while you were working, I could see a point of light in your chest."

I wondered what this bright point of light was. It had punctuated a variety of experiences along the way, but its meaning was still a mystery to us.

As the discussion pulled us into its gravity, Hameed reached over and in one swift, agile move, twisted a knob on the TV with the rubber tip of his rosewood crutch to turn down the sound. Marie chuckled. He had many uses for his wooden pal. We had heard many boyhood stories about it, including how Hameed would use his crutch to hit the ball in soccer games, much to the annoyance of the opposing team. Heated arguments always followed.

"You're using it as your arm—that's not fair."

He would yell back, "It is my leg!"

"No, it isn't! You are using your arm!"

"I always have to use my arm! The crutch is part of my leg!"

I saw this as a testament to his ability to come up with creative solutions to any problem.

Marie popped up from the couch and made a start toward the kitchen. "I'll go make some tea," she chirped.

"I'll be in in a minute to help," I said as she whisked by me.

Hameed continued his monologue without skipping a beat. "So it is not exactly a new state . . . " His brow furrowed in concentration. "That's it!" he said with voltage. "It is an integration that is coming of the Guidance, Brilliancy, and the Pearl. It's all me, as one cohesive presence."

He paused as soon as he noticed I was observing him in *that way*. "What are you looking at?" he asked, searching my eyes for a clue.

I dropped my gaze to the carpet. "Oh, nothing."

The truth was that I was pleased with his new discovery but more fascinated by something unrelated to what Hameed was saying. But I was hesitant to shift the discussion in another direction.

Faisal registered that I might not have words for my musings. "I know you are seeing something. What does it look like?"

Feeling assured that I was not derailing the conversation, I decided to give it a go. I studied Hameed more intently. His upright stature revealed his long torso. With a subtle wing-like motion, his shoulders reached their full span. His straight but relaxed spine supported the pulsing rhythm of his chest as it appeared to be breathed by some force beyond his body. I then peered into the more subtle layer that his body was expressing.

"I see an opening in the Mobius.[1] When I look inside, it opens into a deep black space. It looks and it feels"—I paused and started to feel my own sternum opening up—"velvety and inviting." I was drawn back to the enchanting universe within him. "And there are a whole bunch of twinkling diamond bodies gliding through the silken stillness."

"I thought something interesting was happening," Faisal said with what I can only describe as a charming double-eyed wink.

"I see all sorts of jeweled spaceships of different shapes," I said, almost as though I were alone talking to myself. "It is a gorgeous diamond universe."

Hameed's eyes were open but didn't seem to be registering what was before him in the room. A blank gaze often signaled the intensity of an inner focus taking all his attention. Then his eyes fluttered shut.

"Yes, I can feel some kind of smooth activity." His upper body slid forward as though he would dive through a slit in space at any moment. "There is a graceful sensation in the center of my torso at the diaphragm . . . now I can see them too! They're like many dazzling spaceships hovering in a starless night sky . . ." he paused as he became absorbed into the moment. "It is so vast and deep."

Faisal started to fill in the details. "The shapes and colors are amazing." A staccato inhale punctuated the arrival of each new form as he saw them arise and float in Hameed's inner space. "Every one of them is unique! But they all have bases of metallic gold or silver, with a shining star or a point of light at the top. Almost like sailboats made of many tiny lights . . . Oh, now I see one that's transparent and delicate . . . and there's another one—it's more solid and shimmery."

My body filled up with a bubbly fascination.

The universe that was opening to us was forefront but blended with the voices of Johnny and his guests. Time stretched as the line between the invisible and physical worlds blurred. When Marie brought in our snacks, I realized that what seemed like hours passing had only been minutes.

We settled back into our TV viewing positions, couched in the intimacy of the shared atmosphere as we sipped our tea and munched on Marie's home-baked cookies. The sounds and images on the screen became passing phenomena as we attended to the fascinating new vessels, commenting on both with a fluidity that made no distinction between the inner and outer shows.

The rhapsody of lights continued their display after Johnny signed off. Marie sleepily sauntered down the hallway to bed, and the three of us rose in unison and ambled toward the door. Our words were spare in bidding one another good night. Faisal and I descended the stairs to the driveway and got into our cars to go our separate ways as Hameed watched from the open doorway. I felt connected with them both through our common universe as I drove away, my headlights beaming into the darkness.

✧ ✧ ✧

The brilliancy aspect of essence had been the dominant focus of our exploration three months before this revelatory evening. And I am sure this fluid intelligence had made it possible for us to get that peep into the secret universe of the diamond flotilla. Now brilliancy arose again, but it had something new in store for us. The smooth presence expanded to an ocean of multicolored diamond droplets. Islands of father issues dotted the panorama. We became stranded on one or another until we could understand the barriers to finding our flow back into the sea of fluid light, which was growing in intensity and pleasure.

Because the aspect of brilliancy is often associated with and felt as the quick action of intelligence, its impact on the heart and body is frequently bypassed. But allowing brilliancy to find its way through our consciousness imbued our bodies with delightful sensations. It ushered in yummy "drinks," beginning with a sweet, pink, divine taste of love in the heart. Rather than the thick sweetness of the nectars of paradise, these elixirs were like crisp, refreshing beverages for the soul, issuing from the mountain streams of the effulgent heart of the universe. We barely began to taste one before another flavor would blend in and its taste shade would come forth.

Hameed's subtle palate was very keen, so he could differentiate all kinds of flavors, while my inner taste perception fell into two very distinctive categories: yum and ick. Essence texture, temperature, affect, and the visual and sound components came more easily to me. Unless he pointed out the discriminations, at first I was only able to taste sweet, sour, and maybe spicy as the pleasant ones; or bitter, slimy-salty, rubbery, and plastic-y as variants of yuckiness. It took years to refine my palate while the "taste center," on the left side of the Mobius at the end of the sternum, slowly developed.

As the pleasurable presence of the expanse moved to the foreground yet again, the sea morphed into an intense, ripe tangerine-orange. The taste tickled my taste buds, melding with a hint of prickled zestiness, like Orange Crush soda—sweet, and just tart enough to enhance the exquisite delight. The bursting energy of Shakti added a thrill. Like bubbly water, it was the perfect mixer for the celestial syrup, bringing out the *pop* in the new inner soda of ecstasy.

As we swigged the tangy, mouthwatering sweetness through every pore, we were swimming with pleasure in its quintessence. My heart softened to a luscious sense of rounded, white substantial creaminess that grew and filled my body. The sweet orange-colored substance swirled around me and settled on my periphery, like a gleaming shawl of deliciousness melting the edges of the milky richness. I became a Creamsicle! Who knew? From then on, my favorite color was orange; up till then, it had been purple, orange's complement on the color wheel.

The orange essence is the aspect of our nature that shows us that pleasure is innate to spirit—it is Being itself—and this rapturous awakening to the limitless wellspring of pure pleasure is uncaused by anything in the physical world. Think of it as the noncaloric optimization of spiritual wholeness. *Ahhh!*

There was nothing to move toward, nothing to try to attain. I was immersed in the simple pleasure of Being that is found in the middle of now. But the Shakti drew me out even more—heaven forbid! I welcomed the spunky vigorousness, and soon it felt quite natural. I realized that this energy was the source of what made me feel unable to sit still. Now that I could feel it directly and understand it, meditation became ecstatic. I was moving within inner universes without lifting a finger.

My trips to Berkeley became more frequent and compelling. The magnetic draw to be with my two diamond buddies was irresistible. Hameed wrote in a journal entry around this time: "The three of us being together is more satisfying than being with anyone else and is a catalyst for the teaching. We are spending maybe too much time together and it is making some people jealous and uncomfortable." They could sense the pleasure we had in one another's company.

What they were not aware of—and what we were only starting to awaken to—was the pleasure of Being making itself known explicitly. Our adventures were of unparalleled intensity and delight and richly fulfilling. The relationships we had with each other didn't fit the conventional models. And the inner sweetness wasn't about just feeling good or being bliss-ninnies; it was an awakening brought on by the intelligent heart of Being, appreciating and celebrating itself through our hearts. Our shared delight in the wondrous universe of discovery—this was the real bond of our friendship.

The tangerine tingle heralded the arrival of the next wisdom vehicle that would unpack this view. The orange-colored, tangerine-flavored teachings prepared us by turning us into tasty treats of the universe. But making a shift of the psyche toward the inner nature of pleasure rather than externally oriented gratification is like trying to turn the *Queen Mary* on a dime. It would take more than feasting for a few days at the divine dessert table for the new vehicle to show up.

When it finally made its entrance, we thought, "Oh my, another one!" We hadn't considered that more vehicles would follow the first one, but then we recalled the vision we'd had of a whole realm of diamond spaceships. This new inner vessel brought the teaching that truth and pleasure are one. There is no substitute for the inner pleasure of Being. To know it sets us free from expecting the outer world to be the sole source of pleasure; at the same time, it makes external pleasures even more enjoyable because we aren't grabbing on to the world and squeezing the life out of it.

This vessel has a joyous, celebrative quality as well as a deep inner richness. Its diamond structure sometimes appears like a carousel in a carnival atmosphere. It has two parts, each expressing a type of pleasure. The center is a rich, golden, melting love diamond with the essence of loving, satisfying, nourishing sweetness. The diamonds surrounding the core gold diamond are sensuously textured gems in all varieties of essential qualities. Their textured chewiness is like hard, dense taffy, and they are deeply satisfying and pleasing. Around the entire surface of its structure are lighter-colored diamonds with a feeling of lightheartedness.

Hameed named this vehicle "the Markabah."

"Why call it that?" I asked.

He explained that it was the word for "vehicle" in Arabic, and that he'd decided to use that name after a conversation with his good friend Hameed Qabazard. In the School, we sometimes refer to it as "the body of bliss," which describes its teaching well.[2]

All of the aspects of essence arise in the diamond form, but each differs from the Diamond Guidance in how its particular qualities express the purity of truth. The perspective of the Markabah showed us explicitly how Being, in its very nature, is always a positive feeling, and that the qualities of truth or Being are inherently pleasurable. Peace, clarity, strength, will, power, kindness and, of course, love and joy—are all ways that truth manifests with specific qualities of pleasure.

The Markabah also brought vital teachings about inner truth and pleasure as one unified presence. This is not an easy perspective to comprehend because truth is often equated with unpleasantness rather than delight. But understanding pleasure and its deep-seated connection in the human psyche to the instinctual drives is central for making the spiritual turn inward. This new vehicle gifted us with teachings on how to approach the misunderstandings and barriers to pleasure, as well as the skillful means to understand and work through this tenacious orientation. It also taught us how to decouple the drive toward pleasure from the animal instincts that are deeply ingrained in our physical existence, so that they can be used as fuel for the spiritual journey.

Our physical body is educated from day one to believe that pleasure is the result of sense gratification. For an infant human being, this is as it should be; pleasure is the signal that all is well and that the gratifying act (feeding, holding, changing) has quelled the needs of the body that create agitation in the nervous system when they are unfulfilled. So it isn't surprising that the sweet, golden diamond in the middle of the Markabah is usually associated with the good mothering person of infancy.[3]

Mom is the locus of the infant's attachment and the focal point for the instinctual drives that ensure survival of the body. A baby's heart, mind, and belly are deeply connected to her, and the little one's equilibrium is totally dependent on her as the outside source of good will, health, and well-being. Mother is the satisfying, gratifying, soothing, nourishing presence that is the source of pleasure and the alleviator of pain. Thus, pleasure automatically becomes linked in our heart's memory with Mother.

As the baby begins to separate from Mother, he is also busy becoming an ego and separating from the source of Being. As he grows, the source of pleasure appears to stay with Mother but then moves on to other people, objects, and pleasing situations. The child's orientation toward external pleasure is completed through the solidification of ego as separate from Being; hence, the source of pleasure continues to exist in the other. In order to reclaim the truth that the source of pleasure is an element of what he intrinsically is, the student needs to see through his outer directedness and understand how it was set in place.

This, then, becomes one of our spiritual tasks in adulthood: to discover the true, nourishing, loving, essential mother that is not an *other*. This golden elixir arises in the first months when mother and baby are in a melted, bonding love fest together. When the golden diamond arises in the middle of the Markabah, it is that merging love in its diamond form, highlighting the central issues that prevent us from having a more complete inner orientation. What we discover is that our own heart is the chalice that contains the nectar of melting, satisfying love. The merging gold love differs in tactile experience and affect from the solid gold of truth. While the solid gold of truth feels like the soft metal of 24-karat gold, the merging gold love is a fluid, sweet, honey-like substance.

As this new teaching moved through our psyches, it delivered up its wisdom in the usual way: by evoking tensions in the body that woke us up to the orientations and beliefs that had been stamped with conviction into our fleshy consciousness. As we wended our way through the issues, tasty diamond bits of divine knowledge impregnated our consciousness with a new dimension of wisdom. By the end of 1981, each jeweled morsel had delivered its particular type of pleasure. A coherent understanding arose that our instinctual intelligence stays with the body but we don't have to be imprisoned by it or oriented completely by it. Instinct has its place in the physical realm, but the delights and rewards of all things pleasurable, physical or otherwise, have their roots in the truth of Being.

The cave of delights is not so easily entered, however. Essence protects itself with dragons, they say. And the dragon of pain is the one we encounter at the mouth of the cave. We usually see only the surface appearance of reality, so most of us cannot imagine that consciously entering into our suffering can reveal something wonderful. A student of mine at the time who had been stunned by the challenges of deep suffering but had moved through them and awakened to her heart's deep secret, once said to me, "Wow, I went through hell and got a present!" If we only knew that within discord lies the potential for awakening, the pain of ego would be more tolerable.

Much of my own suffering at that time was caused by an inability to parse out inner truth from outmoded desires. Had moving to Los Gatos been a mistake? The quiet rural setting I had craved was now an isolating gulf between my fellow travelers and myself. I was smack-dab in the middle of the upward draft of discoveries that were shifting the very fabric of my being, yet I still held fast to conventional life as though it were the ultimate goal for me. The conflicting pulls were tearing me asunder.

The world's ways of happy-making were unsatisfying for me not because they were wrong or unspiritual but because my approach to them was not a real expression of whom I had become. I had changed radically—when I returned to California, this was apparent to everyone who had known me—but I hadn't realized the extent of the change. I was living a life that was no longer really mine.

I was becoming increasingly disappointed in who I was when I was with Perry. Like an animal restrained in an unnatural environment, I began to lash out at the smallest provocation. Cool dissatisfaction seeped into my heart, and I withdrew more and more from my husband as our charmed life closed in around me. He was growing frustrated and angry with me as well.

I was even conflicted about my involvement with art. Painting had long been a mainstay for me, a reliable way to express my internal sensate world for which I could find no words. I could speak through the smooth-handled sable brushes that extended my innermost feelings and dreams onto canvas, depositing colorful syllables. Periodically, I would get together with my mother to draw and paint. That, too, was becoming less frequent now, partly due to finding a new vocabulary of light that I could not capture on paper or canvas and partly because there just wasn't enough time for it all.

While I was in the throes of these difficulties, Hameed and Faisal were settling into their own householding. Hameed had been married to Marie for three years by then and, in 1982, Faisal had married a young woman named Patty Walker, now Patty Rice, a private student of Hameed's who was a member of the Boulder group. Because Faisal was a friend of Hameed's and had become more integral to the circle of students in Boulder, the marriage generated a celebrative feeling of promise in our community. Both he and Patty were well loved, and the sentiment was that two fine human beings make for one special bond. One of the blessings of their union was their beautiful daughter, Neda.[4]

I had opened a practice in Menlo Park for seeing students who were dribbling into the East Bay group from the San Francisco peninsula, but I longed to spend more time in Berkeley. When our trio gathered to inquire or spend time in sohbat, it was head-spinning and heart-filling. Everything paled in comparison. The gnarly bits in our personal lives would smooth out, minimize, even disappear during those conversations. I had no idea that the magnetism drawing me to be with Hameed and Faisal would overtake me like this.

I needed a new perspective to help clarify my conflicting loyalties. The state of the Markabah had brought great merriment and celebration in the recognition that truth is the source of pleasure. But spiritual maturity requires a life that is not driven by instincts. Pleasure could align my orientation to truth, but only when it was not under the influence of the conflicts I was struggling with. Redirecting the animal to be in service to the chariot, rather than the other way around, is a long process.

As we had already discovered, loyalty to truth is a prerequisite for obtaining a ticket on this carousel-like spaceship. If I hadn't been driven inward by the magnetic dynamism of True Nature, I wouldn't have come this far. But like the back-snap of a rubber band anchored in the familiar world, I was being yanked away from my inner truth time and again. I knew that my drive to realize my innate nature must at some point outweigh the drive for all of the comforts and securities that, in the end, really came down to ensuring the survival of the body or the self. If my desire for the truth took a back seat, the wisdom vehicle would not nestle firmly into my heart.

This perspective helped me understand why I had been persistently questioning my priorities to the point where my doubt had built to a crescendo. Now I had the Markabah to guide me through the shadowy miasma of my animal self, freeing my heart with fresh wisdom. Even though a scary unknown awaited me, confidence was growing that I could celebrate the sublime nature of me *and* hold my pain with kindness as I was stretched into new shapes. The simple intention arose to understand whatever condition I found myself in. I became less bound by the "pleasure principle" that had been setting the direction of my life. Whether I encountered pain or enjoyment, truth could be found because it lives in unperturbed goodness and pleasure in the heart of everything.

I wanted to follow the pull of my deepest heart's desire—not what made me feel good, secure, and taken care of, but literally what ignited the core of my being with true happiness. But what would this mean for my married life? Hameed, Faisal, and I were having a jolly good time. And Perry and I were fighting like cats and dogs.

19 ❖ Being in Boot Camp

A NEARLY INAUDIBLE rumble pulsed through my body, as though my whole body were a tympanic membrane. The reverberation was inseparable from the immense presence sinking into the room through a ripple in space-time. Hameed's red Persian carpet transformed into a landing pad as the visitor touched down and swallowed us into its presence.

Hameed and I had been engrossed for a couple of hours that afternoon in an inquiry about how to remain in the truth of what we knew and manifest it in the world more completely. How might we engage in life more fruitfully and in a more real way? How could we keep from getting snagged back into actions and perspectives that hadn't matched our understanding of truth for a long time? Why were our lives still so often discordant with our inner experience? We had been straddling the mundane and the spiritual, but we were missing the bridge that could connect the two seamlessly.

Our eyes had been closed as we sat in spontaneous meditation; as we sensed into ourselves more, they opened and met. The fire in the wood stove blazed. Glints of light reflected in Hameed's steady eyes like flickering Morse code, and a slight nod of his head conveyed that we were sharing the experience of the same presence. Also that he knew something . . .

"Wow! What *is* this?" I said out into the room, only obliquely addressing him. "Boy, I feel like the whole earth is in my belly."

My attention shifted to Hameed. "Did you *feel* that? It's like at the movies when you hear that Dolby sound right before the main feature . . ." My voice trailed off as I became aware of his silence. He was motionless in contrast with my animated chattering.

I settled into the floor. My body felt squat as I felt pulled to the center of the earth. Hameed looked rock-like, his brow creased with focus. One corner of his mouth bent slightly upward.

"Yeah, it did feel like a very heavy spacecraft, didn't it?"

We didn't get much further with the inquiry before we were inter-rupted by a phone call he was expecting. It was time for me to make my way back home anyway.

The experience of this massive presence stimulated an uptick in my process. I drove a slow road home to Los Gatos, contemplating the questions about my life that had shaken loose. I felt increasingly anx-ious as I got closer to home. I was afraid of what lay ahead.

In phone conversations with me and discussions with Faisal in the days following, Hameed began to make some sense out of what hap-pened that day. In September 1981, he had reported in his journal feel-ing tension and resistance on the left side of his body, especially in the back. As the content of the blockage became more conscious, he felt a hard defensiveness and hubris. Not long after that, we did a session for him so that he could explore it further.

With my hands on his stomach, I felt receptive and steady. My touch expanded beyond the flesh to include his body of consciousness. "What are you feeling?" I asked.

"I sense a feeling of inflation, almost like a white balloon full of air . . . Now it deflates—like something comes along and pops it."

My hands trembled as his ribs expanded with breath and pushed against them. His exhale stopped before it was complete.

"I feel like your outbreath just hit a cement floor, Hameed." The inflexibility of his chest was notably different from his usual supple breathing.

"Yeah, I feel like I am stuck in the inhale, like I have to hold on to the expansion."

I noted the correlation between Hameed's body and his emotional condition. The sensation of his being puffed up was amusing. It was more than an expansion; I could see a bloating of a barrel-chested de-fensive posture. Quite the opposite of his usual form.

"Now I feel a hole in the left side of the solar plexus," Hameed reported.

"How does it feel? Is it a deficiency of some kind?"

"I am not sure," he said, taking his time.

We remained in the quiet of uncertainty.

"Now the hole is opening, and an opaque fluid is flowing out." A brief silence, and then, "I think the defense was against this hole opening."

A substance of this kind would often show up when a blockage was opening. The consistency was like the slimy stuff in a polluted river, with lumps of discarded artifacts floating downstream in the scum. We understood this thickness to be the actual substance of consciousness when it is conflated with ideas, beliefs, and historical content. It appears in the initial stages of the process of clarification and understanding.

When Hameed picked up the inquiry again with Faisal a few days later, attitudes he was holding that were inconsistent with living a spiritual life were exposed. Over the next few weeks, he stayed engaged in this new inquiry during daily activities such as watching TV, brushing his teeth, eating dinner, and even while working with students.

A journal entry on Friday, September 18—about two weeks prior to our exploration of what it means to live a real life from an essential perspective—reports the emergence of a gold diamond in a new way: "I saw that I was unwilling to let go of sexual pleasure-seeking. The sense of deficiency is created by conflict. I want the sexual contact, but I do not feel I can rely on getting it. So there is resistance around the hole."

Hameed began to call this particular deficit "the survival hole" because it is related to the instincts and their defensive role. Understanding the role of the instincts when they are operating in adaptive, supportive ways moves us through this deficit, but in the process one has to face a palpable sense of defenselessness. Every one of us has the drive to survive, to feel secure, to have connection and pleasure with others. Our animal self needs to be fed, watered, and sheltered. And companionship and pleasure are important aspects of our human experience. But how much food, and what kind, is optimal? Do we need to live in fifty-thousand-square-foot houses? How much money is enough? If we believe that in order to stay alive, we need more than we actually do, we become attached to our body, other persons, and the physical world in disproportionate, unbalanced ways.

Each of us has our top-of-the-list indulgence. As soon as Hameed saw that pleasure was his and that it was connected to security, he felt the hole relax, and it became like a center or an opening. The hole then expanded into deep, black space inside him. In that space appeared what he thought was a new Markabah. The point of a large three-dimensional diamond, which looked and felt like a dense, golden bow of a boat, jutted out horizontally from his solar plexus, while the other end of it remained deep inside. The diamond became bigger and bigger, then turned upward like a whale breaching. Its golden tip moved up into his head. Then the lower half moved into position from deep in the back of his body into his pelvis and became a solid platinum base.

> The upper part [*corresponding to the upper part of his body*] was of diamond solid gold, and the bowl-like base that filled the lower body was of diamond platinum. These two diamond substances turned out to be objective truth [*gold*] supported by objective, universal will [*platinum*].[1]

Hameed saw that it was not a Markabah at all but a new vehicle with a different feel and message. That recognition brightened the significance of the arrival. Hameed started to show signs of the new teachings that "the battleship"—our initial name for the massive presence we had encountered—was bringing to port. From the same journal entry: "I feel quite immense, quite powerful, quite invulnerable."

The deeply rooted strength and powerful heft gifted by this new vehicle rendered Hameed stalwart and warrior-like. He embodied the indestructible quality of diamondness and, with his both-feet-in-the-ground-of-Being approach to the world, became a model for others. Probing the inner drives of the body and the outer pressures of the world had summoned the vehicle that was now showing us how to live in alignment with spiritual truth in the face of powerful but mostly unconscious motivations.

Hameed soon began to call this new vehicle "the protector of essence." As we unveiled its meaning, it changed into a structure that not only defends and protects the truth of Being but also grounds essence as it supports that truth through the ruthless assertion of the real. "The Citadel" became the new moniker of this fortress of truth. It is a diamond consciousness whose main qualities are the fortitude and the skillful means to support the personal life of Being—not based on ideals or beliefs but on what we know from experience to be true. In contrast with the ironclad defensive structure of ego, it does its work in us by revealing the wisdom of right living *in service of* essence.

We had a lot to learn about what that meant down on the ground. We had already been graced with the profound revelation of knowledge, heartful ecstatic discoveries, delight, and wonderment; the Citadel teachings were just what we needed to guide our journey of maturation with one eye on material necessities and the other on the invisible universe of our origin. Rather than succumbing to the forces of the world that support the ego self, we now had to develop the discipline and grounding to support living on the earth plane as Being in even the smallest elements.

The various diamonds of the Citadel showed up one at a time, highlighting how our habits and unconscious desires, rather than our center of truth, usually dictate life choices and establish the status quo that is all too easy to get stuck in. We saw how allowing our indulgences to dominate our choices and actions skewed our priorities. It humbled me to see how I would complain about my husband not being awake enough and claim that I wanted the truth—but I'd then go eat a pint of ice cream, grab a drink, or go the movies to distract me from doing what I needed to do.

Did I really know the difference between procrastination or avoidance versus acting from a normal need for entertainment or other kinds of enjoyment? I saw that I had been indulging in sleepwalking through parts of my life, and the diamond-studded rootedness of the Citadel was there to guide me in prioritizing my activities in a balanced, practical way. Many of the lifestyle changes I started to make were plain common sense. For example, reading while eating was a common blunder of mine, and I noticed how splitting my attention blurred my awareness and made me less present in both activities. The more I saw that the habitual life is largely unconscious, the more I felt the need for support to have a real, awake life.

One night while Perry was working late, I was sitting alone, looking out the back window at the moonlight. This pastime occasionally provided me with clues to my unconscious. I would pretend that the moon was a big eye in the sky, peering at everything she was lighting up, and I would try to see the world from her perspective. I called it "moondreaming." That night, the moon outlined silvery patterns in the trees and hills, and I noticed that she was also casting her light on the furniture and all the other objects in the room I was in. It occurred to me that I had always considered myself to be an organized person—but how organized was I really? And around what principles?

I had to admit that the cluttered little piles I'd collected in almost every room (in the name of tidying up) had become subtle distractions that prevented me from being completely relaxed at home. So I made time to arrange all my papers into one to-do pile on my desk and chose an hour each day to deal with them. Instead of constantly pushing away nagging inner reminders, I could now relax, knowing I would take care of what needed to get done during the allotted time. This one simple change created a lot more space in my psyche.

The dedication and arrangement of living spaces for specific purposes —the wisdom of the household, I call it—can make all the difference. Creating the proper environment is a personal practice, and how one approaches it changes as awakening deepens and the need for refuge develops. Someone else may have an entirely different way to handle such matters than I did or have another area of emphasis that needs attending to. But it is possible to promote a conscious attitude within a conscious environment in any kind of living situation.

Hameed, Faisal, and I regularly made all sorts of inquiries into our life circumstances, but initiating these particular changes was more than inquiring into our inner world and understanding it—it was a support for functioning in the outer world with the fruits of our inquiries. This echoed throughout the teaching field and affected the orientation and expression of the Work. Knowing, feeling, and being real are all great, but they're only the beginning. What's the point of doing all the inner work if we only sit on our glowing essential butts? We can't just *be* something—we've gotta *do* something!

Hameed had always been strongly disposed toward disciplined practices in the groups, but the work periods became more precise. They started with mostly doing ordinary tasks with presence and awareness and evolved to include the understanding of the specific obstacles in our psyche that impede presence from being lived in day-to-day life.

The work periods are still done today in the School; we call them life practice periods. This aspect of the teaching is still the most resisted and the least understood by many students—at least at first. I can see some of them in my mind's eye, rolling their eyes like disgruntled schoolkids and protesting, "What's in it for me?" or "How will washing floors and weeding someone else's garden help my spiritual development?" Gradually, students experience these times as occasions when the protector of essence shows up implicitly; over time, its wisdom carries over into daily life as a supportive strength to do what is needed.[2]

Some people might see structure and discipline as rigidity, perfectionism, or a compulsive need for control. Others may interpret it as an echo of a parental demand from childhood that they no longer have to obey; they have declared themselves free to live spontaneously, with little or no structure, just "trusting the universe to take care." But these attitudes can mask the possibility of living from the true freedom of Being rather than from inner or outer compulsion.

When we are awake in our choices, we are guided by the values and intelligence of Being. Living the truth we know rather than blindly submitting to—or unconsciously reacting against—the conventional truth handed down to us is a form of conscience, but it is not the punitive, critical conscience of the superego. A real conscience does not operate by rote; it responds with awareness and sensitivity to the true need at hand and considers the bigger picture.

Another job that the Citadel was performing admirably was to help us see our limitations realistically. Pretty much everyone tends to overestimate or underestimate their capacities; seldom are we objective about what we can or can't do. It was becoming increasingly noticeable to the three of us, and to others, that we were limited or inconsistent in the expression of our inner realizations.

Many spiritual teachers have reputedly acted out their own needs in ways that their students felt were not aligned with the precepts or values of their spiritual path. Faisal, Hameed, and I were not exceptions. We sometimes struck up conversations, initiated friendships, or participated in social engagements without being sensitive to how the students might respond. The new vehicle brought the wisdom of how to support the personal essence while honoring the needs and limitations within the interpersonal sphere.

The more we slogged through the mud, jumped the hurdles, and climbed the ropes of what life threw at us in the boot camp of essence, the better we became at expressing the Citadel's teachings. The discipline of being present in all our activities started to develop in us the stalwartness that would keep us from being swayed by the forces of the world that wanted to throw us off course. As we discovered, developing this strength is not only arduous, it can also rouse a deep aloneness. I am not talking here about isolation from others—I mean a radical inner aloneness.

All three of us had to grapple with this, but Hameed was the prime exemplar. If he had not been willing to walk in stark aloneness, especially at the beginning and throughout the early years, he would never have discovered truths that no one else had known before. And if he hadn't stood in the strength of his own knowing, regardless of the disagreement or disapproval of teachers who couldn't understand his experiences, the path of the Diamond Approach would never have been born.

The ability to be at home in one's internal solitude is a distinct feature of realization. Now the Citadel demanded that our personal lives be prioritized around a deeper reality. The following story, which is read to students as they enter the teaching of the Citadel, illustrates the challenge and the dilemma for every seeker on the path.

Once upon a time Khidr, the teacher of Moses, called upon mankind with a warning. At a certain date, he said, all the water in the world which had not been specially hoarded, would disappear. It would then be renewed, with different water, which would drive men mad.

Only one man listened to the meaning of this advice. He collected water and went to a secure place where he stored it, and waited for the water to change its character.

On the appointed date the streams stopped running, the wells went dry, and the man who had listened, seeing this happening, went to his retreat and drank his preserved water.

When he saw, from his security, the waterfalls again beginning to flow, this man descended among the other sons of men. He found that they were thinking and talking in an entirely different way from before; yet they had no memory of what had happened, nor of having been warned. When he tried to talk to them, he realized that they thought that he was mad, and they showed hostility or compassion, not understanding.

At first, he drank none of the new water, but went back to his concealment, to draw on his supplies, every day. Finally, however, he took the decision to drink the new water because he could not bear the loneliness of living, behaving, and thinking in a different way from everyone else. He drank the new water, and became like the rest. Then he forgot all about his own store of special water, and his fellows began to look upon him as a madman who had miraculously been restored to sanity.[3]

I felt helpless whenever I caught myself, often in hindsight, accommodating others or doing or being something inauthentic. I felt frustrated that I didn't know how to untangle myself. Even with all the positive changes I was making, insecurity was still a strong influence in my need for relationship, comfort, and marriage, and it often drew me away from the commitment to extend my essential presence into these areas as an expression of something more real. I saw that my behavior mirrored a position I had resisted seeing straight on: clinging to my habitual life while wanting spiritual treasures as well.

The conventional worldview was still so entrenched in me that I had not actualized the inward turn totally. I needed to take bigger steps in my outer world to square with the truth I knew in my heart. I couldn't see how deep the roots of those worldly values and ideals were until the powerful presence of the Citadel challenged everything in me.

We were now calling the hole that Hameed first experienced in our session "the hole of defense." I could see how emotional defenses are conflated with the basic drive for survival: What was once a useful drive for protection of the body had become the need to protect the comfortable, conventional self.

This had become glaringly evident in my own experience. I was being edged to the brink by the sharp diamonds this Citadel was wielding. The question of how to proceed with my life was not simply a matter of how to be with my husband while engaging in my inner work. It was about how I could support the real in me in all areas of my life. In what way was Perry part of that picture? More important and scarier—*was* he part of it? It would mean giving up a lot if the answer was no. If the answer was yes, did it mean giving up myself in some way?

One evening, as I sat alone in my house, watching the sun's rays fade and the valley fill with darkness, I realized that I had to either make the jump or commit to staying where I was. The choice to remain in my marriage seemed like backtracking, but the thought of moving forward made my knees go weak. I felt inadequate, helpless, and full of fear. The helplessness then became a distinct feeling of defenselessness. I had reached a limit of what I could do on my own, or even with Hameed's and Faisal's support. Living from essence, never disconnected from it, eluded me. I fell into a sinkhole of defeat. I simply didn't know how to do it.

I felt a contraction in my back near my left kidney. It opened to reveal a new hole that felt like the back side of a hole of defense that had shown up on the left side of my solar plexus a few days before. This deficiency felt like a basic truth about me. And what was worse—I would be found out! Everyone was going to see that I was incapable after all.

Then I got busted, big time—but not in the way I expected.

When working with other holes—such as the lack of strength or joy or love or will—accepting the emptiness and allowing the missing aspect to arise had been the way through. This hole was different. I was in touch with the deficiency of this particular hole but also with the basic emptiness common to all of them. I was a whole mess of holes, like Swiss cheese. I felt grief about this poor little deficient self.

And then the Citadel showed up.

I had learned long before that ego is a set of historical experiences that are retained in the mind and that we continue to identify with. But then a question arose: How could a set of ideas, memories, and beliefs take action—much less support one to live a real existence?

The answer was so obvious that it parted the fog: *It can't.*

Struggling against feelings of deficiency is futile. Ego is a construct of the mind, so it cannot do anything. Ego is deficient *by its very nature.* The me who was so firmly convinced that she should be able to do anything if she just tried hard enough was precisely the one who couldn't. If I kept going along with the masquerade, I would always feel deficient.

I relaxed as this *aha!* rippled through. The roundness of presence filled out my countenance. I felt the magnificent lift of sturdy support and protection that would guide me through the turbulent seas of the world.

Princess Precious Pearl's vessel was ready to set sail.

20 ❖ Marching toward the Land of Truth

DAY BY DAY, my body thickened with resistance as destiny pulled me toward the step I now knew I needed to take. Perry wanted the conventional married life as the center around which everything else orbited. I now knew that the teaching was my hub and that the spokes of my outer life needed to fan out from that. But I still hesitated to make the break.

As my visits to Berkeley became more frequent, Perry sought the company of a young woman at work. I knew he was seeing her socially, but I suspected that the relationship had become more intimate. To his credit, he told me the truth when I confronted him.

As the words stumbled out of his mouth, a knot twisted in my gut as an image of her jolted me. "She is pregnant, you know," I said curtly.

"She wouldn't do that to me," he insisted. "And how would you know that anyway?" He scowled.

"I don't know how I know, but I do. Did you use birth control?"

"I didn't . . . but she said that she did."

"If you were not using it yourself, you were inviting her to get pregnant."

He tried to convince her to have an abortion. She said no. Her choice to keep the baby blew the last fuse of Perry's and my marriage. He wanted me to stay. I simply couldn't. I was crumbling in pain and raging like a wild animal. In my more sober moments, I was well aware that I had contributed to the situation. Maybe even caused it.

I vacillated between lashing out and self-flagellation. Blaming him or myself created festering blebs on my heart, which I began to anesthetize with alcohol. My astrolabe was broken. My vessel had set sail, but now I was heading straight for an iceberg.

But this was my opening to do what I knew I must. I marshaled everything I had to get back on course. I was grateful when the protective fortress of the essential world wielded its long, sword-like diamonds and cut through the crap. Clarity arose and the thickened false protection of my unconscious thinned. I felt the inner support to design an outer life more consistent with my spiritual one. Wallowing in the suffering halted, and although the pain still was there, I began to find the strength to carry it and not succumb to it.

My inner warrior princess took over the steering. Hesitation was blown to the winds. I took the step of leaving Perry with determination . . . as I cried like a baby. The warrior and the little girl stood side by side in their mission, but my emotional fire was running hot, so a bitch in heels showed up occasionally. Good thing that royalty is more powerful. The princess won out in the end, once she realized that her power had been hijacked.

I moved out of our house in the spring of 1982 with the help of my tiny but sturdy friend Susan McGraw—all of five-foot-two and 110 pounds—and Dave, my six-foot-four, 275-pound big bear of a brother who has the biggest protector heart anyone could ask for. I stayed with my mother for a few weeks, then decided to live in the East Bay near Faisal and Hameed.

When she knew that's where I wanted to be, Susan welcomed me into her home. Just as she had been splitting up with her husband, Michael Torreson, who was also a student of Hameed's, she'd had the good fortune to run into Marie, who had been looking to rent out her house on McBryde Avenue in the Richmond Hills near Wildcat Canyon, which she'd smartly held on to after moving in with Hameed. With her usual generosity, Marie made it affordable and easy for Susan to move in.

Over the next months, kindness flowed from friends, soothing my smarting heart. Faisal and Hameed had each been helpful in my many explorations into what the right life for me would be; they never pushed me one way or the other and they continued to support me in the wake of my decision. Slowly, optimism returned as I saw life offering new chances. A desire to continue my education slowly surfaced. The day I woke up with certainty that I would enroll in school again, I was all a-flutter. Mushka and I made the short trek to Hameed's house and burst through the front door in unison. We took a quick right turn into the den, where Hameed was folded into a book. He looked up and brightened. I blurted out, "I am thinking of going back to school."

"What for?" His forehead crunched.

"I need it for my development," I said timidly.

"No institution is going to teach you what you are learning here."

"I don't expect that." My body stiffened in defense. "I've experienced all this clarity and precision and brilliance, but it is mostly just experience. I need to learn how to put it to good use."

"You can do this if you want to." His forehead smoothed as he started to yield a bit. "But I don't see what the point is."

"For one thing, I want to learn to write. I might need it someday—I just have that feeling. This really feels like the right thing to do."

I glared at him and he backed off, shrugging in neutrality. After we talked a little more, his face relaxed with a dusting of positivity, but I felt far from championed.

On the walk home, my shoulders were hunched in collapse. My thoughts raced to make sense of the juxtaposition of my decision and his response. I realized that I was trying to justify my choice even though I'd had *that feeling*. It was right. Why fight it? This move was not about trying to match Hameed. I wanted to grow, and I sensed that I could approach education again with renewed curiosity. I felt lifted into a growing confidence—with an edge of defiance. My eyes narrowed and my shoulders straightened up. "He'll see," I said to Mushka as we approached our little bungalow.

So, in 1982, I entered JFK University in Orinda. Hameed soon softened around my new venture and took notice that it was increasing my confidence and acumen. I decided to get the necessary credits to complete a bachelor's degree. "Why not?" he said. "You seem to be doing well and enjoying it." He had seen by now that I was not jumping the diamond ship. I was grateful for his support.

As I continued my studies, the Diamond Approach School was growing fast, with new students arriving as if on cue. The only "promotion" continued to be word of mouth rippling out through the spiritual field of consciousness. People would witness their friends going through changes and ask what they were doing. I've heard many stories of students finding out about Hameed while talking with a friend many states away and then deciding to move to be near him. And more than a few discovered him by picking up one of his books in a country across the sea.

Hameed didn't want to push things in any direction; he had no self-interest in making the groups larger, so he was content to see how they would grow on their own. "The Work will take care of itself," he would say.

The thirty-by-fifteen-foot living room was filling up on group weekends and evenings. Students sat along the back and side walls on benches that had been made during the work periods—benches with cushions! Folding chairs were placed in a semicircle in front of them, and in front of these were pillows for those who sat on the floor. The wood stove was in an awkward spot; if the room was crowded, those on the other side of it couldn't see Hameed well, especially if they were on the floor, but we worked around it. He would have the stove lit during the damp rainy months, and we would all be toasty warm.

At some point, membership hit critical mass. In 1980, Hameed had been inspired to think about starting to train teachers in California. After months of thoughtful consideration, he decided that there were enough students with the right attitude and understanding whom he could entrust with the teaching. The vision was not to engineer growth but to respond to it. What was important to Hameed was to create vessels—teachers who would embody the teaching and help keep it alive.

There is a Sufi teaching about the living vessels who carry the teaching of the mystery schools: They might go underground or be invisible for a while, but they are called forth in humanity's times of need. When the demand is present, they take their positions to disseminate the knowledge and serve the teaching. It is true necessity that dictates when that time is, not the whim or ambition of the individuals who carry the knowledge. Hameed anticipated that need and also wanted to safeguard the work that was coming through.

Even though he would say, "Essence itself is the teacher, and that is something we all have access to," it was obvious that skilled guidance was necessary to open the way. Inquiry was, and remains, the central method, and its alchemy relies on presence as the igniting force of awakening. The method would have less blast-off power without the personal attention provided by an embodied essential guide and teacher in private sessions and small groups.

Hameed could not accomplish this all himself without making a significant shift in the format. If the group continued as it had been from the beginning when he taught and led Inquiry during the meetings every other week, he could have possibly taken on more people in increasingly larger groups. For the work to flourish, however, new structures had to be developed. So, in addition to starting the teacher training, small work/discussion groups and private sessions were instituted and soon became effective tools for the personal integration of the large-group teachings. In these added settings, students received more support as they went through their process, and the intimacy of a smaller group afforded a closer sense of connection to those who wanted it.

Hameed's idea was, and still is, that as teachers we are guides and spiritual friends who can assist others to walk the same path and find their way with greater autonomy and self-reliance. He saw the advantage of others presenting the material and had a vision of groups starting without him as the main teacher. Knowing that the development, embodiment, and realization of each teacher differs, just as the needs of each student vary, he had great faith that the Diamond Approach would choose many people as its conduits. The path was still young, and the teaching would choose its emissaries in the way that would serve it best.

In 1981, I had the chance on the first night of the new training in California to scan the group of individuals he found trustworthy enough to carry the teaching. The atmosphere was respectfully low-key, with an underlying aliveness. As the fifteen arrived and quietly assembled in the big room, I took a seat in the back row of folding chairs where I would have a good view of the bunch. I noticed in particular Kristina Bear with her calm, observant demeanor and Jeanne Hay, a scintillating Southern belle whose eyes were riveted on Hameed. Bubbles of excitement filled my chest. I don't think any of us understood the magnitude of the position these folks would be in over the next years.

We meditated as usual and then took a short break before Hameed launched in. The path of the teaching, as far as we had taken it, was alive in me experientially, but to hear Hameed articulate it in all its spectacular specificity tailored to teachers-in-training was another kind of learning in itself.

As I sat listening, out of the corner of my eye I spied the profile of Jessica Britt, who was kitty-corner to my right. I had seen her around at a few of the meetings in recent months, but in this moment her beauty struck me. Slick chestnut hair pulled back in a tight bun made her appear

Balanchinesque—the opposite of the image I expected in a woman living in the counterculture of Esalen. She was serene and receptive, and the openness in her dark eyes, which were fixed on Hameed, took in the presence of every word.

Although Jessica had continued doing private work with Hameed, she had not joined the big group after that first night when she had felt it was "just too weird." Hameed sensed that she would be an excellent candidate for the teacher training, and spoke to her about it. She was interested, but he told her there was one caveat—she had to join the group. So she did. At that time, some of the students had worked with him privately for a few years but had not attended group for very long. This is very different from how it is currently done. Students are now put through the gauntlet before entering the teacher training; years of group work are a prerequisite.

Today, the number of seminarians (as they are now called) at the beginning of a training is in the hundreds, and the few who complete the teacher training and become certified comprise a small percentage of these. Hameed's idea that the training would produce mature vessels for the work was borne out. "It is worth having many to support the few who will arrive to serve truly," he used to say. Back then, "many" meant perhaps twenty, about half of whom completed the training.

The teacher trainees go through a great deal of rigorous training and practice to ensure the quality of their presence and skill. And although not everyone becomes a teacher, the whole training group benefits; those who don't continue have been engaged, committed participants along the way, which supports both their own learning and the learning of those who remain.

In 1978, after the first retreat with the initial group of students he had formed in Colorado, Hameed chose six people who had completed the six-month Returning Process to be trained in guiding others through it. They were woven into the teacher training seamlessly when it began in Colorado near the end of that same year.[1] At that time, the Returning Process was required for all students who wanted to become part of the work group. There were multiple reasons for the sequence of participation and training. First, it was a good test of our students' mettle, preparing them for the longer-term disciplined work of their own spiritual journeys. Second, building the skill and strength needed for the dynamic and confrontational style of Hameed's work was considered crucial before embarking on the road to training to become a teacher. Third, the teacher training was a forum for revealing any underlying difficulties, capacities, and limitations that may not have become evident during a student's participation in the Returning Process.[2]

Marie had several friends who were considered experts in a broad range of bodywork modalities, so I attended several classes with her, eager to learn. Together, she and I taught the bodywork component of the second teacher training in California.

Faisal and I didn't attend the training meetings formally but were welcome to come when we wanted to. He was now living in Colorado about half of the time and his travels to Colorado were often synchronized with Hameed's. The three of us would still convene when we were all in California, but I started to notice that those occasions were becoming less frequent. After a while, I could sense that something wasn't right, but I couldn't put my finger on what it was. Sometimes Faisal would arrange to visit Hameed when he knew I wouldn't be there. At first, I assumed that he simply wanted some time alone with his friend, which was fine with me, so I dismissed the uneasy feeling as simply an overlay from my childhood years of being shunned. But when the distance between Faisal and me widened, it became more difficult to deny the obvious. He didn't want contact with me.

One morning when I called Hameed, he told me not to come over that day because Faisal did not want to run into me.

I was crushed. I started to shake inside.

"*Why?*"

Hameed hesitated before answering. He must have heard the alarm in my voice. "I don't know."

"Whaddya *mean*, you don't know?"

According to Hameed, Faisal had been vague about his change of heart in relation to me. Hameed claimed that he didn't know what was really going on with Faisal; but maybe he knew and didn't want to tell me because he was afraid it would hurt my feelings. In either case, I felt angry that he was trying to steer away from the conflict and hadn't come to my defense. I let him know how much this bothered me. I was aware that he felt himself in a difficult position between Faisal and me, but I didn't care. I wanted him to help us. He didn't know what to do.

I hung up, still fuming with emotional combustion and disappointment. I scoured my mind for my latest contact with Faisal and came up startlingly empty about why he would spurn me like this. I hadn't seen it coming. I was knocked off my axis.

And now I was pissed at both of them.

As I stayed with the anger swimming chaotically inside me, I began to open to the pain and fear under the explosive tension. The shaky ground under me was giving way.

I scrambled to retrieve my connection with Faisal in an attempt to regain my equilibrium. I tried for several days to reach him, but he didn't answer my calls or respond to my messages.

What had I done to deserve this? What about the trust and honesty we had developed?

About a week after my conversation with Hameed, I lay in bed one evening, contemplating my failed friendship with Faisal. It became all mashed up with the recent losses in my life. I blamed myself and then blamed him. Then I just cried and felt the hole in my heart that his image once occupied.

I started to put the equation together. My father's approval and support for me as a woman had been almost nonexistent. Although my stepfather came to my aid in my teen years by acknowledging my budding beauty and womanhood, I sometimes acted out the earlier deficit of this valuable reflection from men via flirtations and inappropriate sexual remarks and gestures. It was all in playful fun, but I had apparently made Hameed's and Faisal's Kuwaiti friends uncomfortable at times. Knowing that it was a sensitive area for me, Hameed had been very kind when he initially tried to communicate this to me, but uncharacteristically oblique. When I finally understood what he was pointing to, I withered with shame. Being unsure whether my behavior was an actual cause of Faisal cutting me off made things even more difficult.

I finally stopped trying. I thought, "If that is what Faisal needs to do—fine, but it is his problem if he can't talk to me." I missed him, but more than that, I missed the three of us being together.

Two of the most important men in my life, and I was having such a hard time with both of them—from opposite directions: Perry, who loved and wanted me but got someone else pregnant and, in any case, couldn't understand or enter my world. My friend Faisal, whom I thought really understood my world but didn't want me to be in his. Different issues, but both breakdowns were frustrating and agonizing. And then there was Hameed, my best friend, who didn't know how to deal with the situation regarding Faisal.

It would have been very easy to blame all three for just being men and leave it at that. But I got the message loud and clear that it was time to take a hard look at my own part, since obviously I was the common denominator.

I did appreciate Hameed for understanding my difficulty around the losses I was feeling and for being straight about the complex and delicate issues that he saw I needed to deal with. With his support, I was able to take a deep journey through my sexual development, which helped me grow into myself with more confidence as a sensual being.

Perhaps Hameed had some sway in getting Faisal and me together in the same place again, but he never took credit for it. A couple of months after the initial break in our friendship, Faisal and I ended up at Hameed's house at the same time. Hameed told him I was coming over, and apparently Faisal decided to be there.

I didn't know this, so I was surprised to see him. I joined them in the kitchen and then Hameed disappeared from the room, leaving Faisal and me awkwardly in each other's company at the kitchen table.

"I didn't expect to see you here," I said. I contracted with protection, uncertain what his response would be.

"Oh, you are talking about the last few months." He paused. "I am sorry . . . I was cruel." He sounded soft and earnest.

I was astonished that he used that word, "cruel." But that's how it had felt. I relaxed, disarmed by his acknowledgement.

He didn't explain to me why he had not wanted contact with me, but he did get me to look at my anger at him for shunning me. We spent the better part of that afternoon investigating what had arisen for me over the prior few months. It was a clearing, at least on my side. I left that marathon interaction feeling a watery, undefended clarity and sweetness. Faisal did not reveal much about where he was. I trusted that this would come in good time. But I didn't wait for it. Over the next few months, I continued to investigate my relationships with all the men in my life. I was determined to stick close to my own reactions and understand what I had contributed to the misunderstandings and rifts.

Good thing that the vehicles of the teaching were all-terrain equipment. The road I was traveling included some jarring off-road topography. Difficult as it was, and would continue to be, I was better prepared to traverse the bumps and bruises than I would have been without their guidance.

The warrior princess bundled up the frightened little girl and held her securely to her chest with strong, loving arms. And together they strode off into the next chapter of life with a sturdy gait and a golden heart.

21 ❖ Love and Peas

By the end of 1982, an entire fleet of diamond vehicles had shown up in rapid succession. We called them "vehicles" because they were sacred modes of presence that carried both the wisdom and the methods of the teachings. We were enthralled with the discovery that each diamond vehicle was unique and perfectly designed for its particular function in guiding a person through the inner layers of psyche, using the human mind, heart, and body as portals to the unknown.

These vehicles are living files of essential knowledge that can be unlocked only by individuals who have the correct orientation. Each vehicle is connected with a presenting issue; when this issue is seen and resolved, the psyche opens up and her orientation is adjusted so that she can assume the necessary attitude and state for that particular vehicle to descend. For instance, love of the truth for its own sake invites the space for the Diamond Guidance, or the heartful desire to be personally intimate with the truth, which opens the heart's deep spaciousness to receive the teaching of the Stupa vehicle.

Buddhists have dakinis and bodhisattvas; Christians call on angels to deliver guidance, protection, and wisdom. Perhaps angels, dakinis, and the like are similar to the vehicles that are our emissaries from the unseen world—except angels do not become part of you, as I understand it. And diamond inner spaceships are not personifications; they are forms of presence that influence the psyche according to their particular wisdom. In any case, it is known that meditating on certain deities or messengers enables the blessings, presence, and teachings they embody to affect consciousness, transporting a person to numinous realms of experience.

We refer to the vehicles as wisdom vehicles not only because they are the direct and extensive source of knowledge of our nature but also because they can transform individuals into functional instruments of knowledge, love, and action. The diamond presence of knowledge, in its various qualities and configurations, opens the student to understand experientially how the logic of the Diamond Approach flows. As a student realizes the aspects and dimensions as who he or she is and becomes increasingly able to integrate them, it becomes more possible for truth to be actualized in daily life.

One aim of the Work is to find the inner teacher through the skillful means that is first offered through an outer teacher who has realized his or her own essential nature. As students practice with a private teacher and engage in large-group teachings, small-group meetings, meditation practices, and Inquiry with their peers, the capacity to deepen on their own is kindled and further developed. Hameed, Faisal, and I hypothesized that most students would be able to experience the vehicles, reducing the need for private teaching sessions over time as the inner teachers were discovered. But the teaching ignites and takes hold differently and in various degrees for each person; although some students need less personal contact with a teacher as they progress, complete autonomy is not something I have seen.

We also thought that some individuals, particularly the teachers we were training, might "specialize" in one of the diamond vehicles, embodying its perspective and knowledge. This didn't happen as we had envisioned. What we discovered over time is that people don't need a full-scale experience of every vehicle to gain the perspective of the overall teaching. A general feel for and knowledge of the vehicles is sufficient for establishing them in the consciousness of those who have a sincere commitment to practice. The comprehensive knowledge that the diamond vehicles offer is probably necessary only for the few who will carry the teaching and keep it alive for future generations.

With few exceptions, Hameed's process of understanding and integration was smooth and thorough. He ingested his experiences with an attention to detail that one would expect from a connoisseur of fine dining. He took in the experiences he found distasteful in the same way as the ones that pleased him—absorbing the flavor, texture, scent, and nutrients at his first sitting. Understanding was the spice that sated him until his natural hunger for truth began to rise up once again—very like in life, where only one course in a meal of many excellently prepared dishes will not suffice. He thrived on new knowledge. Pauses were times to abide, reflect, and savor—a palate cleanser between courses.

In addition to having a complete initial experience of each vehicle, Hameed could discern its presenting issue, the type of space it arose in that opened to its specific perspective, and the architecture of the vehicle from its contours to its core. Although subtle seeing was not his strong suit, it would be activated to spectacular perfection during these occurrences. The unique shapes of all the diamonds in each vehicle would show up with vivid taste, texture, sound, and visuals.

After Hameed's initial experience of a particular vehicle as a structure of multicolored diamonds of a specific body of knowledge, the complete form of its presence would wane. The component diamonds would then show up in his awareness, one by one, like forms floating to the surface of a lake. Each brought its specific contribution to the teaching of the vehicle, neatly unwrapping the layers of the psychological issues specific to that diamond. When understanding clarified one layer, the next colored diamond would present another issue for understanding, and so on. Eventually, the vehicle would arise in its totality once again, with all its component diamonds.

My process was the opposite of Hameed's in some respects, and our experiences provided us with a confirmation from two different but complementary angles. He was mostly gliding through space—and states—in an orderly manner. I felt like a little shuttlecraft zipping around hither and thither—going on side trips, finding shimmery new things and bringing them back to share, and bumping into emotional squalls one after the other along the way. In one act, a vehicle would instantly light up in its sublime form, replete with its particular presence plus the wisdom for understanding the related issues.

Although Hameed's pathway sometimes had the appearance of a tidy linearity, as I reread his journals I saw that his process was not always that ordered on the first pass. Many seemingly disparate insights had to be connected; but when the connections became obvious, it was as though he were reading from an illuminated tablet that lit up the correlates. Hameed's entire body and consciousness were imbued with each diamond-decoding device. He *became* the illuminated guidance.

Hameed's ability to see and synthesize the patterns of our experiences and the correlate issues was a function of his brilliant intellect, but the copious notes he made along the way played a huge part as well. The entries he made in his journal helped us discern which experiences were universal to all ego structures (these we referred to as "diamond issues") and which were specific to an individual or group of individuals based on their particular history or tendencies. Appreciating the unwinding of our unique individual processes made it natural to honor each student's way of opening to and discovering their essence, and their own work filled in some gaps in our understanding as well. It was a dynamic, mutually influencing dance of interactive inquiry.

The discoveries and experiences that Faisal and I were having often lent a new interpretation to the aspect of presence or vehicle we all were currently exploring. That was the beauty of our trio—we saw, felt, and opened to things differently and could discuss the variations; we were also able to catch one another's states, which further elaborated our own experience and understanding.

I was amazed by how easily Faisal could pierce many layers of a student's defenses and resistance to view what lay underneath. He seemed less interested in the process of understanding the issues involved, although there was acknowledgment of what those were. His greatest gift seemed to be in helping people access the treasures of essence. I felt quite plodding in contrast to his sleek ability to swiftly shift a student's consciousness to essential dimensions. It seemed like magic.

I was not aware of the details of Faisal's unfoldment regarding these vehicles, and I can't comment with clarity on his interior process during this period. Sometimes I found his insights profound, and other times I couldn't tell where he was coming from. He was spending more and more time in Colorado, and the inconsistency in our friendship and his desire for a closeness with Hameed that excluded me made him more and more an enigma to me. At times, I felt our trio to be off kilter, like a broken wind-up toy, but then things would smooth out and move along without a hitch.

My trust had thinned, but I came to accept that there were limitations to our friendship and that our relationships with Hameed were our common thread. I had no idea how this triple-reeded instrument of Hameed, Faisal, and me would play out. Whatever the outcome, I knew that the symphonic intelligence of Being was the force behind whatever was happening. And when the three of us focused on the miraculous journey we were on rather than the difficulties between us, we could appreciate the resplendent creativity that was articulating itself through each of us. Throughout the continuous flow of revelation, Hameed was steady as a flagship, resolute in his mission. With unfailing consistency, space seemed to unfold in front of the ship's diamond nose cone as we kept traveling to new universes. I never took issue with the fact that Hameed was the head of Starfleet. I felt secure knowing that he was.

❖ ❖ ❖

The vehicles continued to whittle away at us like the great artist Michelangelo, whose tools carved away the outer marble, revealing the true forms within. On one of his trips to Colorado, Hameed engaged with Faisal in exploring a new set of issues. These arose as the felt sense of a thick rubber cloud surrounding his head. Hameed called it a "dull dome"[1] because that precisely described the sensation he was having. The following journal entry describes his struggle as the next vehicle of the teaching was approaching and, at the same, triggering the barrier to its arrival.

> August 16, 1982
> Letting go of my mind so that the teaching will be an embodiment
> is now an important part of my process. I am afraid I will lose the
> diamond knowledge.
>   It seems that more particularly, the fear is of letting go of the dull
> dome.

As the leaden clouds dispersed, his head lightened to a bright openness that made way for the entrance of a dome of diamonds. It descended in a display of transparent, mind-bending jewels of many colors and qualities, just as all the vehicles do. The gorgeous dome of diamonds topped the neocortex and extended outside the boundaries of his head. Imagine yourself in a transparent geodesic dome . . . but instead of triangles there are diamonds of light that leave your mind open. Hameed named this vehicle "the Diamond Dome."

If the Diamond Guidance is the intellect, then the Diamond Dome is the essential mind that brings about a precise understanding of the levels of knowing. There is the usual learned, discursive knowledge based on memory, which is necessary for functioning in our daily life, but basic knowing—knowing the presence of Being—is not a reflective knowing; it is the knowing of Being, which is knowing by direct experience.

True teachings must begin with this undiluted experiential knowing; otherwise, the concepts taught are abstract ideas that are not based in a reality beyond subjective mind. When a teaching is grounded in the true felt known, then its conceptual models are accurate pointers to the realities that underlie the teaching.

The knowledge we accrue through education can peacefully coexist with a more basic, direct, essential knowing, but the trick is knowing when and how to use each of them. The Diamond Guidance is an adjunct to our ordinary intellect and can navigate any kind of knowledge. That is what gives it its power. An intellect that can use mental knowledge while also having a foot in the universe of presence can conceptualize all kinds of knowing—whether mental or direct—with exactness.[2]

We know Being by *being* it, not by looking back on it or viewing it from outside. And Being is only now, so we must be the now to know it. This fresh, in-the-now knowledge challenges the stale state of ego, which is patterned by memories, images, and past experiences. Like a Chinese finger puzzle, ego binds itself tightly in the endless pursuit of some ideal, spiritual or otherwise. Even spiritual seeking itself is the expression of that striving.

The central issue for the Diamond Dome to settle is the incessant activity of the ego in its attempts to free itself. Ego identity is a wound-up ball of activity that can be experienced directly. This becomes obvious when you sit to meditate and the "monkey mind" takes the opportunity to swing from one distraction to another through the mental canopy, or you start itching like crazy as you get closer to the direct experience of agitation.

The more solid the foundation in the belly, the more the mind can let go, and the monkey's activity is seen for what it is from beyond the jungle. So, Hameed introduced a nondoing meditation that enabled the mind to settle while the belly was grounded in concentration practice. He was not teaching that we should try to get rid of mind. The point was to not be its slave.

But monkeys are tricky, so we needed to follow the symptoms to their source. We found a small structure about the size of a BB. The closer our awareness came to it, the harder the sensation became. Its home seemed to be in the spleen area when it wasn't buzzing around in our consciousness, creating havoc. Inside this BB, Hameed felt an agitated ball of energy. This not-in-the-now self-structure sometimes looked like a hard, shriveled-up little ball. I called it "the pea." The name stuck, and we use it today as shorthand for this core of our patterned sense of self.

Even though it is constantly displaying itself, it doesn't want to be found out. The main principle of its activity seemed to be, "Stay in motion! It's too scary to stop . . . I might disappear!"

One day while Hameed was relaxing in the bathtub, he discovered the engine of this perpetual-motion machine. The frenetic swirl slowed down just enough for its components to become apparent to him as a cycle of rejection, desire, and hope: *rejecting* what is now, *desiring* something else, and *hoping* for something in the future—even if that future happens to be a second away.

The desire to be in a certain state that he had experienced before and hoped to move toward again was a subtle rejection of where he was in the moment. It had been obvious in our Inquiry practice all along that when we sink into our present experience and understand it, the next step reveals itself; nonetheless, this subtle activity of rejection, desire, and hope had not ceased completely, and the descent of the Diamond Dome was exposing this incessant ego activity.

The presence of essential knowing of the Diamond Dome delivered the wisdom that illuminated and dissolved, one by one, the ideations and adhesions of the ego self—for example, the ego's inflexibility and rejection of self and others, its fierce grasp on its limited point of view and, of course, its suffering and ignorance. We also discovered the importance of forgiveness, which was a step into the Diamond Dome. If we do not forgive the past fully, we adhere to it in our minds, and our present awareness is clouded with grudges. We began to understand that acceptance is a necessary step in order for the ego to surrender to the moment.

In a series of journal entries, Hameed delved more deeply into his experience of the Diamond Dome. In the first entry, he reflects on the feeling of the Dome descending into his belly before rising in the morning:

August 18, 1982
There is another reason for the feverish activity. There is the question of identity. To know the teaching or have the teaching is acceptable to the pea. It makes the identity feel special. But to become the teaching

is conflictual for the pea. Embodying the teaching in a real way means to become essence completely, which transcends the sense of self.

The purity of presence itself challenges the ego identity. It is the very *not*-doing that exposes how the pea is always messing with itself so that it can continue to exist. We discovered that it takes a long time to learn how to let ourselves be.

The Diamond Dome's message that *knowing is immediacy of Being* brought additional skill to our practice of Inquiry. The more immediate our knowing, the more deftly the blade of truth could penetrate the historical knowledge of the familiar self. As we applied this understanding, the endless cycle of rejection, hope, and desire began to unwind. It was a relief to see it for what it was—but even then, we could do nothing to prevent or completely stop the relentless activity of the ego. Here Hameed recounts another important part of the teaching of nondoing—helplessness.

August 23, 1982

I woke up with contractions at the left side. I felt deep sadness and my eyes filled with tears. I did not know the cause. In meditation, I wanted to just be aware. After a while, I saw the futility of this. Even paying attention is effort and based on desire. I do not always pay attention with this kind of effort, but this time I was controlled by my desire to be free. I felt the deep tears again. The sadness is connected to a longing and a yearning. The longing is for a completely free condition, where there is no need to even be aware. Where being itself is enough.

I decided not to do anything. I didn't know what to do to reach such a state. There is nothing I can do in this situation. Everything I do is effort. Effort does not work. I want to be effortless and carefree. I gave up trying. I gave up everything. Even awareness.

I just let myself be there, and whatever happens, happens.

I decided not to work on myself for a week. I felt frustrated, sad, and helpless.

He then began to feel the "light of enlightenment"—this is what we used to call a substance like liquid, sweet light that we felt as divine. It flowed into his head and into the chest.

I decided to take a drive to Estes Park. I got deeper into the
sadness. A longing for release and a deeper recognition that I
cannot do it.

I got engaged in fantasies and daydreams about enlightenment.
I noticed that it was dependent on an external agency, a teacher
or God acting on me. After a while the fantasies stopped, the
tears stopped, the feverishness of the search stopped, and a plastic
structure emerged. No emotion, no search.

Then came a heartfelt sincerity to know the truth of this experience,
to understand what was happening. He saw that even though he had
given up effort, he still had hope that enlightenment would happen.

I believed that freedom would come if I gave up efforting. I see from
my experiences that my efforts worked, or at least that is how it
seemed. I kept receiving more understanding and more essence. I see
now that my past experience gives me the hope that it will happen
in the future because that is what happened in the past. I see that
I then desire the same thing to happen again. And I use my will to
make it so.

Hameed and Faisal had a chance to talk the next morning before
Hameed had to get to the airport to return to California. As they were
exploring together, Faisal saw in Hameed's heart a diamond-gold
wheel. All around the perimeter were diamonds. Hameed and Faisal
named it "the wheel of time." It is a significant part of the teaching
of the Diamond Dome, and its presence becomes obvious when it descends to the heart.[3] The primary teaching of this wheel is that the cycle of suffering must be released from time—from any past and future
orientation—for liberation to happen.

August 24, 1982
I am still wondering what will erase the hope, which indicates the
presence of hope.

the past experience leads to hope
hope leads to desire
desire leads to effort

> effort leads to rejection of what is
> rejection leads to suffering
> suffering leads to hope . . .
It seems that the way out is not to want a way out but to love truth
for its own sake.

Only the grace of Being and a pure love for truth can quell our feverish activity; we cannot stop it through our efforts. Trying to squish the
annoying mind bug is just another kind of effort to get somewhere—
which is inevitably according to some idea of what that place would be.
And that always makes a mess.

The freedom to be in the now is vital for knowing the truth of presence itself: that there is no need to hope for better or different experiences in the future, *because the essential truth is right now*. The
immediacy of now is a slam-dunk into a timeless domain. Here we can
relax into a felt sense of fundamental goodness and an absence of desire
for what we're hoping for.

Hameed's process of seeing through his own ego activity and recognizing that the real way out is *in* made him acutely aware of how
important it was to establish in his students a deeper level of the love
of truth for its own sake—and as the real key to freedom, not as a way
to get out of jail. Our method of Inquiry had become so effective that
experiences of essence were becoming easy for the students to access,
and he felt that some of them were entering into essence too quickly
and having many spiritual experiences too close together. He skillfully
reoriented people away from merely acquiring new states without sufficiently loving or valuing truth and worked to instill in the students a
firmer foundation of awareness and detachment.

All throughout this period, new vehicles kept showing up. They
didn't always finish completely downloading before another would appear; it was as though Being were running several computer programs
in us simultaneously. Yet whatever themes they brought carried through
in logical sequence.

In discussion with Faisal on November 4, 1982, Hameed reported a
new blend of states materializing in his awareness. "I feel like there is
truth and will in me. I feel personal intimacy and a sweet contentment
also."

During that conversation, Faisal saw in Hameed a diamond structure —a new kind that is like the shape of a stupa, with a solid silver base, a turret of solid gold, and a point of light at the top. The stupa shape of this new vehicle provided its name.

Whereas the Diamond Dome deals with the core of ego identity and its ego activity, the Stupa deals with the rind of ego and its separating boundaries. It is the key to the heart and its secrets for traversing the path. It became known as the Diamond Body of Love because it brings the teaching that only through love can the ego surrender its boundaries.

As I was to find out, an intimate love, along with a stillness of heart, is necessary for it to arrive. One morning many months later, as I lay asleep on my futon, the sun's rays filtered through the trees and danced in bright patterns through my closed eyelids. "Oh, jeez," I growled, "time to wake up." I rolled over onto my stomach and dug my face into the crook of my arm. Mushka stuck her wet nose into my ear to rouse me.

I peered out the three long, vertical redwood-framed windows and into the little canyon beyond the deck. The sky was so thick with blue that it looked unreal against the greening hills. A flock of sparrows circling at eye level swirled lower and shrank to a single point, disappearing into a small opening in a sun-silvered shack. I felt a longing to be like that—flying free, then disappearing into nowhere.

"Alone again," I sighed. My voice sounded damp and low. The white fluff near me was sweet company, but . . .

Mushka looked straight at me with her glittering eyes as if she knew what I was thinking. "But *I'm* here!" she conveyed with a lick on my face, followed by a piercing, affectionate yelp. She eased her body down to the floor beside me, her head cradled in her ample paws.

"Thanks, girl. I love you too."

I didn't always mind living alone—well, mostly alone—but there were times like this morning when I felt an emptiness filling with unhappiness. I wanted a lover—human comfort, intimacy.

I wandered through the billowing fog of ideas, hopes, and desires and sifted through my sensations. Some tension at my sternum and the left side of my diaphragm drew my attention, and I breathed into the area. Yearning swelled, then crested in the center of my chest. Tears spilled out of my eyes. I suspended my ideas of what would quell the pain and simply felt the yearning.

The sadness felt heavy at first, but as I let go into it, I felt the release of pressure. The tears pooled in my ears and flowed down in delicate salty trails to the pillow. The emptiness grew, and I wailed and moaned in primitive, unrecognizable sounds. The release relaxed my body into a deepening quiet, and a softness filled my heart. Warm, green compassion soothed my aching being.

Then I felt my heart flowering from the center of itself, rooted in silence.

A quiet, black, velvety space opened and invited me into its depth. Nourishing nectars streamed, melting me into a simple solitude. I continued to soften as the space around me deepened with richness. I was touched in an exquisite way by the spacious darkness inside every cell of my being.

I realized I had always thought of intimacy as a romantic encounter, a candlelight-and-roses kind of thing—and, most important, staring into another person's eyes. This new, sweet interiority made it apparent how *being* in love was the very essence of intimacy.

In the middle of my chest, every kind of love arose as different essential aspects. Will, strength, kindness, brilliance—even power—existed in my heart as diamond love. Each gem was rounded in the middle, with a pearly fullness. It was remarkably impersonal yet personal at the same time. The pregnant love diamonds in the black expanse revealed that this structure was the treasure of my own true heart.

I felt rich, whole, and beautiful. The longing to find another person to complete me evaporated. I had found an intimacy and love of incomparable grace. My heart was so smart!

I got up off the futon and floated to the back door to let Mushka out for her morning rounds through the neighborhood. Inhaling a deep breath of fresh air, I found the freedom of movement in my ribs and torso a sensual pleasure. I drank in the sounds of the birds with their lively banter, the scolding squirrels scurrying through the thistles. The world was vibrant and alive, and I felt in personal contact with it all. Weightless, flying free like those sparrows, I began my day's activities.

As I made my way over to Hameed that afternoon for our daily check-in, I was still feeling the deep intimacy of loving space and plump diamonds. It seemed to take a sweet eternity to get to his house.

Hameed met me at the door. I was touched by the immediacy of our interaction. I felt deep personal appreciation for him—the man, the friend, the teacher—in all his unique preciousness. I saw that my heart had never faltered. I was just afraid sometimes. I felt the steadfastness of my commitment to truth and how it had always been a driving force in my life.

We went into the den, and I told him the story of how my heart had become a diamond portal of love. Tranquil gladness filled his eyes as I spoke. I felt his appreciation for the truth of what I was. He didn't have to say a word.

A new level of our friendship was opening, even more real and human. I saw our personal differences as the interesting, distinctive qualities of what we each were. This personal intimacy and our love for the truth was the essence of our relationship. The rest was peripheral.

And me? I felt deep appreciation for myself as well as for Hameed. I felt the simple, open truth of a woman inseparable from Being. There was no little girl to be found, for she had dissolved into my heart. The sweet, innocent love qualities she held within her small frame had become part of me. I was contented with my aloneness as I sat in profound intimate contact with my friend.

"Would you like some tea?" Hameed asked. He looked royal.

I paused to feel the rich simplicity in the atmosphere.

"Sure."

22 ❖ A Star Is Born

HAMEED HAS ALWAYS claimed that he is not really a storyteller, but actually, he is. I love listening to his stories. We were in our office at the Ridhwan Center in Berkeley, and I looked up in the middle of writing a paragraph in this chapter to ask, "Hameed, when did you first see or feel the Point?"

"I saw it years before I knew what it was," he responded, and, without any prompting, jumped into the story of what happened. "I was in my apartment one evening with a friend. We had dinner and then got stoned on marijuana. We smoked together but then went off into different rooms to do our own thing. I found myself at the dining table, staring at a plate in front of me. It transformed into a round opening that became the entrance to a spacious sky. I felt the urge to jump into it, so I did."

I relished his enjoyment as he continued.

"Yeah, I felt I was zooming through space. Initially, it was like a clear blue sky of day. Then it became darker as I left Earth's atmosphere. I looked ahead of me and saw a brilliant star in the distance. I was curious about what it was, so I approached it and saw that it was like a binary star—two points of light had appeared as one. I don't know why there were two, but I knew that one of them was me. I believe this was my first conscious encounter with the brilliant Point of Light."

Hameed's dinner-plate jump gate into the starry night appeared in 1967, about a year into his college days. He had been experimenting infrequently with pot and hallucinogens for a few years. These magical mystery tours were more like research expeditions than social entertainment, however. Fun has always meant learning for him, and inquisitiveness infiltrated everything he did.

He had no idea that this sighting of the Point of Light—which resembles a star appearing in a luminous night sky—would reappear fifteen years later as a major contribution to self-realization and psychospiritual discourse.

By the early 1980s, it was notable that the Point was often the punctuation mark at the end of a comprehensive essential insight, frequently accompanied by a jubilant spontaneity like that of a child engrossed in unselfconscious delight and play. It sparkled like a firefly, with weightless freedom, and each moment was a surprise.

Hameed's journals are filled with queries and connections that reveal our mounting interest in exploring both the usual sense of self and the "real" self. The insights and experiences of presence that Hameed, Faisal, and I had over the years had put ever more pressure on the ego. The Stupa and Diamond Dome teachings challenged the separating boundaries of ego and the deeper core of identity, catching ego with its pants down and leading it into a certain kind of death. The question *Who am I?* had been answered in part by our recognition of the personal essence. But the question of identity—*What am I?*—had not yet been solved. The false identity as an activity had been neutralized, but what it means to have an authentic core was still a mystery. Hameed made this journal entry in August 1982, as he was beginning his inquiry into the essence of identity:

I have had experiences of the Point but I do not know it completely.
I have not become it. I feel deep tears and longing and a desire to
just Be. Being should be enough.

He deeply wanted to know himself, to be himself, in this totally unrestricted manner and wondered what was in the way. Faisal was particularly enamored with the state. I wanted the feeling of freedom that the Point afforded, but I did not long for it, at least not yet.

Essential prerequisites started to show up to supply us for the work we were to do. On August 29, Hameed wrote:

This afternoon Faisal discovered that the aspect of essence that
erases ego pride is honey. He felt and saw essence descending in the
form of honey in various densities. He felt that honey is the aspect
of essence that is humility.

I am pleased with Faisal's discovery. It makes quite a lot of sense.
I experienced it some but not fully. I don't think I see the issue of

pride fully for myself yet. I saw before that honey is surrender, and I also know that ego finally melts in honey. But I had not seen that the issue for the complete surrender of ego is specifically pride. Now I see that the pride of ego is based on the separateness of ego and its adherence to this belief in its separateness. Ego is proud that it can exist on its own, do things by itself, and even achieve enlightenment and freedom.

Faisal's discovery had put a missing piece in place: Pride is the kingpin of the ego's separate existence. Funny thing is, the crown of the ego's fashion statement is a false hood, or cap, at the top of the head. It often starts as a hard spot of tension in the middle where all the sutures come together, and it blocks the crown chakra. In the Hindu tradition, this chakra is the connection to the higher realms beyond individual consciousness. Its opening is considered the turning point leading to freedom from the ego.

As Hameed worked through the issue of pride, I witnessed the shift in his countenance—from being a separate, hidden guy to a more inviting presence. The bow to essence from within the ego itself delivered the rescue remedy: Any remaining whiff of arrogance was being dissolved by sweet surrender. Simultaneously, he discovered another feature of the essential aspect of brilliancy. He fell in love with its majesty and beauty and realized that what he was in love with was its exquisite preciousness.

Bowing to Being had shown us that although the fancy costume that the ego dons might look good, further scrutiny reveals cheap material and shoddy workmanship, not the outstanding appearance it attempts to show off. Understanding pride exposed the ego's sense of having a separate existence, which is the feather that adorns ego's hat—pride. This took us straight to the crossroads where all signs pointed toward the Land of Narcissism.

Being properly outfitted for the journey required profound respect and appreciation for the preciousness of Being and a deepening of our sincerity, humility, and steadfastness.

Hameed came to pick me up for lunch one afternoon in March of 1983. The Mercedes hummed as we passed by daffodils dotting the semiwild front yards of the small cottages in my neighborhood. As we snaked our way on the narrow road past the fragrant blooms, sunlight filtered through the deep-shade trees, dappling everything in its path with yellow neon. It had been a rainy winter, and everything was alive with fecundity. The vividness was a stark contrast to my gray mood.

I peered out into the world from a heavy quiet as we drove down the street and finally spilled onto the freeway toward Berkeley. As we zoomed along Highway 80, Hameed turned toward me without losing sight of the road.

"So, how are you doin'?"

"I dunno. I feel kinda depressed. Oddly unlike myself."

"Yeah, you seem a little low." He gave me a quick glance and an "I'm listening" gesture, but I said nothing. We spent much of the drive in silence, both sensing the bleakness in the space.

We pulled up in front of Solano Café—still our favorite place to hang out and talk—and wrestled with the car doors on the incline of the avenue. Finally winning over gravity's grip, we hoisted ourselves out. I lumbered and Hameed plunked and shuffled his way up the stairs to the deck of the restaurant. Once we were inside and settled in at our customary table, he cocked his head to the right and raised his eyebrows slightly, a silent invitation to talk.

"I actually feel rather empty in a funny way," I began.

Before I could say more, I spied the waiter coming toward us and put on my happy-face mask as he strode up to the table. We ordered the usual tea for me, a latte and croissant for Hameed. He loves almond croissants.

We sat in motionless silence for a bit, and then Hameed started to talk about what he had been reading lately. One after another, he had been consuming books about Vedanta teachings and in-depth self-psychology. He is a slow reader but very persistent. He had completed reading *I Am That* by Nisargadatta Maharaj[1] in the '70s, handing it off to me in 1982 because it had some relevance to our experiences.

In the book was a description of the Self as a deep identity of the Absolute ground of Being, which, as I understand it, is the ultimate Self-realization in Shiva Advaita. Nisargadatta also described the existence of a point of light with a striking resemblance to the one we knew that had often shown up in the context of deep, black space. We wondered whether this was the same space that Nisargadatta called the Absolute.

He often spoke interchangeably of the Point and the Absolute, as though they were two sides of the same phenomenon.

In addition to reviewing Nisargadatta's teachings, Hameed had been reading James Masterson,[2] Heinz Kohut,[3] Otto Kernberg,[4] and others, studying how their theories shed light on the psychological issues that our experiences of the Point had evoked. Hameed was intrigued by theories of the self. What stood out most prominently for him were Kohut's discussions of narcissistic transferences whose features resonated with Hameed's observations of his, Faisal's, and my processes over the past few years, as well as those of many of the students. He had been looking through his notes and noticed the steady progression of these issues lighting up over time, recently culminating in an increased sensitivity to perceived slights and to others' misattunements.

We had recognized these sensitivities early in our explorations but didn't have a way to identify them precisely, nor did we have language to describe what we had observed. Now, as the vortex of the Work drew us into deeper realities, the personality was being peeled closer to the core. The categories of symptoms that Kohut was pointing to were useful discriminations; especially relevant was the craving to be seen by others or to feel connected to people who were shiny (in our estimation) in order to bask in their radiance.

As Hameed spoke, I continued to be aware of my state and the shifting reactions moving through me. I noticed that many of the things that Kohut described fit me well. I cringed to hear them put so crisply: *hungry for reflection . . . need to be special . . . overly sensitive . . .* The emptiness I was feeling was not merely about missing some*thing.* I was missing value, meaning, aliveness. I had been heading in the right direction, but the Point brings out the crisis of meaninglessness at a new level. So my being on track may have been instrumental in bringing it out even more.

I finally found a word for it: "despair." The earmark of an existential crisis. I had recently read Kierkegaard. That didn't resolve it.

Hameed kept reciting descriptions of the narcissistic character. His voice droned on in the background of my mini-drama. My self-esteem-o-meter bottomed out. I felt worthless. A gap in my core pulled my awareness to its hollowness. I felt like I was standing on a cliff looking into a huge abyss.

The Sufi story about the water reaching the edge of the desert came to mind. The water longed to get to the lush land on the other side of the parched sand, but it had to surrender totally and evaporate to be capable of making the journey.

Hameed looked straight into my eyes. "To be able to say 'I am That,' one must know what one is in a palpable, felt way."

I squirmed. His completely here presence only exaggerated my lack of it.

"But the barriers to this recognition appear to be quite the dragon in front of the jewel," he continued.

"Yeah, but my dragon is a cliff. Some scary monster would be easier than this empty place," I said, smirking. "Makes me want to run and hide under my covers."

My chest ached and my eyes moistened as the raw understanding of my dilemma spread through me. Hameed was speaking to the issues obliquely, so I assumed he was being careful to not throw me into deep process in the middle of the café. Sometimes it is better to tread lightly and let things develop.

My gripping need for him to focus on me and validate my experiences and contributions to the teaching forced its way into my attention. I contracted, and my humiliation swelled. I got how important it was for me to be seen, admired, and reflected by him. I knew that Hameed loved and valued me, but I wanted more. I wanted to feel that my relationship with him was extraordinarily special. Rather than realizing that our friendship was unique and served an important function, I had been using it to buoy my sense of value and importance.

My attention was split between listening to his Cliff Notes version of *Narcissism and Vedanta Readings*—which I was actually quite interested in—and my inner litany: "Why isn't he paying attention to me? I am going through something here—where *is* he?" I wanted him to notice where I was in my *very interesting experience* that would be oh-so-meaningful for us to understand. As he continued to speak, I felt as though a big fat red arrow were manifesting above my head, aiming down at me for all to see.

"The unrealistic expectations of oneself or another are bound to disappoint," he tossed out.

Was he reading my mind?

"We want our essence to be seen and known. However, the need is due to the gap in our own awareness: We're not seeing our true nature."

I mumbled a listening noise. All of a sudden, my pelvis had started to feel wobbly.

Hameed expressed how this dilemma had played out for him with Henry and other teachers. He got brighter and more focused as he then began to share some of his experience of his own family. "What I saw was that I wanted my mother to see *me*, not just what I meant to her. I wanted her to see me not as her son but as what I am, independent of her relationship to me. I knew she loved and valued me—but as her son, not just for what I am."

His eyes darted about the room as his mind began to relate his early experience to the thoughts he had been having about the subject. "Ultimately, it is the parents who didn't see our essence. No matter how much they love us, they cannot see our essence if they cannot know it directly in themselves. But even if they *could* see us, it seems to be part of the human condition that as we grow, we move away from Being."

"Bad design," I said flippantly.

The café was filling up now. Our waiter delivered the check and hurried off to the next table. The room blurred as the recollections of slights, devaluation, and the wounding in my own life began to cut into my inner atmosphere.

Hameed stood up, signaling that it was time to go. I pulled myself together and ambled along behind him on wooden legs. As we drove off to do a few errands before taking the short drive back to Richmond, I drew into myself like a folded blanket, trying to protect my vulnerable underbelly. I felt like an impostor. "Who killed me and left this one sitting here?" I thought. Then I got curious about a strange hard sensation in my chest.

"Hameed, what is this hardness I feel? I feel so weird. It feels like a hard walnut!"

"You *are* a hard nut to crack," he said impishly. He knew that would get me.

"Hey, watch it!" I snapped, pretending to joke.

"Yep, it does feel like a shell."

"It is growing as I pay attention to it, Hameed . . . I feel like there is nothing real here at all—only this fake hard thing with no substance. I am a big, empty shell!"

No response.

When we arrived at my house, Hameed gave me a reassuring pat on the leg. "See ya later."

"Okaaay," I said, hinting at annoyance. "I guess I gotta stay with it, right?"

"Yep." A toothpick angled in his mouth wiggled as he spoke.

I waved a limp goodbye and trudged up the stairs without looking back.

I spent the next few weeks moving through the hollow shell of ego. Finally, I came upon the enormous, deep wound that revealed the gap in my consciousness between who I thought I was and the reality of what I am. This time, I jumped off that cliff into a deep chasm of blackness. Whirling in space, I felt frightened, disoriented, and alone.

A turning point came one evening as I witnessed the work of a woman in a small-group meeting that seemed to pick up from where I had left off. I noticed a weighty but earnest sincerity developing in each person who brought their questions into the room that night. I felt myself easing into a field of support and simplicity.

Not a word had been taught yet about the narcissistic transferences and the brilliant Point. However, many of the concerns and questions that evening related to what Hameed, Faisal, and I had recently been exploring. As usual, when the three of us went through something, the students would catch wind of it and sail directly into the wake of the teaching's unfoldment.

A young woman, whom I will call Cheryl, was sitting directly in my line of vision in the circle. She seemed agitated as she waited her turn. Hameed worked with one student after another, overlooking Cheryl's gestures for recognition. Her distress grew into obvious annoyance. Hameed was tinkering with his beads, acting as if he didn't see her. She finally caught his eye and shot her arm up into the air like a flare.

"Hey!" she called out.

"So you want to work?"

"Yes I do." The edge in her voice sharpened as she struggled to stay in control. "I *hate* you." Cheryl had the look of cold rage. "I think you are an asshole."

I watched to see what Hameed would do. His interruption was strong but not harsh. He became the grand presence of an emerald mountain of compassion.

"Okay. You can feel the rage, but you can't attack me. Just tell me what you are feeling, not what you think I am. What do you hate me for?" he asked, looking interested.

"I hate that you didn't pick me to work. You were ignoring me!" Her fuse was burning hot. You were not giving your total attention to *me*!

He held her in supportive tenderness as she expressed the hot mess of her experience.

"I am now."

The responses in the room ranged from fear to kind awareness. Even Cheryl seemed struck by the unreasonable exaggeration of her reactions, which are typical of narcissistic rage. She stared for an infinite second into space and then crumpled into a heap on her chair.

"I feel such a hurt," she howled. Tears of sheer desperation smeared her cheeks. She cupped her drenched face in her hands. "I feel a wound the size of the Grand Canyon."

Hameed eased her into the wound and stayed intimately present with her, as though he was sharing the space on that kind mountain with her. "What is happening, Cheryl?"

"There is a black"—she hiccupped a cry—"a super-black emptiness."

"What does that do to you?"

"I feel disconnected from my self." Looking up from her collapse, she stared at him, pleading. "I need your help."

"I am here," he said softly.

"It is like a huge, empty space. I am falling through black space. I don't know where I am. I don't know what I am doing . . . Where am I going? I have no direction. My body feels like it is fragmenting." She paused. "I am scared."

Cheryl whirled in black space, vulnerable, disconnected, disoriented, and helpless. Then the most amazing thing happened. A softness appeared in the room from no particular source. And a yearning to be herself emerged from the depth of Cheryl's being. I saw that the source of her yearning was the very darkness she was swirling in. It was as if it were drawing her toward itself. I am not sure she felt it that way, but that was what I saw.

"I just want to be myself, even though I don't know what that is," she said earnestly. The tears stopped. Time halted. The sunlit softness receded, and the dark emptiness became brighter, like moonlight on a black lake at night.

Cheryl's back straightened and her eyes widened, as though she had been shaken awake. "It is like night . . . and I see the sparkliest stars ever!"

The blackness deepened into the room.

"Do you feel drawn to one of those lights?" Hameed asked.

"One stands out. I feel like it is mine." Cheryl paused. "I feel something in my heart . . . glittering light."

Another pause. "No, it is not *mine*—it is *me*! I am here!" she announced.

Mirroring her tone, Hameed simply said, "Yes, there you are! I see you."

"I feel simple and pure and alive. I am happy."

Her voice turned coy then, but with a blush of innocence. "I feel like I wanna play with you."

"Okay, what do you want to play?"

Cheryl giggled. "It is enough that you feel playful, too. Actually I feel we *are* playing. We are frolicking in space."

Hameed's nod was all the acknowledgment she needed.

As I was tracking Cheryl in her process, insights were going off like fireworks in me. I appreciated the nuanced skill that Hameed was exhibiting in his work with her. This, blended with her willingness to be exquisitely vulnerable with the whole group, invited not only my silent participation but theirs as well.

I'd had peekaboos of the brilliant Point over the prior weeks, including feeling its definite presence in my chest just as Cheryl did. By the end of this evening, however, I realized that the Point of Light was no longer showing up in my chest. A mountainous density much like what I had seen in Hameed had risen up my legs and filled my belly, then my entire body, with its gleaming, supportive strength. Its base seemed to be far lower and deeper than my feet. My legs no longer felt like two distinct parts of the body; they were now blended into an enormous pyramidal structure of diamonds. The Point of Light crowned it like a lighthouse. And I became its radiance.

The sense of having a real self vanished. Yet it remained implicit as the mountainous support brought the specific quality of being authenticity itself. The feeling, or even the concept, of self became irrelevant. I was emanating light without self-reflection. I felt the stark yet grounded solitariness of just being. No mind noise, images, or ideas could influence this simple purity.

This state lasted for weeks. There were times in those days when I felt as though I had entered a mountain. It was very like being inside a massive European cathedral—a silent spaciousness with a holy openness pervading it.

The diamond vehicle that arose for me that night was the Diamond Will, which is the sixth of the ten diamond vehicles. The Diamond Will is the wisdom of nondoing as the true support for the shift of identity from mental content to Being. Being then arises as an immense mountain-like solidity, and this has the effect of stabilizing realization.

The related primary issue is the narcissism inherent in the ego self, which is nothing but the expression of the soul's alienation from her precious nature. Hence, the sixth vehicle is the wisdom of self-realization of True Nature—recognizing this as our real identity and abiding in it as what we are.

The brilliant Point is the quintessential exemplar *and* understanding of what realization is in the Diamond Approach.[5] Seeing ourselves for what we truly are and having the felt-known recognition *is* self-realization. The Point of Light specifically and precisely differentiates *experiences* of True Nature—for example, of presence, essence, space, emptiness—from *being* True Nature. Some paths make no distinction between awakening and realization, but we find the term "awakening" too broad as a category. It does not clearly differentiate between waking up to what True Nature is on one hand, and, on the other, recognizing this nature as being what we are. The meaning of being realized is that we awaken *in* Being *as* Being and recognize that there is no distance between self and Being. I am not merely present or experiencing presence—I *am* presence.

The cliffhanger was finally solved when the diamond support healed the rift between me and my real identity. The two sides of the cliff became the gleaming rock walls of the mighty cathedral supporting the "I" of light. I no longer needed to attempt to construct a bridge to some shiny object on the other side of the crevasse. The leap of faith into the emptiness turned out to be the way to go beyond the mind and toward the self-recognizing brightness of my own being.

23 ❖ The View from Beyond

PERCHED ON A CLIFF at Pomponio State Beach, Hameed and I took in the ocean expanse. We had come for no other reason than to find a good backdrop for colloquy. He had popped over to my house, and we'd decided to go for a drive with no particular destination in mind. The ocean is simply where we ended up . . . not unlike what often happened on our inner journeys.

Apricot-mauve clouds blended and morphed in the darkening sky. I basked in the friendly, spacious atmosphere with my buddy. A gap in the clouds immediately above the horizon exposed a crisp edge. Crepuscular rays streamed through stretched, puffy clouds and onto a patch of water below as the sun squatted in position to lower itself beyond the horizon.

"It is almost as beautiful as the real thing," Hameed said quietly. He saw the material realm as a representation of the essential world. "No matter how picturesque the physical world is, it doesn't compare to the beauty of the inner universe."

To me, the sunset appeared to be sublime reality in resplendent display, blurring the boundaries between the heavenly and the mundane. We were drawn into the finale as the sun, like a bald guy's lit-up head, descended from view.

"Did you see that?" I squealed.

"Yes. I think so! It was a spark."

"Yeah. And it was neon green!"

"Oh wow. I've never seen that before." Hameed's enthusiasm was innocent, childlike.

Maxfield Parrish shades of blue on the horizon gradated to blackness, and a few stars peeked out.

"It is late," he said. "I guess we should head back. Marie will wonder what happened to us."

We headed north on Highway 1 in silent contentment. Hameed found the turnoff, and the car whined as we rounded the hills from Half Moon Bay on Highway 92. I had been wondering what was happening for Hameed after we attended an evening talk by Krishnamurti a couple of weeks earlier, and I decided to ask him about it.

"Hameed, how have you been since we saw Krishnamurti? Last time we talked, you were feeling so tired and heavy, and you suspected that something was coming up in response to his state."

"Oh yeah," he said. "I was meaning to tell you . . . I really liked seeing him. He had such clarity, didn't he?"

As soon as the words came out of Hameed's mouth, I sensed faceted light dancing in my forehead. "Hameed, I am feeling the clear Diamond Body as you are talking. Just like what happened when you, me, and Faisal debriefed a few days after Krishnamurti's talk. Remember?"

He nodded. The transmission from that evening had begun to unfurl within our consciousness almost immediately, and I noticed a new version of the Diamond Guidance as a body of transparent, colorless diamonds. We didn't know whether Krishnamurti had experienced this state, but his talk seemed to have stimulated the diamond clarity for us, whether he knew it in this specific way or not.

"I am pretty sure his clarity affected what followed for me," Hameed said, and then he paused. I could sense his mind reaching for clues. "But I am not sure how yet. Anyway, remember that about three days after we saw him, we started experiencing lead."

We were beginning to understand that the leaden state of consciousness has to do with inertia. Not merely contraction, but inertia from remaining fixed in a particular position concerning the nature of reality. Krishnamurti was an example of enlightened teachers we encountered who had a propensity for remaining on an established course even after having experiences that challenged their own views.

"I saw that I was feeling the conviction of being an individual with a personal life of my own," Hameed continued, "and that I believed the diamond knowledge belonged to me as an individual. So there was inertia in my fixation about knowledge. It occurred to me that I was seeing the part of my personality that wasn't changing. Maybe it was the lack of fixation we experienced with becoming the Point that made this obvious, now that I think about it."

I nodded. "Yeah, that makes sense."

"Anyway, I started to feel existence as a dense presence. It was the feeling of existence itself as an essential quality. It was an intense, compact density, but not a blockage. More like a neutron star."

"What did the presence of existence have to do with the fixation?"

"I felt that the Point was the true core of myself, but the lead arose as me clinging to some kind of conventional existence. This compact star presence showed me explicitly that Being gives everything its existence and meaning. It is the Point of Existence."

"That's funny," I guffawed. "When I was feeling so bummed out a few weeks ago, I was crying to you, 'What is the point of my existence, Hameed?'"

His teeth shone white against the night. My mimicking the whine of my own voice amused him.

He refocused and continued. "Remember a few weeks ago when you, Faisal, and I were investigating permutations of the Point? When I saw that the Point could shine with any quality of essence, it became like a point of space—witnessing everything from a totally disengaged vantage point."

"So you're saying that the Point became a little bubble of perception that was a witnessing awareness. Uninvolved. You mean that, right?" I asked.

"Yeah," he said, nodding. "Well, it developed further."

"What happened?" I tugged at my seat belt to loosen it, twisting toward him with curiosity.

"This point of space opened up to a more expanded witness."

Hameed began to appear super dark to me. I couldn't tell whether it was because night had descended or because the state was manifesting as he voiced it. I was a little concerned that he would witness us right into the side of a hill. "Are you okay driving?"

"I am fine. But I notice that when I get into deep states, you get all nervous that I won't be able to function."

"Well . . . to be honest, I trust you in *nearly* every way. Driving—not so much." He couldn't see my squinty-eyed grimace as we swerved around a hairpin turn at what felt like Mach 2. "It is your state mixed with the ton of steel you are piloting that makes me feel a little squirrelly."

"Don't worry, Kran."

Hameed blended into the darkening atmosphere as he continued talking and gesturing. Intrigued, I put my nervousness about his driving aside.

"I felt like I was the Point witnessing at first; then I became a vast, silent, dark emptiness. Deep gray, almost black. I saw my personal life as a dream I don't have to be involved in. I can feel that even now—it is like a movie that has a beginning and an end, but it's not me. I feel I am beyond the totality of my personal life. The concepts of life and death don't apply to me; they are a process of constant transformation happening within me in a way I'm completely disengaged from. All existence, from the lowest to the highest, is in a continuous state of flux, but I am the background against which this flux is seen."

He took a breath. "Who I am is static, unchanging, unreactive. I am beyond time and timelessness. I am the silent witness beyond everything. Anything that can be an object of perception is not me."

"So you are not the content? And the witness is free," I concluded, surprising myself with my certainty.

"Yes, exactly. I don't need to be freed or enlightened. I am always free, always have been and always will be."

"This dark gray space feels a little spooky," I said.

Hameed shot me a flash of recognition. "The silence *is* eerie, in a way . . . but not bad. It is just so beyond anything we have known before. It feels ultimate because there is nothing behind it. The silence is beyond sound or no-sound."

Light from the occasional passing car lit Hameed into form. Then he would recede into darkness, save for the highlights on the contours of his face, lit by the dim glow of the dashboard.

His presence was beginning to pervade me. After some minutes, my body loosened as the unrestricted freedom and depth of space backed us out of an earthly orbit and into the farther reaches of the universe. A reflexive sting of adrenaline drew me back. As my mind clung to the edges of my body, I noticed that my vantage point continued to remain outside the contraction, watching the animal part of me as it recoiled in fear.

I felt my eyes widen. "It *is* a big perspective. Maybe it wasn't only the driving that was making me uncomfortable," I confessed.

We rolled into the Richmond Hills and were soon weaving our way back to the safety of our little compound.

The next days produced more insights as Hameed discussed with Faisal and me how movement toward a more impersonal, broader perspective was challenging our vantage point that was centered within the small view of our personal existence. Hameed wrote in his journal on May 17, 1983:

> The clear Diamond Body is the guide to the impersonal by
> understanding the Point. It has the teaching of the Point and how
> that points the way to the Brahman. The experience of no-mind and
> no-time is the realization of the Point. But it is also the exit out of
> personal life and into the impersonal Brahman.[1]

Experiencing either the Point or the Brahman does not bring the understanding of how they are linked. This new kind of Diamond Guidance, comprising only completely transparent diamonds, provided the synthetic capacity of mind to make the necessary connections between the two.

Although the Point does not feel bounded, neither is it experienced as extended in space. Imagine yourself as a point of gleaming light on the infinite ocean and becoming the light itself. The luminosity spreads over the surface, and now you are the infinite, radiant presence at each drop in an ocean of profound depth.

Experiencing the connection of the Point to the Brahman showed us how the Point is the individual expression of the deepest ground of Being. The Point is the spark of that depth. Thus, the realization of the brilliant Point became the exit from a more located individual to the universal nonlocal witness. In this state, perception remains local—I still see the table and chairs in my room—while the presence of the witness is infinite, perceiving from the deep vastness that is everywhere and everywhen. It is at once outside of time and space *and* viewing all of creation.

After recognizing the connection between the personal and universal witnesses, Hameed felt a deep sorrow and grief: *How can I leave the world when there is so much suffering in it?* As he felt this depth of heart and sincere desire to be of service, a hard pebble emerged in his chest. In a process that took a few days, it became a glassy obsidian rock that looked like it was hurtling through deep space. It was so black that it radiated blackness.

This meteor-like phenomenon he simply named "Obsidian." When experienced completely, its hardness reveals the nature of the absence of existence coemergent with pure existence. This paradox confounds the mind. The effect was to remove all self-centeredness from the motivation to assist and serve. Hameed no longer felt any impetus from his "self" to help—he couldn't *but* help. He saw that it is not—and never was—he who could do anything to aid in liberating the suffering in the world. This is always the action of True Nature itself.

The state of Obsidian had presence, absence, depth, and clarity. The universal witness became the backdrop from which all the boundless realms emerged. In our Work, we see that boundless reality is experienced in five ways—love, knowledge, awareness, spaciousness, and dynamism. Each of these dimensions is one component of an indivisible truth, and each reveals more of what we are as the vastness and develops our experience and knowledge of the nature of all manifestation. It is like diving deeper into the sea; at each fathom, another color drops away from perception, until all that is left is the fathomless depth itself.

Boundlessness, or nondual reality, is where the Diamond Approach overlaps with many other spiritual paths. The boundless dimensions are equivalent to nondual realization in other traditions, but our understanding differs from those in several significant ways. For example, nonduality in a more classical sense is the underlying spacious unity of Being and of all manifestation as one: The sky knows itself as the nature of all the stars. In the Diamond Approach, the Point is considered nondual because the individual consciousness and essence are one. Each star knows itself as the immediacy of light.

The boundless dimensions most often emerged for Hameed, Faisal, and me through portals that spontaneously opened in the midst of ordinary life situations. We saw how the five dimensions of love, knowledge, awareness, spaciousness, and dynamism are categories of experience that are always a part of life in this world—and we were starting to see their origins. This helped us understand how the vastness of the inner realms informs individual existence.[2]

The five dimensions appeared in succession over the course of about two years. Our growing capacity to differentiate these ways of experiencing nondual reality exposed the building blocks of ego in increasing subtlety, providing a delineated understanding of the layers of self that obstruct the realization of nonduality. This was vital because bound-lessness impacts the boundaries that comprise the ego self, hence putting pressure on the conviction of the dual perspective.

Hameed, Faisal, and I had each entered many expanded states over the years, but now boundless Being was exhibiting itself in specific ways relative to the map of the Diamond Approach. This might appear to be a brilliantly thought-out, systematic approach to peeling the onion even further, but in fact, it was not. Following our guidance into unknown territory was what brought us these experiences and the understandings that followed. Our experiences were the traces of ink on the pages of the teaching that was writing itself through us.

One example of how the script was playing out occurred when Hameed was on a trip to Maui with Marie in 1980 and Boundless Love first infused him with its presence and perspective:

"I was settling in at our little cottage in Hana, and I turned on the TV. Some kind of western was on. I felt I was in the TV. I thought this was interesting, and it felt very good. I decided to go outside. When I looked around, I felt I was love seeing everything, and then I realized that everything was love, made of love. I was surprised. It was quite unexpected."

Up to that point, we had experienced love as a quality of presence. We had discovered many types of love—tenderness, sweetness of all kinds, nectars of the heart, and so on. In the late '70s and early '80s, prior to the realization of the boundlessness, we also had felt a light coming into us through the Path center, at the top of the forehead at the hairline. At first, we called Boundless Love the light of enlightenment, and other times we referred to it as the light of love. The name "Loving Light" (also referred to as "Living Daylight") settled as we recognized it as the love of God, or Divine Love. We call it "Loving Light" when we feel it as a holding environment around us that allows us to release our bounded sense of separateness. We experience Divine Love as a ground when we recognize the spacious nature of it beyond individual existence.[3]

It is a holding, sweet presence that enables individuals to feel safe and to trust in the process of unfoldment.[4] We felt it around us as a soft, loving presence but not yet as what we are. It led, however, to some very important insights about the individual consciousness and its relation to the divine.

The bathtub has always been one of Hameed's sacred contemplative places. One afternoon in November 1982, when Hameed was having a bath, the Loving Light started to flow from above his head and down through the Path center, infusing the Diamond Guidance with its delicate presence. A download of information poured into Hameed about the various ways that the individual consciousness is torn from the loving holding of Being and becomes the seed of ego. This illumination became the teaching of the Holy Ideas and formed the basis of his book *Facets of Unity,* a significant contribution to teachings on the Enneagram.

The soft sweetness of Divine Love took us through some jarring turbulence. As our small flock—Hameed, Faisal, me, and a few unsuspecting students—took flight into boundless skies, we were confronted with earthbound trusses that were limiting our freedom. To cruise beyond Earth's orbit, we had to deal with the darkest of feelings: beastly hatred, mistrust of God, and the pessimistic outlook of ego toward this underlying positivity we were now present to. Also, being in touch with the vast generous and regenerative nature of unlimited love highlighted the ego's greed, avarice, possessiveness, and disharmony.

It takes time, but when we see that we are ultimately a benevolent presence, and that the true nature of all and everything is good, we understand that we cause hurt to ourselves and to others if we don't know love as a ground of reality. When we have embraced that new perspective, generosity becomes our way of living, and we have a more comprehensive view of the world and its pain. The strife and discord of ordinary existence is no longer the only or truest reality for us because we now have the correct outlook: Our disconnection from the ground of love is the main source of agony, and we have ways to find our way back to it.

Each of us was dealing in our own way with the issues associated with Divine Love—for example, the belief in individual boundaries, which is the main obstacle to boundless realization. As Hameed's ego boundaries re-formed, the graceful Loving Light ebbed, and he recognized this reconstituting of his ego as the willful reassertion of a separate self. He felt the suffering and persisted in his inquiry into what had triggered the resurgence of the separate self. As the restrictions of his perimeter resolved, he once again knew himself as the rich, generous nature of love—just as when Divine Love as a dimension showed up for him in Hawaii.⁵

Faisal, on the other hand, began to communicate his interest in God as an entity separate from himself. I also saw God as an entity at that point, and appreciated the perspective. I liked the idea of a bigger, responsible party I could count on. But I was puzzled by the fact that I was also experiencing boundlessness, which meant there were no boundaries around anything. So, what was the relationship between those two perspectives?

It took a while before I could feel myself as part of the Divine Love, much less as the expanse itself. I rebelled against it because what I took to be the unlovable in me was secretly alive and still controlling the edges of my existence. I could feel my center of gravity as essence and presence, but to know myself as the divine goodness of the universe . . . well, that was a whole other story. It would require yet another shift from individual-centered identity to a more universal presence.

All of our questions regarding boundaries and boundlessness, and what these new experiences meant to each of us, led to animated discussions. In a conversation we had around that time, we saw that my capacity to let go of boundaries was greater than my ability to let go of my identity. For Faisal, boundaries were more of a challenge, and it was easier to lose his identity. Hameed toggled back and forth but seemed to be fairly fluent in both directions.

Our strong suits, preferences, or personal orientations were never the determining factor, however. The movement into the boundless dimensions was a shift that we needed to understand for the sake of the Work. We had to discern the universal principles that were operative beyond our subjective experience—what was the *teaching* trying to convey?

It was necessary to point out to most of our students that because boundaries are central to our ego experience, they often go unnoticed. We can feel consciousness extending beyond the body, the walls of a room, or even outside the solar system, and still retain the sense of being a separate entity. Instead of moving through boundaries to subtler and novel realizations of what we are, we can easily become a new-and-improved, bigger self.

I first became aware of this while talking with Hameed one day in his den. We were discussing the Divine Love, and I could feel myself as a greatly expanded presence of pink, fluffy sweetness. Extended through-out the cosmos, I could feel the world and all of humanity as part of the vast field of my presence permeating everything. All was included in this field of oneness—except for a particular person I was miffed at. The door was shut to her.

When I reported this to Hameed, he posed the obvious question: "How can you be the nature of everything and see her as outside it?"

Yes, I was huge—but bounded nonetheless. My little "I" was wear-ing a beautiful cloak of the universe! It now started to tear and shred as the sword of scrutiny ripped through it.

Very humbling.

Even though I'd had experiences of being an individual without a boundary, I still somehow believed that the boundary demarcating me was what had created the feeling of being a personal self. I saw that this belief wasn't just a fear-based attachment to my entityhood. I loved being a person, but I also yearned to be part of the ground of love. Still, I didn't want to be a generic drop in the ocean—even if that ocean was love. I did not want to dissolve into that vastness. I wanted to be myself *and* be dissolved in the love.

The process of understanding this apparent conflict took some time and contemplation, but eventually the longing strengthened until I sim-ply let myself go into the expanse at any cost. The boundary of the ego self dissolved. And I was cheerfully surprised to find that I had not disappeared. I felt buoyant in a vast field of sweet consciousness. The Stupa teaching about the intimacy of my personal relationship to the Divine came back to remind me: I am the individual consciousness coalesced within my natural surround of Loving Being.

Ahhh . . .

We now understood our personal presence from a larger point of view. All three of us had experienced the Pearl beyond Price for years, but now the loving expanse was the center of identity and the Pearl its divine progeny—a form within the formless. We then knew ourselves as the graceful presence of boundless love morphed into human form while never leaving that formlessness. We saw that we do not disappear as a personal presence, after all; we simply come to know a larger per-spective from which we as individual beings have arisen.

As our students began to recognize themselves as the offspring of a ubiquitous field of nourishing love, pearls were being birthed more often in the groups and sessions. Watching as the blessings of this teaching were being digested and embodied was even more satisfying than our own fulfillment.

24 ❖ Tapioca Supreme

ON A CRISP SUNNY November morning in 1983, I headed out for a day of private Inquiry sessions with students and lunch with my friend. I breezed in through the front door of the Ali house and made a quick right turn to the den. Hameed glanced up from his desk with a pleasant look as I made a beeline for my spot on the couch.

"Guess what?" he asked, looking back at an official-looking type-written page in his hand. I could see the watermark, as well as the periods and the dots over the *i*'s where the typewriter had poked little holes in the thick paper.

"I can't imagine." I paused, squinting my third eye. "What?"

"We got our 501(c)(3)," he said with lighthearted matter-of-factness.

"Great," I said, reflecting his apparent satisfaction. "But what is that?"

"It is our church status. I just got the letter from Morton today. It finally came through."

"So we are legal now?"

"Yes, the teachers will have legal protection as ministers of the Ridhwan Foundation."

As the footprint of the Diamond Approach teaching sank more deeply into the world, Hameed had felt compelled to create the cor-relate legal supports. The laws governing the practice of counseling and psychotherapy were being revved up in reaction to the personal growth movement of the '60s and '70s, which had spawned many teachers and facilitators with questionable training. Our knowledge of the psyche and how psychology intermingled with our spiritual practices put us at risk. Hameed felt fine about continuing without legal structures if the situation were to remain the three of us working with students, with Marie offering the Reichian breathwork as a support. The driving energy behind the new idea was Hameed's sense of responsibility to protect the teachers he was training.

He turned to Morton Letofsky, who was, and still is, a big force in a small package. Morton had been an attorney in a small mountain town in Colorado and was now in the Colorado teacher training. By combining his many skills, he could achieve a new aim. In 1980, Morton began the search for an attorney to establish a nonprofit church status for our spiritual organization, since we had been advised that this was the ideal way to go. The Ridhwan Foundation had been established in 1978 and had purchased the building in Boulder that became the main center at the time, so it was logical to have our 501(c)(3) set up in Colorado.

Morton's Citadel fired up and supported him on the highways and byways of red tape and detours; his wife, Deborah, who was well equipped with her relational intelligence to interview attorneys, was right by his side. Fortunately, they found Bob Lees, whose good counsel provided us with a healthy legal foundation on which the Work continues to thrive. We are grateful for his wisdom as he keeps us up to speed on any relevant legal nuances or changes in the law.[1]

We don't forget where our home is, but when in Rome, we do as the Romans do. As I sat contemplating the implications of our new status, however, I felt a pang of concern. We were becoming a visible establishment. "The world" was beginning to feel like an encroachment into the relatively simple, unstructured ways of running the School. Were the Romans taking over?

Soon it was time for my session with a student, so I pulled my body up from its comfy scoop in the couch and exited the den. When I turned left toward the front door, I nearly stumbled over a squat little being about two and a half feet tall, with pigtails high on either side of her head. She was bending and straightening her cherubic knees in an excited dance, which made her tails bob up and down like blond wings that were too small to allow her chubby body to take flight. In her left hand she brandished a baby bottle half filled with milk. Like a tiny soldier, she raised her other arm, her index finger pointing up at me as if to ask, "Who goes there?"

I greeted her with a chirpy "Hi, there!"

"Aaa! Aaa!" she replied in her fifteen-month-old sound vocabulary.

Marie, watching from behind her, beamed with motherly delight as she responded for her, mimicking a child's voice: "My name is Sandy." Then, back in her adult voice: "And this is Aunty Krannie." Marie and

I exchanged a wink of gladness for this first encounter between the wee one and me.

Sandy looked directly into my eyes. Fearless. Then she promptly jammed the nipple into her mouth and strode off into the kitchen, with the bottle hanging out like a stogie. I liked her right away.

I made my way to the refuge/workspace that Hameed had built up on the hill. Sweetness and a vague sense of unease sparred with each other as I climbed the stairs. The recent changes in the School and in the Ali family, plus my divorce from Perry, were a lot to absorb all at once. My heart was happy for Marie, but my mind was abuzz with images of what having a toddler in the house might be like. It wasn't as though we'd had nine months to prepare for the shift. She had arrived ready-made.

Marie had wanted a child for some time and, for various reasons, that had not happened. But the little girl was kin. Marie's brother had married very young, and by the time Sandy had her first birthday, it was becoming obvious that he and his wife could not provide a good life for her. Hameed had already fathered two children, and the main focus of his life was the Work. But he loved Marie and wanted her to have what she wanted, so when the opportunity presented itself, they adopted the little one. Sandy collected several "mothers" after that, of which I am one.

Not long after I met Sandy, her name was changed to Natasha Ariana Ali to go with her new life, but everyone called her Tanya. She was quite a dynamo, and Hameed's nickname for her was "Turbo." Once she was old enough to use the words she overheard in our conversations, she would often traipse through the den and ask in passing, "What color is the diamond today?" A chuckle would erupt from whoever happened to be in earshot. We had no idea that she had been paying such close attention.

The intelligence of Being was also reshaping reality for most who were in the School now. Students were fluidly breaking through to new realizations of all kinds. We had been graced with six diamond vehicles thus far, and the seventh came along in parallel process to our awakening into the boundless dimensions.

Picture a chandelier with crystals of delicate, semisolid water, almost like melting ice, but not cold. Imagine a sense of graceful and subtle presence that imbues your consciousness with an exquisite, refined precision, both by its direct feel and by the sound of tinkling diamonds as if stirred by a breeze.

It was more difficult to conceive of the seventh vehicle than the ones that had arrived before it because it was subtler in many respects than the more earth-shaking and pyrotechnic spiritual experiences. When this vehicle of watery ice diamonds descended, its refinement and tenderness were gracefully divine. We called it "the Water Chandelier."

For all its delicacy, it has the power to defrock us of our defenses and open us up to the wisdom of our ordinary, undramatic humanity, with all of its vulnerability. Being vulnerable is the watery way to Being because transparency in our individual consciousness in its sheer state is necessary for the consummation of the marriage of individual consciousness to its true nature. Defenselessness is threatening, even seems foolish, when all we want is to survive; for spiritual awakening, however, it is a necessity. Without total vulnerability and openness to essence, there is no essential development and no essential marriage and hence no possibility of attaining nonduality.

I believe that it will be a long time before humanity understands that indestructability is innate to our humanness and cannot be won through war or bought with any form of currency. Only through the refinement of the very fabric of consciousness will we be absorbed into the imperturbable ground of Being. For those who are on the way, the subtle presence of the Water Chandelier is a welcome but challenging friend that highlights the opaqueness and isolating thickness of ego structures and defenses.

Ample opportunities to work through the issues and receive the gifts that spilled out onto us from the watery Chandelier would present themselves in our daily lives and during retreats. The vast, substantial ground of Being began to reveal itself over the course of the summer, peeking through consciousness to culminate in a remarkable opening within a few weeks after the retreat in Gualala, California, in July 1983. We didn't have a name for it yet, but we soon recognized it as the highest state and fundamental to all the experiences we'd had thus far. So we named it "the Supreme." Around August, Hameed reported the realization he had while in Colorado on a work trip:

I don't remember where I was coming back from. I opened the door to the house that I share with Faisal and Patty and stepped over the threshold. Suddenly, everything became pure translucency. I had already recognized that awareness is always the same awareness, but now I was seeing the nature of awareness itself.

The Supreme is the nature of our usual awareness, which is always mixed with knowing. At first, we saw it as pure awareness because it was not yet separated in our experience from the presence of knowing. The Supreme does first present as pure awareness; some Vedanta teachers, in fact, speak about everything as knowing. This was true for us as well at the time the Supreme first appeared; we didn't know anything more basic than this way of knowing pure awareness. That is why we thought of it as an ultimate state at the time. As Hameed wrote:

> Ordinary awareness is the same awareness as this translucency, but we are aware of its functionality rather than the presence of the limpid clarity that is the nature of awareness itself.[2]

Later that evening, a conversation with Faisal helped unpack the experience. The writing inquiry that followed clarified things for Hameed even further.

> It was all and everything. Describing the transition from witness to the Supreme presence of all related how the nothingness opened up to reveal the fullness as its other side. Not as two distinct phenomenological discriminations exactly, but as two sides of the same thing. Being and nonbeing as one. Fullness as its front, and nothing, or the emptiness, as the back. The distinctive emptiness of the Supreme is a pure openness. Each point in space is the interpenetrated fullness and emptiness of this Supreme beingness.
> This is not meant to be descriptive of an entity that most people call the Supreme Being. It is to say that the Supreme Being is the ultimate ground of Being as pure presence. The presence of paradoxical nature of all that is. Fullness and emptiness.

Various traditions discern the dimensions in different ways. For many, the vastness is one undifferentiated field, referred to as spacious emptiness, self-knowing awareness, pure awareness, or boundless compassion, to name a few. Some traditions emphasize one dimension over another and dismiss or minimize the importance of the others. In the Diamond Approach, our experience is that the dimensions arise in specific discriminated ways, with their own significance, as fundamental elements that underlie ordinary experience. These differentiations arise in a natural unfoldment as we discover deeper truths about reality in general.

Some states of consciousness, especially as we entered into the boundless dimensions, were initially conflated for us. Imagine a view of Earth's atmosphere from space. It is all one atmosphere, but scrutiny reveals various interpenetrating layers, each with its own characteristics. The more we explored the sphere of experience in the interior cosmos, the more discriminated each layer became.[3]

Because our teaching values the individual consciousness and living an ordinary life, it makes sense that the realization of our nature would occur in this way. The boundless dimensions of love, knowledge, awareness, dynamism, and emptiness therefore not only reflect the various facets of True Nature, they are the basis for the capacities of individual consciousness—such as awareness, knowing, feeling, and action.

The spacious fullness of presence progressed to a dense, vast spaciousness pregnant with diamond indestructibility. Further examination continued to reveal a sense of empty openness and presence at once—awake, luminous awareness *inseparable* from Being.

Several weeks of discussion, contemplation, and Inquiry revealed that rather than a background witnessing or an experience of mysterious depth, the Supreme is the basic, clear, shoreless ocean of consciousness and the ground of all existence. As a dimension of reality, it is the oneness wherein all things arise as discriminated forms within the field of Being. Hameed sometimes spoke of the forms of manifest reality as concepts in the mind of God, although, as indicated in his journal entries, he did not view God as an entity.

Throughout the following months and into 1984, the Supreme unveiled the mind's reification process and further developed the understanding of basic knowing. In the Diamond Approach, the Supreme is the dimension of direct knowing, or gnosis. This limpid clarity of awareness and inherent self-knowingness is called *jnana* in Sanskrit and is described as a "cognitive event that is recognized when experienced. It is knowledge inseparable from the total experience of reality, especially of a divine reality."[4] It is self-knowing, pure awareness, and

Being, completely coemergent. Being that knows itself by being itself. It is also the basis of the cognitive capacity of mind at all levels.

We spent most of 1983 and 1984 moving through the process unleashed by the Supreme insinuating itself into our consciousness. The revelations produced detailed understandings of the mental process of reification and the concepts that underlie the structuring of ego.

Sometimes we would feel stoned during our explorations as we were stretched by and into another reality. In one conversation, I felt the state of the Supreme for the first time and began to understand that Hameed had opened to the fundamental ground of reality. I could feel the indestructible nature of the Supreme presence, and its pure openness as well. When I looked out my window, I perceived everything as full, like an overstuffed couch, bursting forth with vivid Beingness.

Another time, when Hameed and I were talking about the Supreme, it became so rich that it felt as though we were immersed in tapioca pudding. We went on a pudding binge for a long time after that. We just couldn't get enough of it. A perfect personification of the two sides of the Supreme would be Karen lying on the plump-cushioned couch, eating her rich, delicious dessert, while Hameed writes about the Supreme in his journal with lucid, crisp, spaciousness.

March 14, 1983

I am everything. I am always like this and always will be. It is a matter of just waking up to the fact that this is me, always has been—a simple awareness that is there all the time because I am the very nature of everything. There is no separation between appearance or essence or nature. I am both and beyond.

I am pure Being. I know myself because I am myself. It is not an event. It is not an experience. I am nothing and nothing happened. I am happening all the time.

It was now apparent that Being was pure awareness and knowing. We began to see the aspects as a kind of spiritual alphabet arranging itself as words, sentences, and paragraphs coming into form as volumes of knowledge flowing through our being. This confronted the reified concepts of a jigsaw-puzzle universe in which all the bits appear to be delineated from one another.

As always, the events of our lives, expected and unexpected, provided new doorways to pivotal understandings. In June of 1983, Hameed was summoned to London. His father was dying. Mute and filled with painkillers as he faced the end of his life, Muhsen watched everything around him with alertness and clarity as he sat upright in his hospital bed. He and his son met in that space and shared the presence of pure Beingness that was both of them and beyond them. Having this opportunity to be together was a completion, and the time Hameed spent with his father helped develop a profound inner support for the Supreme identity.

As for me, I was subsumed more into the Supreme over the following year. I rippled throughout the ocean of consciousness in an infinite trajectory in all directions. However, it would be a while before I recognized that I am the nature of every wave in the sea of consciousness. It was the same for my comrades. The Supreme had some big shoes for all of us to step into.

As my realization became further integrated, it needed to become more actualized in all parts of my life and work. In 1983, I completed at JFK University the few credits I still needed for my bachelor of arts degree, supplemented by a few evening classes at the California College of Arts and Crafts. I then decided to continue on and get my master's in psychology. Watching Hameed work was, of course, fabulous instruction. And the strand of Inquiry in the Work interwove with the interpersonal perspectives and methods I was learning at JFK, creating a specialized skill set in service of the discovery of essence.

My schoolwork was fascinating, but the innocence of not-knowing, so important for curiosity to function most sharply, kept getting eclipsed. I had to continually review my orientation in order to hold my school knowledge lightly and as a supportive guidance, rather than a determinant of how I viewed myself, other people, and the world.

An internship as a volunteer at Community Mental Health Services across the Bay, in Novato, Marin County, taught me a great deal about the difficulties facing young adults with mental illnesses and disabilities. I communicated with them through activities such as art projects and day trips into nature, which provided structures for discussing their inner worlds. It was difficult and tiring. It was also meaningful—and yet I felt I was not being used in the ways I was meant to be.

I had lofty ideas about healing and helping people who'd had difficult childhoods that left them relationally challenged; I felt that the Pearl would be the perfect antidote to the personal struggles of those with moderate-to-severe personality disorganization. Since the personal essence is the quintessence of integration, someone with a weaker foundation would surely be assisted by experiencing their own essence. What better time in life to catch them than when they were teenagers?

My mentor and supervisor in the program had supported me to think about how to help these youngsters get in touch with essence, but he warned me that it might not be so simple. He was right. By the end of my internship, I felt I had failed. When I bid the kids goodbye, I was sad to leave them and disappointed that I hadn't been able to do more for them. But when I recognized that what I had experienced was the failure of a hypothesis, not a waste of time, I learned an important lesson: that awakening to essence is not what every individual needs or aspires to. Essence can fortify skill sets in all walks of life, in the right situation at the right time. However, what those kids needed was support to develop the most basic skills for functioning in their immediate environs.

The value of this lesson continued to inform me throughout my subsequent internships. I became less ambitious but still open to how essence could aid me in my work with many different kinds of people. And my experiences in these other venues benefited the work of teaching the students and training new teachers in the Diamond Approach. After the second teacher training began in 1984, the large group, which met on weekends, had split into two small groups for evening exploration sessions. One group, which consisted of all the teachers and teachers-in-training, was led by Hameed. I led the group of students who were not in the training.

Developing teachers to be vessels for the teaching was a priority; over time, the School became much more rigorous about supervision. We instituted procedures for giving effective feedback to the teachers, who were learning the skills for providing private Inquiry sessions. More was expected of the second tier of individuals in the teacher training than the first—and even more of the third set of teachers.

Hameed began to consider what structures would be optimal for presenting the teaching in the future. What formats would most successfully support the students' orientations and maximize their progress?

How could the skills of the teachers who were being trained best be used? What kinds of programs would support the overall development of the School going forward? These deliberations would result several years later in a new program structure called the Diamond Heart Programs, delivered through the Diamond Heart and Training Institute (DHAT), an educational arm of Ridhwan.[5]

With Hameed's help, we made some general outlines for the group meetings, but it was more or less a leap into the unknown. We spread our wings and fluttered in the currents of the teachings. Some of us learned to soar gracefully through trial and many errors. We each found the niches where our skills could shine to benefit others.

Doing private sessions and teaching small groups felt natural to me, but taking on a new set of students in a large-group setting in San Francisco was a stretch. Although more extraverted now than when I was in smaller gatherings, my shy roots still had a hold. It took a while to find my own voice in articulating the teaching.

The curriculum was designed to extend over a period of seven years, and it would be focused on the recognition and development of the individual consciousness through the teachings on the essential aspects, including the Pearl and the Point. Students would then determine if the desire to continue was still alive in them, and they could choose to do so if it was their path.

As the groups grew and expanded, we had to continually update our understanding of what our students needed. Initially, for example, we did not want students to be involved simultaneously with other teachings because Hameed felt that this would be too confusing. We still believe that it can be problematic, but we have no hard rules about it; such situations can be discussed and inquired into if questions arise.

We also thought that therapeutic work was a helpful preparatory step for those who were not ready for serious spiritual rigor; we decided that therapy should be done prior to entering a group if needed. This proved unrealistic, since healthy, resilient egos turned out not to be the norm. Also, a student might be resilient at the start, but as the Work gradually thins the shell of the personality, layers that need therapeutic attention might surface. We have become much clearer about the focus of the Diamond Approach, as well as its limitations. This work is not for everyone, and it does not address every type of psychological condition or issue.

So we see it as a positive move for students to seek out whatever other support and guidance they need as they pursue their unfoldment in the Ridhwan School.

Each summer, all the students from both groups would gather for a residential retreat—sometimes in Colorado and sometimes in California—and we would live and interact as a group for seven to ten days. In the early years, we cooked, cleaned, and ate together. Sometimes the sleeping arrangements were rustic, to say the least—at Boy Scout and church-owned retreat sites, for example, we were many to a room, stacked on bunk beds or laid out on the floor in sleeping bags. Later, when we had to seek out convention centers and hotels that could accommodate larger numbers, we unfortunately lost the group practice of doing life tasks together, since meals and other amenities were arranged as part of nonnegotiable packages in those venues.

In any setting, however, our time together was rich on many levels. As with all groups in close quarters, issues arose between members and living together made those more prominent. But we didn't have the attitude that we should all love one another all the time. The truth was, and is, paramount. Working things out is part of the journey, and taking responsibility for one's actions and feelings is required inner work. Learning when and how to communicate has always been an important aspect of this. The model of etiquette Hameed emphasizes is to not act out on negative emotions: "Feel it, don't necessarily reveal it."

As the years passed and the retreats increased in size, we all felt a more palpable, robust presence as each participant contributed to the field with their maturing consciousness. By the end of a retreat, we were a field of thriving oneness, very like bees in a harmoniously functioning hive. Even the most basic accommodations were transformed into a palace through the sweet honey of Being. Each palace revealed its own majestic halls, secret tunnels, and portals to other universes. Jewels arose within each type of space to refract the light of the teaching into the world through our humanness.

I saw us as the rose window in a cathedral of Being, permeated by the rays of a numinous sun that casts no shadow.

25 ❖ What Did You Say the Name Was?

JOGGING ONE HOT July morning with Mushka as my partner, I was feeling the enjoyment of our pleasant tandem existence. She sprinted ahead, steering me off the road to the shortcut to Hameed and Marie's house. Contemplating the empty nothingness within the pure awareness of the Supreme as I ran, I noticed the moment-by-moment changes in the landscape and in my own body. But they were merely shifting images on a movie screen, not objects in motion through space. I felt oddly less than nothing. I decided to run this by Hameed to see what he thought.

Mushka disappeared into a grove of trees and a cluster of nearby bushes thick with tea roses, emerging onto a lawn that was slowly shrinking due to Marie's planting mania. White fur flashed through the montage of leaves, branches, and rich splotches of Mr. Lincoln red, Brandy orange, Monet yellow salmon, and the pastel-cream, pink-edged Peace rose, among many others. I delighted in Mushka's puppy-like frolic at her ripe old age of twelve as she sent the butterflies aloft and chased them in spiraled revelry.

I popped my head in the door of the workroom. "Hey. Gotta moment?"

"Hi there. Yeah, but just a moment."

"Meedle, I am experiencing the nothingness in a different way."

"What way?"

"Still kind of an empty nothing but . . . well, less of it."

One of his eyes seemed to peer straight ahead and the other narrowed quizzically. "How can there be less than nothing?"

"I dunno. It is so nothing that I can't even call it nothing. Like really nothing is there—not even nothing."

Mushka's shrill *arf, arf* and the sound of approaching footsteps announced the next student arriving for a session with Hameed. "Keep looking," he said. "We will talk later."

The day passed fluidly, with no time marking it. This new space felt so clean of mind that I had difficulty using it to probe. It seemed remarkably unknowable. In the following months, it became the territory for many of our conversations, which wove between the expanse of pure awareness with the presence of knowing and, on the other hand, a dimension of awareness that had no discrimination or recognition. When we look at our usual experience, that awareness always includes knowing, but it had not occurred to us that it is possible to experience awareness apart from knowing.

It took some time to wind our way through the Supreme and into this new state of awareness that we had yet to name. These two states could be easily conflated, and we toggled back and forth between them for months before they became accurately distinguished. The new dimension had an emptiness that was more rarified than the nothingness we had understood as the nature of the Supreme; it was the experience of the absence of anything, including nothingness. It was so empty that it didn't feel spacious or even empty. Hameed began to refer to it as "absence." I experienced it as a state of pure, unobscured clarity that was empty of all concepts.[1]

We soon started calling this new dimension of nonconceptual awareness "the Nameless," which seemed like a perfect fit. If you don't recognize it, you can't name it!

As we ventured further into the more rarified spacious clarity and absence of the Nameless, we continued to struggle for many months to integrate the supports needed to maintain the Supreme identity and stabilize in that realization, which turned out to be important wisdom for all the boundless realizations that would arrive in the future. This landed us smack-dab in a number of pivotal interlocking issues. Primary among these was a new and more fundamental type of narcissism than we had encountered before.

Each dimension, as it arose, had exposed another layer of accretions. I was beginning to feel like a set of Russian dolls. The vastness of Divine Love challenged the illusory boundary of our individual consciousness, while its cocoon of loving goodness provided the holding support that eased us beyond the borders of our internal and external representational worlds. The Supreme revealed a new level of narcissism by shaking the tectonic plates of a self that is conceptually based, exposing the insubstantiality of the reifications that underlie all self-images.

The first round of narcissism, which had occurred around the time of realization of the brilliant Point, had already cracked the shell, so we were familiar with the hubris that manifests as the need to be seen as special. It is like the wave in the ocean that says, "Look at me! See how wonderful, unique, and special I am?" Now the arrival of the Supreme was raising the question of what it means to be a unique wave in the ocean of humanity, and what our relationship to one another was from that larger view. In Supreme narcissism the wave insists, "I am the *best*, the most wonderful—the supremely special one!"

The Supreme also began to challenge the ground that the three of us stood on with one another, with the Nameless adding even more pressure on us. Wanting to be the first to have an insight, grasp an important concept, or discover a new state—and then be validated by Hameed and get the credit—became more of an issue for Faisal and me.

Competition is normal and can be a healthy, positive motivator—and even fun in some circumstances. But in the context of inner truth and realization, it is not useful except as fuel for the process of understanding. From the perspective of nondual reality, everything and everyone is connected as true forms within a field of unity. However, the Supreme is an intensely powerful experience of expansive Beingness. So envy, rivalry, and competition become amplified if the underlying unity is not completely realized and integrated. Through the veil of ego, we can fool ourselves into believing that we are the best, unsurpassed by others. Because the Supreme's robust, aliveness is the stuff of all manifest existence, we *are* the best—but so is everybody and everything else!

Faisal and I were not immune to that particular siren call. Hameed understood this and would let us go on excitedly about our breakthroughs, even though he occasionally got tired of having to give us credit for recognizing some truth he felt was self-evident or that he knew he had realized first. But he always dealt with his reactions as his own issue, looking into them with a magnifying glass that Sherlock would have been proud of. He used everything that happened in our triad to understand himself and, more important, to understand how it related to the teaching.

Grandiosity was just as likely to surface as competitiveness; I began to see how I was wearing my sparkly light as a badge over an increasing sense of inadequacy. Entangled with these difficulties was the need for validation—the issue of support. I was still seeing the vast, undifferentiated field of awareness through the lens of being a single entity existing among other entities. It takes time to understand that the aloneness of the Supreme is a oneness of infinite unity, not a social aloneness of the individual self. Until then, the fear of loss of another person's support stimulates a strong urge to connect with others in order to maintain a sense of inner equilibrium.

This unconscious draw toward a special connection to another person as one's basic support is one of the deepest and most difficult issues to resolve, and we began to understand how it is often used to fortify a shared ego identity. As our ego identity is deconstructed through experiencing deep states of nondual awareness, one way it expresses itself is as the need to be the same or similar to another person or to other people. When the identity of the personality gets conflated with the Supreme identity, the need to maintain relational stability with others who have the same experiences or orientation becomes more pronounced, and differences in perspective are experienced as a lack of support. Our identity and the sense of mutual support remain centered in the relationships themselves rather than in knowing that we are the identity of the Supreme expressing itself through each one of us. If not understood, such a tendency will limit, or even completely obstruct, nondual realization. This harkens back to the early dual unity experienced by an infant, when the sense of self is undifferentiated from the mother and her functions of feeding and soothing.

One way this issue shows up is in codependency. Some of us try to be the tit of the universe and force-feed others with what we actually need ourselves. Not recognizing our own need to be loved and supported, we may offer advice, opinions, and all manner of help that may or may not be needed. What we're really saying is, "I can relax if you are okay."

The real question isn't whether or not we should support or seek the support of another person but rather what is the relationship supporting? When support shields somebody from necessary challenges, it is limited and will eventually break down. Encouraging another toward being more real is true support and love, the authentic basis of an enduring connection.

After every realization, each of us is thrust out once again into the relational field and must be able to apply our inner knowing to the complex difficulties that arise between individuals even when there is a shared understanding of certain basic principles of reality. The three of us were no exception. When Hameed wrote in his journal about his explorations with Faisal during that period, the entries toggled back and forth between nothing being problematic between them and things not going well. To me, this meant that he was holding the hiccups lightly.

Hameed's first inkling of anything more serious than their usual divergences in viewpoint or style came at the entrance of the Supreme in 1984, gaining momentum through that year and into 1985. He and Faisal seesawed between maximizing sameness and being dismayed by the breakdowns that occurred again and again when their differences flared up. I wanted to fix things, but I had only a partial view of what was going on. Watching the balance tip back and forth, I would either withdraw or try to clarify what was happening between them. Neither tactic was useful. Still, I felt it was important for them to have each other, even if I sometimes felt like an interloper in a guys' club.

Case in point: I never quite understood a story line that Faisal would weave into our three-way conversations. It was something about one of them being the Mehdi, who is an important figure in Islam, and the other having an important role in relation to him. Faisal brought this up a couple of times when the three of us were discussing other things, and I found myself receding into the background as though I didn't exist.

One day, after listening for about fifteen minutes to the Mehdi story once again as we sat together in Hameed's den, I decided to ask why I didn't come into it at all. "So, who am I in this tale?"

Faisal's answer, with a hint of wryness, was, "You can be Mary."

Not my idea of a good time, I thought. I felt offended and belittled. But I also was perplexed by the story. I wondered what it really meant and why it was coming into our conversations. I thought that maybe I just wasn't seeing what Faisal was pointing to because I didn't have the cultural background to understand the story. Maybe it was a deep metaphor of some kind.

Hameed took it all with a grain of salt. When I asked him if he was that guy Faisal said he was, he responded, "I am just myself. I don't want to be anyone else." The subject never came up again in my presence, but other indications that things were out of sync cropped up. We noticed that Faisal was not showing up in the usual places. He and I crossed paths infrequently when he was in town. He rarely attended group in California anyway, but his appearances were even fewer now. And he started missing retreats as well. That was new.

"Of course we will get through this," I told myself. "We are all earnest and truthful." As it turned out, we returned to some measure of good will as the vortex of revelation kept pulling us together into its center.

This journal entry from February 1984 gives an indication of Hameed's process as he inquired into the issues around the loss of his shared support with Faisal and his feeling he could not fully rely on me either.

I was feeling a small hole in the upper solar plexus [*he called it a universal deficiency*] just below the Mobius. I have been alone. I cannot depend on either Faisal or Karen to know my state. The aloneness meant no merging gold [*love*]. The merging gold here means the support of the self-object [*another person*] to be myself. The absence of the merging gold in aloneness meant also the hole of the Diamond Will, the support to be oneself. The result is an emptiness in the belly. So I am both alone and don't have a self, which is the emptiness I have been feeling. And I am unhappy about it.

After that, I started to feel the dense diamond state of the Supreme will. Support for the formless identity. This aloneness here is the absence of the support to be. Then it became the merging gold's connection with the Diamond will. However, the will that arose is the Supreme will. The Diamond will is the support for the Point, so it seems the Supreme will is the support for the Supreme identity. The Supreme will hole means dealing with early transferences.[2]

The support for the individual consciousness to abide in the certainty of the Supreme identity turned out to be the Diamond Will vehicle arising anew within the Supreme. This time, the mountainous presence of the Diamond Will manifested as an immensity of dense Supreme diamonds out of the field of Supreme consciousness. The transparent openness at its center, which is a spaciousness that has more the feeling of pure openness than in any other dimension, showed itself to be the nature of Being. The Supreme Diamond Will brought the wisdom of not needing the support of anything or anyone in order to be the boundless being that we actually are.

Hameed had faced aloneness before, but it comes up in many different ways along the journey. Each inner death introduces the soul to another level or kind of aloneness. I watched how Hameed used the loss of his friend to realize and integrate the presence of the new level of Diamond Will. As for me, my internal support was becoming more integrated, but I also realized that how I behaved in relation to others would speak far louder than the silent abiding within. Amidst all the relational uncertainty, Hameed and I continued to deepen our understanding of what it means to remain steady in the realization of the Supreme identity.

As the nonconceptual awareness—the other way we referred to the Nameless—came more to the fore, it divested us of other cherished ideas. Even the concept of Being couldn't be known in the ways we had formerly understood it. Conceptual mind, real and imagined, was being deconstructed like so many cardboard boxes left in the rain.

The transition from the ground of the Supreme reality to this more nonconceptual awareness of the Nameless revealed itself more entirely to Hameed, Faisal, and me within months of the experience I had on that hot July day. When the cognitive mind fell out from under us, only pure awareness remained. In this state where there is no discrimination, the mosaic of manifest reality appeared out of pure awareness as patterns without separation or recognition of the meaning of any differences. A fresh field of awareness, absent of concepts of any sort, permeated everything. We woke up to the underlying unity whose forms are made of a transparent clarity of awareness that is awake to itself.

Because the capacity to differentiate is prior to the conceptual dichotomy that characterizes discrimination, I could see the differences between things, but I couldn't access what their meaning was, although I could draw upon my learned knowledge to function. When I relaxed into the direct quality of pure awareness, I felt sheer, spontaneous happiness and delight.

We were obviously having insights and understandings in retrospect, but the inevitable question was, If there is no recognition, how are we ever going to know something without leaving this state of nonconceptual awareness?

Then Hameed discovered that the Diamond Guidance had transformed. The diamond quality had become something more like a natural crystal: less translucent than a diamond but bringing wisdom about the dimension of pure awareness that precedes discrimination. All the aspects and vehicles now manifested as crystals instead of diamonds. It seemed that the skillful means to understand the teachings of nonconceptual states and their concomitant barriers without leaving pure awareness was arriving.

Comprehension while in an experiential state of no-mind seemed counterintuitive to me, yet it was obviously necessary not only for articulating the teaching but also for living in this condition. I had my doubts that this was possible until I experienced it myself. It happened one day in a café in San Francisco, where I was having a glass of champagne with my mother, who had recently experienced some of the boundless dimensions during her continuing private sessions with Hameed. We clinked our glasses with a toast to our blessed life, then took a sip or two. The searing freshness of the Nameless radiated through us. She looked at me, wide-eyed, and asked, "Is this supposed to happen?"

I knew exactly what she meant. We giggled as our minds dispersed in the bubbles. Her eyes were fountains of light. I was right with her. My consciousness expanded and dissolved into the infinite spaciousness.

A more substantial, discriminating layer of awareness seemed to manifest ever so subtly within that thinner atmosphere. This more discerning layer then manifested as a form of consciousness—a crystal emerged. In that moment, I was not only gifted with the capacity to know within the nonconceptual dimension—I knew that I *was* the Nameless.

I recalled what Hameed had been saying about knowledge being possible in the nonconceptual. Imagine a rarified sky forming itself into a bird that flies through it and yet is inseparable from it. The bird peers with great precision, through its discerning eye, from and into its sky medium. In just that state, Mother and I left the café and walked around the transparent-looking streets and buildings. People also seemed less opaque. Everything was a color in the fabric of transparent clarity.

After an hour of walking, talking, and enjoying each other in this new state, June and I hugged goodbye, and I took the on-ramp to the freeway beyond time. I seemed to know exactly how to operate my car while centered in not-knowing. Musing on our experience as I drove, it came to me that because all the dimensions are coemergent—even though a particular one tends to dominate our experience—they manifest in various ways to help us understand the manner in which the others are operating at the same time.

That made sense. If it were not true, how would it have been possible for any of the teachers we had seen over the years to talk about their ineffable realizations?

No-mind had made a way for a new kind of freedom in me. In the days that followed, awakeness consumed each moment into itself, completely disappearing and being reborn into the next, leaving no trace. There was no holding on to actions or events and no memory of them. Performing ordinary tasks such as cooking eggs, making the bed, or even carrying on a conversation was undramatic. Witnesses reported that I appeared to be attentive to whatever I was doing. I knew I was awake, but that was the only thread that carried through my experiences. The searing awareness was more like pre-mind than no-mind.

As the three of us watched functioning continuing throughout these erasures of ourselves, the question of just who was the doer of this or that activity percolated in the back of our minds. We all recognized that we were operating in a new dimension of True Nature.

The same force that had taken us into its vast skies had landed us on the ground with all the other Earthlings, and we started the long course of learning how to relate personally and function more skillfully from the invisible. Much tougher than soaring free in the infinite sky.

26 ❖ The Absolute End

"*WHEEE!* QUITE A RIDE here in the back! Could you slow it down a bit?"

As I slid around on the bench seat in my white cotton dress, Hameed whizzed around the curves on Arlington Avenue as it snakes along the Berkeley hills. I could see peeking above the two headrests part of the curly, black head of Faisal to my right and Hameed's black straight-haired bounce to my left.

Hameed had recently told me about some fruitful discussions between him and Faisal; being truthful with each other about a number of emotions and misunderstandings had improved matters between them. Hameed still didn't completely understand why their relationship had become so rocky, but he seemed to feel that things were resolved. His relief had shone through his relaxed expression all afternoon.

I was glad that the three of us had returned to some measure of homeostasis, yet I felt a mild tension in the air, like one of those teeny gnats that disappear when you try to see them straight on. But the familiar friendly atmosphere buoyed my hopes, eclipsing the niggling sensation.

We had just lunched at our usual café on Solano, discussing our latest understanding of yet another, deeper nonconceptual dimension of our spiritual nature. The Absolute had taken center stage, revealing the most mysterious fundament yet. Although this black vastness was not entirely novel for us, it was emerging anew as it situated itself within the Diamond Approach. Wonderstruck by the sense of magic and profound depth that had descended during our conversation thus far, we decided to continue our exploration elsewhere.

Hameed and Faisal tended to be sedentary, but being an energetic sort, I needed a lot of physical movement. I knew I would soon hit my limit of sitting around. "You guys!" I growled. "Let's make sure we get out and *walk* today." I was hoping they would humor me, which they sometimes did, sauntering along and conversing—an Arabic word thrown in here and there—and stirring the air with their hands as if scribbling a secret language in the atmosphere.

As Hameed's aging white Mercedes grumbled up Wildcat Canyon and veered left at the fork toward Alvarado Park, I glided portside and planted my espadrilles firmly on either side of the transmission hump to steady me around the turn. After a quick left into the lot near the trailhead, Hameed pulled the car up to the dusty log that marked the parking area, and we sat for a few minutes without talking. Hameed's question, musing and crisp at once, arose out of our shared space: Who is it, or what is it, that is having all these experiences?

I could see Faisal's profile as I scooted up to rest my chin on the back of the front seat between the headrests. He had turned toward Hameed, offering me a three-quarter view. His eyes narrowed and darkened as they often did when he was peering into another dimension.

My first response was that it was obvious. "Me," I said matter-of-factly.

"Yeah, but what *is* that?" Hameed countered. "Not only that—how is it that one person might be in an experience of the boundlessness as love and the next person in boundless awareness, or depth, or pure Being? And they are all correct in saying that it is the most fundamental—the way reality is."

We had wondered about that for years, but the query was becoming more precise and seemed to press in on us for an answer. My eyes fixed on the dry brush visible through the windshield, then my view expanded to include the many thin trunks of baby oak trees under their mothers' shady embrace. I let go of the walk for today and leaned back against the seat. My mind went blank with a cool relaxation that dropped me into my inner landscape.

Velvety quiet permeated the car. It felt as though a secret were near, whispering, and adjusting us to the right posture to hear it. Time stretched, then vanished. Slowly, words emerged. Perceptions, interpretations, and conjectures drifted hither and thither. We could feel the code starting to be cracked, but it could not be opened with force. Only the gentle yet precise queries of the loving sleuths would gradually disarm it.

The questions remained, like friends accompanying us home. Soon our heavy carriage was humming around the bend to Hameed's house. As we approached the driveway, short, simple words were exchanged. We eased out of the car and headed silently toward our evening destinations. The three of us were never together in this way again.

My last discussion of any substance with Faisal was during a phone call in which he earnestly reported his experience of how deeply meaningful it was to know God in the way that he was now experiencing it. He saw God as a divine being on a throne. I found his view puzzling, especially after what we had come to understand about the nondual unity of the Absolute, which is beyond all concepts.

We had experienced ourselves in so many ways over the years, and all of them were possible real experiences of True Nature and its personal essential expression. So it seemed helpful to review in my own mind how our understanding of True Nature had evolved in the teaching. The boundless dimension of Living Being had already been revealed. Living Being is the dynamic force of the universe, a presence whose felt sense is pure primordial aliveness. It is magnificently birthing everything at each moment as a morphing organic flow from nonbeing to Being, at each point of the universe. Our discovery of it was one of those eye-openers we all took part in uncovering, although it was Hameed who named it. Hameed called this dynamism the Logos to describe its logic, reason, and functioning as the Absolute manifesting itself into being.

We were using the term in two ways. The first, "logos," refers to the particular logic and reality view of a teaching. The other, "Logos," refers to the very substance of a universal creative, self-generative force that can be experienced and known. In the latter context, we understood the Logos to be the initial utterance of the universe manifesting— both the original creative force and that which is within all natural creative processes.

At first, we experienced this creative force of Logos as an entity. It felt like a substance of living presence that would descend into us in various ways. But our sense of a divine being who is conceiving and reasoning creation changed over time. Creation is neither chaotic nor random; it is inherently ordered, and its evolution moves in a dynamic, optimizing way. We came to see this dynamism as the flow of natural law, just as the sun and the stars function according to natural law. Hameed described the synthesis of his understanding of the Logos in these journal entries from February 28, 1985:

I was starting to have a succession of insights, experiences, and perceptions that led me finally to see that this living dynamic thing is best called the Logos.

I saw that the new Diamond Body in the Supreme that exposes all essential aspects as concepts is the realm of original concepts or Absolute ideas.

I saw that the entity is universal mind, or "big mind," which is always creating the universe through thinking or conceptualization. The dynamism is the thinking into creation, but it's not a mental thought process; it is the emergence into manifestation from a Platonic idea. The dynamism is the potential for form to be created out of the primordial concept.

Both these realizations, plus Karen's perception that the diamonds of the Supreme were emerging from this entity, plus Faisal's perception that this entity is the source of all essential states, led me to see that it is the Logos that is the source of creation itself.

Hameed describes the culmination of his understanding:

Then we started to see the whole constellation of issues related to the Logos. As Karen became the black nothing [*one of the ways that the emptiness of the Absolute had manifested*], the Logos descended from the top of her head and down over her forehead. Then her line came back [*the ego line indicating separating boundaries*]. This made her see the Logos as an object [*separate from herself*]. The moment she let go of needing the object—that ultimately supports the sense of self—we had the perception of the conditions that promote the view of Living Being as another or as connected with her.

At first she felt connected to God. She felt some kind of umbilical cord. She felt that God is some kind of intelligence someplace far away. As the Diamond Will appeared, she started becoming the Logos. She felt it dripping down as a pearly-like substance. [*The Logos can manifest any aspect, quality, or dimension. What I was experiencing felt like a personal relationship with God, inseparable from Living Being, but I had not yet extended into the entirety of the ocean.*]

When she first embodied it, she felt that God is in everybody and that she has a connection to everybody. Then she experienced the state of oneness, what I call Divine Being. And she then knew herself as that.

Hameed saw oneness as the state of any of the boundless dimensions, where no form is separated from any other and each arises within a particular medium. This is classically referred to as nonduality. In some journal excerpts that followed, Hameed wrote about God as a concept he no longer related to as a separate entity. He did continue to use the word "God" occasionally to refer to spiritual nature, but the term was reserved for the individual consciousness in relationship to its larger ground, not the realized condition of being the expanse itself.

As I listened to Faisal's voice on the other end of the line, the progression of all these realizations ran through my mind like a movie in fast-forward. He knew that this was how I saw things, so it seemed natural to me to ask, "How can God be a separate entity, even a divine one, when we are coming to know everything as *not* entities?" I felt the edge of challenge cut as it flew out my mouth. I wanted to unsay it, but it wouldn't stuff back in. Faisal fell silent.

I stared at the receiver in my hand, waiting for a response, a question, even a sound—anything that might give me another chance to begin again with the love I was feeling rather than the insistence that he see it my way. I was afraid of what it would mean if he didn't feel aligned with where the current was taking Hameed and me. I wanted to know how Faisal saw it, but my mind froze with my own agenda. I didn't want him to leave us.

The call ended with a polite but strained goodbye. "So maybe he is off to another kind of awakening," I thought as I hung up.

I felt shaky. I had been clunky and inelegant in my response to him. Faisal had reached out to me, though it was uncharacteristic of him to do so. His desire to share ideas and experiences that were precious to him touched me, but I was also confused. How had he reached a conclusion that was so contradictory to what I thought we all now understood? I didn't see how our views could reconcile to become a foundation of one teaching. And I thought there must be more to this than his relationship with God.

Then came the letters. Faisal no longer felt he could continue on the same path. The nature of his disappointment with Hameed seemed to morph with each letter. Hameed was surprised at the intensity of Faisal's feelings and surmised that he must have been going through a lot that he had not told him.

I was rarely mentioned in the letters, except to say that he felt that I had aligned with Hameed, as if I were simply choosing sides. It pained and angered me that after all that the three of us had been through, Faisal could not see my integrity or trust that my views were based on my own experience. I always knew that he didn't hold his relationship with me in the same light as his connection with Hameed, but now I saw that our bond might never have been for Faisal what it was for me. Maybe I didn't know him, or he me, after all. I felt the ache of empty sorrow.

Quite a bit of back-and-forth between Hameed and Faisal occurred via letters over the next few years. Some were not dated, so it is difficult to know exactly when they were written. The correspondence included personal issues plus discussions of their views about the Absolute, God, and the Mehdi story. Faisal and Hameed were "both bruised by this rift," as Hameed wrote in his journals. His sadness and sense of loss trickled off the pages as I reviewed them in preparation for writing about the events of that period.

We came to accept Faisal's claim that he was going in another, more correct direction for him, in order to do the Work in the way he felt was right. When I backed up a bit, I could see that a greater force may have been instrumental in this course change. The teaching has always seemed to optimize itself through its own devices. The apparent dynamics that caused this bifurcation might have been flotsam and jetsam distracting us from the undercurrents that were moving us along with a deeper purpose and meaning than any of us could have known then.

In any case, sometime early in the spring of 1985, the trio disbanded and a new configuration was transpiring. Faisal had been working privately with some individuals in the group, so Hameed turned his attention to them; more than anything else, he was concerned how Faisal's departure might impact the students he and Faisal had shared.

Hameed's anger, grief, and sense of the loss of support was worked and reworked throughout the rest of 1985 and into the next year. During that period, the Diamond Will appeared again, this time as a mountain, stabilizing Hameed in the realization of the Absolute.[1] He was an unshakable, dark expanse, more alone with the alone and more open than ever. The sturdy throne of diamonds kept him from being yanked from his equanimity by the pressures of life and the growing needs of the School. To my regret, I was flooded with my own reactivity about recent events and couldn't be there for him in all the ways I wish I could have been. Regardless of external losses or gains, Hameed's focus on the inner universe remained steady. He kept our ship cruising into further reaches of uncharted territory, minus our former crewmember.

❖ ❖ ❖

In May 1985, I moved into a small annex up the hill from Hameed and Marie's home. It had formerly been our workspace and was affectionately known as the tree house. To make room for me, they had turned the garage into a new workspace that we all could use. This arrangement gave Hameed and me even more time to inquire and develop the Work together, and Marie and I sprang into a new level of friendship as we discovered more about each other's creative visions and interests. Living nearer to her and Hameed but not in the same house hit my sweet spot of optimal distance. I was close enough to feel connected with the family and far enough away to enjoy my own space.

One mild day in May, I was sitting on an old folding chair on the redwood deck outside my little one-room home. The deck, which was bigger than the house itself, spread neatly around the house and the sturdy oak tree right next to it; a six-sided bench wrapped around its trunk like a collar. My sprawling, limbed friend was standing sentry to witness, protect, and shade me, as it would for the next four years. I inhaled deeply and felt touched by generosity all around. I was drawn inward. It was time to meditate.

Hameed had reminded me once again that I needed to meditate more regularly to realize the depth we were venturing into. Even though I could easily sink into the black spaciousness under all kinds of circumstances, he had stressed the importance of just sitting and not doing anything: "You are a dynamo! And you like to move. What is pro-pelling your physical movement is the same energy that will fuel your spiritual voyage. Harness it and let it do the rest."

I was absorbed into the silence for forty-five minutes. With mind out of the way, no effort was needed to allow the depth to reveal itself with great potency. After the sitting, my body felt indescribably light, nearly sensationless. I drifted down the stairs, which were almost not there either, then across the backyard, and slipped through the open sliding glass door into the main house. Hameed was reclining on the sofa in the den in a position long familiar to me: on his left side, the upper part of his torso propped up with pillows, left hand cradling his head.

He appeared to be permeated by an essential watercolor-like sheen of purple-y indigo darkness, which was seeping through his skin from the depths. His crystal beads were shiny and black, like his eyes. Even the delicate click of each bead as it flowed through his nimble fingers seemed imbued with tranquility. He made a waving invitation with his free hand to summon me closer.

"I have the feeling I am at an end." His voice was low and thought-ful. He looked straight at me with penetrating expressionlessness.

"End of what?" I said, curious and nervous at once.

"My life," he replied.

A dart of fear shot through me, reconstituting my body to its earthly density. Was he sick? Then I settled inside, remembering that this would not be the first ending, death, or disappearance. We'd had so many of them that I had difficulty recalling them all. Every aspect of essence, each vehicle, each dimension, brought about a death of some kind. And each death was more profound than the one before it.

"Okay . . . what life is over?" I asked drolly.

If he was aware of my initial anxiety, he ignored it. "Like I have done what I set out to do, both in realization and in my personal life. I have achieved my purpose."

"Yes. I get that."

"I formulated the teachings, taught them, wrote books, established the School, trained the teachers. Students are learning what I want them to know, and the teachers are good now."

"True. That part of it is pretty complete," I said slowly, "but not over. There is room for improvement!" I added, more upbeat. I was trying to talk him out of disappearing physically, as if he could fly off at will—which he threatened to do at times.

"My life has been a success in terms of the Work, my marriage, and creating whatever wealth was needed, but this feeling is about more than specific accomplishments. It is a sense of finishing a phase of life."

Although he was decades younger, Hameed occasionally spoke as if he were eighty, expressing that he had lived fully and that he could die without regret. At other times, when he was weary of this world, he would announce that it was time to go. But neither of these statements were an indication of depression. The impetus to leave came from a wish for a complete freedom that he was uncertain could be attained in this physical existence. When he said such things, Marie would roll her eyes and tell him to be quiet. She was *not* ready for that. Neither was I, but I felt empathy for the longing and came to understand it as simply that.

As we explored the depth further, it opened into the room. I felt like I was dropping from the surface of a dark lake at night, descending slowly until the moonlight of awareness became merely a glimmer on the surface. I was absorbed into its fathomless bottom and disappeared. The light faded to a point, then ceased.

When awareness emerged from the vastness, it felt similar to waking from a refreshing, deep sleep, but I knew I had not been sleeping. From its black source, the intensity of searing perception penetrated throughout my body. I saw now that this is what I had perceived in Hameed.

Black spaciousness pervaded the atmosphere. "I don't want to fill this with anything," he said, looking serious. "I want to see what comes."

I tried to see into the openness and perceived a depth of nothing. Absolutely nothing. I felt nothing, I saw nothing—and I had no idea what would happen next.

I began to feel the endless possibilities inherent in this deep openness. The Absolute as the formless ground of fundamental reality spawned a new set of feelings and perceptions. This ground now felt like a teeming potential of depth and clarity at the same time. The light of the awakened Absolute made it possible to look with the eyes of the universe into the secret of its existence. Manifest reality appeared as an enchanting dark beauty. But behind everything was the dense emptiness of the unity of Being and nonbeing. My mind went silent and my heart relaxed. I closed my eyes and soaked in the dark that was beyond darkness.

When I peered out from the deep, I saw my friend sitting there in his simple splendor. "I am home," Hameed said, looking transparent yet rock-like. "There is nothing I want and nothing I need."

A crystalline, infinite spaciousness and depth pervaded the room. Total contentment exuded from him as I watched him become the dark grandeur of divine ipseity. He felt finished. There was nothing left for him to do.

The days following passed in a silken flow. Dinners were consumed, tea shared, TV watched, students seen. The inner silence, unbroken by the sounds of the world. The profound depth, a sanctuary that no dissonance in the world could rupture. We started to appreciate the value of cessation of consciousness in the darkness as a cleansing experience.

Through it all, I pondered where I was in my own life. At thirty-four, I had a ways to go before I could say I had fulfilled my purpose—in contrast with Hameed, who, at the ripe old age of forty-three, seemed to feel he had fulfilled his.

I was becoming interested in having a relationship and had been dating off and on, although it was not satisfying. I recognized that my relationships with men were not evolving at the same pace as everything else in my life. I could sense that my householding days were not over yet and I had the feeling that there were issues keeping me from finding a mate. I already had easy access to presence, so I did not need an analyst to provide that perspective, but I felt I could benefit from some type of formal context to explore the relational complexities that the therapeutic alliance is designed to delve into. Plus it was a training requirement for school to engage in psychological work from a client's perspective.

Working with Hameed in that way was not an option. He wasn't a blank enough screen for me to project on; I knew him too well and trusted him too much for certain issues to surface. And because I felt completely and unconditionally loved by him, there were fewer hooks to trigger a transference to explore in relation to unresolved family issues. So I jumped on an opportunity to enter Eriksonian Analysis. As I worked through the issues of my personal history with my therapist, Hameed and I kept our attention on the new territory of the teaching. We discovered something new about our relationship that neither of us could have expected.

A few months earlier, when the Logos that I had formerly seen as "the entity" descended down from my head to my heart, it infused my body with its brilliant dynamism. Then a pearly intimacy in the heart materialized that created a new kind of unity. As this developed over the next weeks, I felt myself becoming the dynamic expanse, but I was also a located individual inseparable from it. I had a vision of a huge living organism in which cells naturally morphed to serve a specific function and were drawn to other cells to create subsystems for functioning together. I felt connected to all of humanity in a universal way, but could see specific links to particular individuals within my own human life. These were not generic or casual relationships; they were with people I had developed a deeper personal connection with and understood to be significant in relation to my life purpose.

Sitting under the shade of the oak trees by the house one mild afternoon, Hameed and I sipped our Perrier and discussed the experiences that had whirled in over the past few weeks. I looked at Hameed and felt curious about the energetic pull I was feeling again, which was now like a magnetic force. I was moved to relax into the sensation, which was a more explicit sense of what our relationship had hinted at all long.

I felt an intense connection, contactfulness—and something else at the core of our bond that defied definition. It was not friendship alone, and certainly not coupling. Hameed and I were one field of presence, one pearl, one being as two, galvanized by our love for the truth, whatever that might be. Hameed referred to the experience as an expression of *monajat*.[2]

From this, a new facet of the teaching was spawned about human relationships and the mysterious unknown forces at play within them. Not only did this dynamic presence bring revelation about our relationship to True Nature, it also revealed the potentials in relationships between the human organisms it creates. We had understood the Pearl beyond Price as the capacity for true contact and the skillful means for relating interpersonally, but we had not fully comprehended the force of attraction between individuals and the purpose of those precious connections.

Each one of us, as singular expressions of Being, is a gem. What we are together in twos or in groups offers myriad, novel ways for our nature's potential to display its treasures. Nowhere was this more evident than in the lives of our students. Hameed was happy to see how well the logos of the Diamond Approach was taking hold in them and expressing itself. Individuals were mastering Inquiry to a remarkable degree, deepening in their understanding that wherever they were in their experience, that place held the secret of the way to the next realization of truth. Dipping again and again into the ocean of presence, many students were blending their inner realization splendidly with their worldly maturation as well: Marriages were entered into, babies born and raised, careers undertaken and expanded.

When Hameed was hit by a motorcycle while he was a university student many years before, he had to choose whether to leave the world or come back. What drew him back to life was his love and the desire to open for humanity a gateway to the enjoyment of freedom. Now he was seeing his vision being actualized.

What we were all learning and experiencing was not only for Hameed and me and the few in our little School at the time. As requests for the teaching began to flow in from near and far, the jeweled portal of the Diamond Approach was opening to points beyond Colorado and California. Over the next decade, diamond ships were launched to deliver the sacred cargo of living knowledge to those who desired it. The bright lights of the Work were beginning to pop up throughout the United States and Europe.

27 ❖ Soul Dancing

ONE DAY LATE IN THE summer of 1985, a few months after the naming of the Logos, I passed Hameed in the kitchen as I headed toward the laundry room. I could hear squawking and pecking in the background. Not only had Hameed named the infinite throbbing, living presence "the Logos," he had given his pet cockatiel the same name. "The bird is loquacious—makes all kinds of sounds," he explained.

From his small cage in the den, Logos would make the lighthearted, chirpy announcement of each arrival at the front door. Hameed could often be heard whistling in ebullient conversation with his little winged friend. Oh, how he loved that bird. He has claimed on more than one occasion that he doesn't have pets and doesn't really understand the point of them.

"So what about Logos?" I asked him one day.

"He is not a pet; he is one of the family. Like Mushka," was his reply.

I loaded up the washing machine and headed back through the kitchen. Hameed had that "I am waiting for you to notice that I feel like talking" look on his face. When our eyes met, he responded to the questioning in mine.

"I am learning more secrets about the mystery of our individual consciousness," he said, as though he were talking about the weather.

"Sounds interesting!" I felt a swell of fascination and redirected my plan for the afternoon. "I'm all ears. What are you finding out?"

He took his usual seat at the kitchen table. "I woke up a few times last night and found myself having a flash of the libidinal ego. It seemed to be fearful, but I could not tell of what. It felt quite fine and smooth. It moved like delicate mercury."

I nodded and slid onto the padded bench by the window, eager to hear more.

"It was really interesting, Kran. It was like I was the blackness of the Absolute, perceiving this thing pass before me. This manifestation of the libidinal ego is quite amazing. It is the most alive and vigorous thing I've ever experienced, much more than any essential state. It feels like an alive creature, and it's changeable in terms of state. It is very dynamic regardless of whether it is positive or negative."

"Wow. So the libidinal ego seems to be evolving in some way?" I offered.

"I am not sure. I've never heard of such a phenomenon, and it is difficult to believe that it is only ego—it seems to be pure consciousness that is totally alive. But I see it only in flashes. I don't get to experience it long enough to understand it because it always runs fast into hiding."

We had borrowed the term "libidinal ego" from Fairbairn[1] to describe our experience of a living formlessness that contains all kinds of raw, instinctual energies. We thought of it as a manifestation of personality or ego in a primitive form.

Hameed and I talked for another hour. My body was electric with excitement. This was usually a sign that we were onto something. We parted company, and I ascended the stairs to my tree house, eager to see what the night would bring. Marie, Hameed, and I would be meeting later for dinner, and *Star Trek* reruns would be on after that, so we could watch our show and continue pondering our long-held query of who or what was having all these experiences.

Weeks later, after many *Star Trek* episodes and a few Johnny Carson reruns, the unifying breakthrough culminated in the first use of the term "soul" in a succinct, defining statement about how all the parts of self—from the mundane to the sublime—function and interconnect. This entry from Hameed's journal notes, made on July 14, 1985, explains:

> The libidinal ego is the soul. It is who the individual is under the usual circumstances of functioning. It is what makes ego feel alive and functional and able to think and feel. Ego feels real because the soul is alive and giving it such possibility. The soul is the ego.
>
> The soul is both the personality and the essence, but as a unified whole. The soul is capable of transforming into any aspect of essence when the issues about that aspect are resolved. But the soul can also exist as a unified mixture of personality and essence.

The surface part of the soul is the personality, the ego, the character. It is the part that is conditioned due to contact with the world. The deeper and inner part is more essential and more real. It is the source of the deeper feelings and desires. The process of realization, or metabolism, is that of transforming the surface part, or clarifying it.

He went on to say how the soul is focused on and captivated by the external world, believing it to be the source of fulfillment. As the consciousness matures, the soul turns more inward and recognizes its nature as essence. At some point, the boundaries between the soul and infinite, boundless reality dissolve, and the soul is recognized as being an individual extension of boundless truth.

This picture is so much more inclusive and broader than just personality and essence. Now we can see the human being as a unified whole, which we are! The soul is the unifying insight of so many things. The individual soul is like a Riemannian manifold.[2]

Many Western traditions honor the individual and have the concept of soul, but before now we had not experienced anything that pointed to the soul—at least, we had not correlated the concept with the experience yet. It had been so close in the ocean of consciousness that even we diamond fishes could not see it for years.

Hameed, as usual, was exploring Eastern spiritual traditions for any correlations with our own experiences in the nondual dimensions. Many of those teachings were useful for conceptualizing some of our experiences of nonduality, but individual consciousness was seen, for the most part, as an illusion. The common view was that you are either ego or you are pure, essential nature. We had already understood throughout the boundless realizations that we are an extension of each formless nondual state—as a personal presence within it, as a true form of Being. But this didn't explain everything. And we were certain that there was more of a continuum than what the traditions of the East were teaching.

If Hameed hadn't had the precision of subtle sensing that led to the recognition of this blobby substance as it passed through his awareness in the middle of the night, it could have gone unnoticed or perhaps been seen as something else entirely. Once again, his interior vision was 20/20. He always seems to be equipped with the tools he needs for the terrain he is exploring; but what makes this particular insight so perfect is that it explained *what* changes, transforms, grows, contracts, gets enlightened, has experiences.

We had understood the Logos as the process of manifest reality being created. But we didn't understand what that means for the individual who is in a process of unfoldment. Now the connections between the soul—the individual consciousness—and the Logos were coming into focus.

It was a stunning revelation to see what had been hidden in plain sight. The soul is the consciousness that experiences the continuum of our experience from the most superficial to the deepest; the most contracted to the most expanded; within space and time and beyond. The Logos is the living potential of the universe that creates all forms of experience, including the experiencer. So you could say that the soul is a "mini-me" Logos teeming with the infinite potential of experience.

Thus, the individual consciousness *is* the soul and the living presence that animates the body during physical life. We also saw that it is what leaves the body at death. While it is completely interpenetrated with the flesh in life, it is discernable as its own presence. "Most of the time, whenever I feel the substance of this soul, I become the Logos," Hameed wrote in his journal, having understood through the entrance of this flowing substance into his own experience that it naturally leads to the ocean. But the stream itself remains a unique current within the ocean. That explained why as many times as I had disappeared into the dark ocean, I emerged as me, not someone else!

Ibn 'Arabi's words came to my mind in a flash: "God needs the individual as much as the individual needs God." The infinite and the finite meet as what we are. The soul is to the Logos what the eye is to the body: an organ of perception and experience. The One manifests into every form, and it functions through the myriad organs of consciousness it has created. We are both the infinite nature of Being and the one who experiences it as a located consciousness.

The continuum of consciousness that we had posited earlier was becoming crisp. It was becoming obvious how our method of Inquiry had been working all along. It is the nature of the soul to unfold and reveal its nature effortlessly when there are no hindrances. Our investigations had shown that opening up to our potential is like the flowing of a stream toward the ocean that it is inseparable from.

Gradually, our knowledge of the soul's properties of permeability and impressionability revealed how people learn, and are changed by what is learned, in ways that either restrict the flow of consciousness or enhance it. Later, this helped students to have a more direct understanding of what is conditioned and structured in the fluid substance of our soul consciousness and how we can open to being structured and impressed by True Nature instead of by rigid patterns from the past.

We realized that it is possible to teach about the soul before students come to an inner realization of any kind. Introducing this material closer to the time when we introduce the process of Inquiry helps students experience the soul as the very substance of their individual consciousness as well as the context in which all their experience occurs. They can grasp from the start that the soul is who and what is practicing and what is realizing her nature through the process.

Now we found ourselves starting to raft down several interconnected streams in the relationship of the soul to the Absolute. Hameed and I had already settled into the Absolute as home and recognized our ultimate nature and selfhood as that. But that raised the questions: Whose nature? Whose home? In a more classical realization, we had first felt ourselves as the Absolute, as the deepest nature of individual consciousness. When we discovered the soul, another process illuminated the individual consciousness as the functional arm of the Absolute in time and space.

As the emptiness of the Absolute began to reveal the more primitive layers of structuring, we discovered that the nonconceptual[3] dimensions correlate to the neonatal consciousness. Primary among the issues that surface are what we call Absolute narcissism and soul, or oral, narcissism. These can be deeply interrelated, and both concern the inability to recognize our true nature, though from slightly different angles of misperception.

It is possible, even necessary, to know the Absolute in its purity, beyond the individual consciousness, and to become the emptiness that reveals the true nature of the soul—but the fear is that if we do so, we will die as a consciousness. We are afraid because we do not know that realizing the Absolute will allow us to emerge again as the true form of Being we have always been, and that our soul will retain its individuality in a state of unified wholeness with True Nature. Once the soul recognizes her nature as the One—the Absolute nature of all—she is united with the many and with her deepest self.

In order to truly know what we are as both sides of the equation—both soul and True Nature, as the One that has an individual location yet is inseparable from Being—it is necessary to work on both forms of narcissism. For the soul, this requires discovering her inherent wholeness so that she no longer needs validation by anyone else. This is not an easy task, because one of the indicators of soul narcissism is a vigorous, insatiable hunger for the totality of what we are to be seen and acknowledged by someone else in order to feel whole.

When I was still in that stage, one day a friend told me that I was clever, and I was pleased by the compliment . . . for a few moments. Then I felt unseen. She had missed something very important—I thought. "So, do you mean that I am clever but not loving?"

When you are on the other end of such a transaction, you get the feeling that however many strokes you give someone for one attribute or quality after another, it will never be enough. The person is never satisfied because she doesn't recognize the true source of all her qualities and capacities or the fundamental ground that provides her very existence.

Absolute narcissism also involves a surging need for mirroring, but it is not a hankering to be seen as special or the best or even for all of our qualities to be acknowledged or admired. It is an intense desire to be—and to be regarded as—the *only* One, in contrast with another or many others. But the true oneness of Being is the One, the only that is *everyone*.

These two forms of narcissism set in motion the struggle to know the two sides of our consciousness: the immanence of the soul and the transcendent nature of which she is the instrument. For the soul, the necessary work is to reclaim and know her wholeness; working through Absolute narcissism is about understanding and realizing the singlehood. Only when we are certain that the Absolute is our core and source as well as the ultimate ground of all existence—including our individual soul existence—can we rest in our personal consciousness and our place in the scheme of things, even as we recognize that our nature is the nature of everything.

Understanding our fear of disintegrating or being annihilated by the Absolute is necessary before this can happen. The annihilating absence inherent in the Absolute is so not there that it appears as black. At first, this mysterious emptiness—which is a sense of indeterminacy and wonder when experienced without any obscurations—is interpreted through any remaining veil of identification with our located soul. As human beings, we are both our individual soul *and* True Nature—they are inseparable. But as the soul consciousness is increasingly imbued by the Absolute, the soul can still falsely see herself as being the central identity. In soul narcissism, one keeps oneself as the center of Being, not realizing that the true self is the Absolute. When you're centered in the soul, you're identifying with the located consciousness, and that identity keeps you inside a limited view.

Seeing oneself as a located soul is not the same as seeing oneself as a separated soul. The located soul is identified with its location but doesn't necessarily have a separating boundary. A separated soul always has both a location and a separating boundary. The identification with being a located consciousness prevents you from being the complete freedom of your nature because True Nature is outside of time, space, shape, size, or location no matter how you may be experiencing it. Although True Nature has no specific location, your soul is the locus of consciousness that makes it possible for you to perceive. That comes in handy for living your life, but the soul can be completely free only when you are not bound to the perspective of your location.

Tremendous fear can overtake us as we face the loss of anything that we believe we possess—including ourselves. The terrified animal in our belly rebels when our imminent dissolution is interpreted through the instinctual urge to maintain our very existence. But it is inevitable that the soul, who is striving to maintain her unique existence by pulling that larger self into its personal location, will be sucked into the event horizon as the next to go.

When this happened to me, I obsessed for weeks about my finances and my health. I was terrified that I was on the brink of joining the ranks of the Berkeley bag-lady battalion and would die destitute on the streets, alone and in pain. This was not a logical fear, and it didn't take long to understand that I was projecting outward the impoverishment of the soul that was emerging as my materialistic attitudes were being exposed.

The good news is that when we realize true poverty to be an inner state of emptiness that does not need any filling, the attitudes that led us to claim even the qualities of True Nature as our personal attainments or property drop away. As we approach that point, however, a deep discontent with our attachments and achievements is bound to rear its head. This can rouse the desire to fill the maw of discontent with more stuff—but it can also offer the opportunity to dive in deeper.

In the spring of 1986, Hameed wrote in his journal about just this type of dissatisfaction—not only about the security, comforts, and pleasures of life but also all the inner riches that he honored as blessings. The dissatisfaction created a sense of inertia in him; he felt thick and leaden, as though some part of him were going to sleep at the expense of newness. This was different from his previous sense of completion for accomplishing all he had set out to do. Now he was acutely aware that everything he had achieved and everything he had come to enjoy was binding him by patterning his life. Having fulfilled its purposes in him, all of that needed to give way to new horizons. "I just want to be free of it all," he wrote in his journal.

One naturally has no attachments as the Absolute, but it was not easy to let go because he was being divested not only of comforts, pleasures, and deeply satisfying attainments but also the qualities of True Nature that we understood ourselves to be. As usual, Hameed was open to any source of knowledge and experience that could shed more light on his current situation. He was drawn to the writings of St. John of the Cross on the experience of inner poverty of the soul as it is understood in some of the monotheistic mystical teachings.

As both worldly and heavenly attainments were challenged and removed, a deeper dark night set in—the dark night of the spirit, in which the heavenly attributes of the soul and the magical gifts bestowed upon us along the way had to be released in the forms we had become attached to. The era of collecting glittery and marvelous things on the shores of Being was over. The benevolent thief had stolen our bags of goodies and taken them with him back to his abode. We slowly came to the understanding that inner poverty is the portal to the Absolute dark night. Actually, we saw the Absolute as the dark night itself, which became more searingly radiant as the annihilating depth absorbed us into its mystery.

We had the direct knowledge that the Absolute is what we are. But some dissatisfaction would still arise in our soul consciousness, signifying that the soul needed to become more refined in a new or different way. When the Absolute expresses through the belly center, for example, issues regarding inner poverty and the instincts have to be faced. In the mind, it's about dealing with blocks to pure perception. Through the heart, it's all about coming to understand what keeps us from recognizing that we are both the lover and the Beloved. The ongoing process of clarification and refinement shows we can be centered in the Absolute while all kinds of other things are stirring in the soul. This simply means that the soul does not have knowledge of all the ways it is in relation to, and in service to, the Absolute. So the next thing to be understood or relinquished arrives, and fear might take hold at any point.

The Absolute didn't disappear as the work dispersed cloud after cloud at the soul level; it was always our ultimate reality. Whenever the soul reacted with some form of dissatisfaction, we could have transcended it—there's no fear when you're sitting in the pure Absolute, so it's much more comfortable to hang out there. But that was not what was happening for us. We let ourselves be pulled into the locus of the soul to face each issue that arose. And our valuing and appreciating the individual allowed the soul's process to continue in concert with the transcendent realization, so that each of our students could also move through the process in their own way and at their own pace as they become more transparent to True Nature.

Around the end of 1986, the relationship of the soul to the Absolute took on another angle. Hameed felt deep sadness for a long while but didn't know why. It was reminiscent of feelings he'd had when he first began his journey. Nevertheless, the intense love for the truth that had been a driving force since blast-off led us to its source in a new way. The heart, now fueled by a powerful, surging love, took command of the ship. Hameed's heart was set ablaze with the burning love for the One, the only, the Absolute Beloved.

It is such majesty and such an amazing beauty that intensifies our love into a deep and consuming passion. The Stupa may transform into a pomegranate diamond heart, deep and passionate, sweet and zesty, intensely loving the Absolute.

The most important thing is that the Absolute is perceived in the heart by the heart. It is perceived in the ego by the ego. The heart is the abode of the Absolute. More exactly, the heart is the window to the Absolute. I have experienced the Absolute many times before, but not in the heart, and not through the ego person.

The dynamic process of our Work that would not let us tarry in one spot for long had once again reinvigorated the soul to develop her heart realization. Hameed's heart was burning with a furious passion while I flamed, and sometimes smoldered, as the twigs and logs of my personal history got piled onto the heart fire. Many beloveds from the past showed up in my psyche, exposing how my prior love relationships were conflated with, and at times dampened by, the occasional upsurges of ecstatic passion that would overtake me.

Therapy had helped me to deal with disappointments in relationships and my apparent attachment to being rejected. I understood how even the Absolute had begun to wear the faces of beloveds whom I had felt rejected by. In the past, I would completely give myself over in a love relationship, desiring to be consumed into its enchanting beauty, only to feel that I had been spit out. The sheath over my heart that I had been wearing as protection against external snubs and rejection by those I cherished had closed off my innermost sacred space from my own self, severing me once again from the Absolute.

How could I have reduced this bedazzling formlessness into an actor in my little play? This saddened me deeply.

My yearning for the Absolute persisted. It dawned on me one day, as I sat in my little house and stayed with this longing, that there was a sweetness in it. I could feel the love within the unhappy emptiness. But there was something else. Something unpleasant. Like bitter saltwater. It was the *taste* of rejection. I was astonished to realize that I was attached to loving the Beloved as something outside of myself, thus resisting the depth of my heart's desire for complete union. I was stuck in my belief that I needed to create distance in order to feel that I could love and know this mesmerizing Beloved.

In wanting the Absolute for myself, I was actually rejecting the Beloved's loving action of eradicating anything that would distance me from its embrace. Yet I saw myself as the one who was being rejected!

I loved beholding the awesome wonder of this perfect lover and longed to be in its sweet, intimate embrace—but not so close that I would be swallowed up. I didn't want to disappear.

Sincerity arose to fuel the furnace of passion. I had arrived at the Beloved's doorstep, empty-handed and in rags. I began to speak as if in the presence of the one I loved. "I do not know how to divest myself, but take it—take me—if you will. I offer myself willingly as the last and only gift I have."

A vacant cave opened where my love and heart once were. The dearth of my heart lacked even the angst of longing. The protective shield over my heart became a diaphanous curtain, which my Beloved parted like a wedding veil. Brilliant flashes struck with thunderous power, ricocheting throughout my heart's chamber. It was the most gorgeous thing I had ever seen.

The marriage consummated. All of me was taken in—the clarified, the sullied, the mature, the young, the occluded, the essential. Nothing left out. The Absolute exquisite majesty of the Beloved took its rightful place in the throne of my heart as the true heart-dweller.

It is said that God spoke this through the prophet Muhammad: If you want to look for me, do not look in churches, mosques, or temples; do not look anywhere in the manifest world. If you want to find me, look for me in the hearts of my lovers.

28 ❖ Down We Go

THE COLORS OF MY surrounds are richly saturated as night descends. I am looking into my tree house as I stand on its ample deck. The sliding glass doors are open, so I walk through them.

I am curious about the back wall, so I move closer. I see that it is constructed of redwood. I vaguely remember it as drywall painted white but pay that little mind; something else has caught my interest. I stretch out my right arm to touch the wall, and when my fingertips make contact with the wood, I realize that it is not as solid as it appears. Using only slight pressure, my hand enters the wall, which feels like thick, spongy air. My hand feels different from the wall but does not have the density of flesh. It passes through the porous material, interpenetrating with it yet retaining its own shape.

My eyes remain fixed on my arm disappearing through the wall as I reach back with my other arm and gesture to Hameed, who is about twenty feet behind me, to approach. "Hameed! Hurry. We don't have much time!"

He moves toward me as swiftly as his crutched run will allow.

My arm is sliding in up to my elbow now. As Hameed gets closer, I stretch out my other hand for him to grab. He reaches out and grabs it firmly, without question.

I have no idea what is on the other side of the wall. I am not sure we can come back. But I am not frightened or concerned. I know that our bodies will follow if we move swiftly, but I sense that his crutch cannot make it through. "Let go of it," I say with firm assurance. "You will be fine, Hameed."

The dawn awakens me. The sensation of my arm moving through the open wall is still vivid. As I contemplate my dream, the bookshelves and ceiling start to quiver, and I realize that everything in my view is vibrating. I jump out of bed and attempt the same moves as in my dream. No luck. The wall is as impenetrable as it ever was. I am under the governance of material law again. Logical in one way, and also perplexing, since what I experienced felt so real. Obviously, I'd had another dream in which I felt that I had entered a different realm through a slice of space-time.

Before I had gone to sleep, I had been talking with Hameed about the material world being even more mysterious in some ways than the inner realms. From the perspective of Being, one perceives the world as not physical and feels the body as having no mass, but matter itself remains in a solid, unchanging state. In light of the emerging quantum physics of the 1980s, the constitution of the world as merely material particles was in question for us. Hameed agreed with the view that physical substance is energy and consists more of space than of particles. So why, we wondered, aren't physical objects permeable?

Our discussion added mind food to conversations I'd recently had with my friend Linda (who had changed her name from Linne around the time I made the move to California) about what it means to embody the infinite boundlessness. She had explained that the body expresses all the states of the soul, even the formlessness. In the boundless dimensions, the body appears to be contiguous with the atmosphere in which it operates, and moves harmoniously through it. This corresponded with Hameed's discovery of the soul and how "the most surface level of the soul is the body"—which Linda had intuited long before.

But this did not adequately explain the interpenetration of my arm with the wall—solid forms occupying the same location simultaneously. Anything is possible in a dream, but I still couldn't shake the feeling that what I experienced reflected a truth about the material world: I was convinced that it pointed to a potential that we all have under the right conditions.

The dream conveyed another message. My taking the lead to move through that wall with a composure that felt natural expressed a growing confidence in my relationship with Hameed. We had been experiencing greater symmetry in our explorations and contributions to the Work. Verbal accolades were not Hameed's style, and their infrequency made me rely on self-assessment, but I could feel his respect for me in his gaze and demeanor.

Hameed's own self-assurance was gaining more heft, but it remained in balance with his humility. He had settled into contentment as the black, crystalline absence of the Absolute that had set his heart free. He didn't need to post a flag announcing the end of his expedition up the mountain; instead, he sat at the top with a quiet confidence that what he had found had quenched his soul. He felt no need to venture further. He thought he would stay there forever.

I, too, felt the Absolute as my home base; whenever I meditated or made time to sit and sense my experience, the depth and stillness dominated. But I could be pulled to the surface by a flurry of reading for my coursework, writing papers, and seeing students. I was still more expressive of the dynamic side of the Absolute than the quiet side, although over time, I learned that "quiet" didn't mean "mute," as it had in my younger days, and that the lively and the still are complementary sides of my being that can creatively dance together.

The discovery of the soul as the agent of the Absolute showed us how the alchemy between the soul and her true nature had been the source of the revelatory processes all along our journey.[1] The journey of ascent emphasized the not-of-it part of our be-in-the-world-but-not-of-it approach. However, the in-the-world aspect was revving up and was about to move Hameed to engage in new ways, as he described in a journal entry from October 4, 1986:

Yesterday I started to feel that what I want is to live in the Absolute. The rest of my life is the exploration of His kingdom. My function is to express the Absolute. To be a mouthpiece for it that reveals it.

Tonight I saw that all the knowledge I am receiving about the soul—its capacities, its functions, its realm, its development—is secondary to living in the Absolute.

I am quite aware that I don't feel personally invested in any of it. My love is for the Absolute.

I remember that in my experience of arriving home, I felt my life was over. I didn't know what to do with the rest of my allotted time. The Guidance is showing that it will be spent in developing and purifying the soul to be a true and complete expression of the Absolute. The knowledge gained is to be used for the guidance of others toward the same aim.

Hameed's desire to serve inspired a number of new activities, including the formation of a group primarily for individuals in the helping professions—doctors, therapists, attorneys, nurses, and even a minister and a Zen abbot. Since they already had expertise in working with people, Hameed thought they would absorb the teaching efficiently and could apply the Diamond Approach to their professional knowledge and skills.

A dramatic shift was about to shake up how the teaching had been done so far. Hameed had been the only teacher of the large groups until that point, but our first batch of new teachers, who had just completed the training, would now share that responsibility. Folding new students into the existing group had become problematic because understanding one step of the teaching was required before going on to the next. So Hameed and I started to plan a new format called the Diamond Heart Programs, which would begin in 1988.[2] He and I discussed what the curriculum would be and which teachers would be best suited for the task.

Most of the training focused on becoming grounded in the teachings in greater detail and more skilled at guiding private Inquiry sessions, with some direction for leading small group work. Hameed didn't focus the training on how to lead large groups—unless you call him putting teachers in front of a room of people and saying, "Just do it," instruction. He figured that presenting the teachings in the larger setting would be a natural outcome of being proficient in the other modes of teaching.

I would be involved in some way, but we were not sure how yet. Although I had substituted for Hameed on occasion in Colorado and taught the training once in a while in California, this was different. The training groups were small, and I knew most of the students already. My stomach twisted into a knot when I realized what a stretch it was going to be to lead a large group. But I had a year or so to get used to the idea.

The new venture was more or less a leap into the unknown. When my time came, I finally stepped off the ledge. I hit the ground a few times, feathers flying—at least it felt that way to me. Eventually, I took flight and found my own warbling voice. All of us in the training spread our wings and fluttered in the currents of the teachings. Through trial and many errors, some of us learned to soar gracefully while leading a large group. Some would turn out to have skills more suited to conducting small groups or private sessions. All of these skills are equally valuable, and we eventually found the niches where our skills could shine to benefit others.

Hameed also ventured out into the public eye. Although this was not his comfort zone, he felt that people who were not seeking an entire teaching would find a taste of the Diamond Approach a thought-provoking experience, and this could plant new seeds in the soil of current spiritual discourse. He gave a few public talks to jump-start the new groups in Colorado and California that other teachers would conduct, did talks for his new books, which were being published every couple of years,[3] and taught some classes at the Melia Foundation in Berkeley, which had been established by his friend Larry Spiro.

Larry, a tall dark-haired man with a happily filled-out belly and an erudite, philosophical mind, was intrigued by the new perspective that Hameed was presenting, and they became lifelong friends. The foundation's mission was to bridge Eastern and Western spiritual traditions. Larry gathered people for presentations, classes, and discussion to cross-pollinate their spiritual, psychological, and philosophical perspectives.

Hameed enjoyed teaching at Melia, but preferred to take a back seat in spiritual or religious conversations with most of his friends who were not participating in the Work. When he did take the risk, he chose his message carefully. He was sensitive not to challenge their ideas about themselves or their views about spiritual work overtly. He didn't want to hurt anybody by piercing their illusions. I felt that he was being too soft and not being true to either himself or them, and I thought I could make a good case for sharing himself more. "I am not saying that you should announce yourself as the one in the know, Hameed, but why not ask your other friends some provocative questions, like you do with Larry?"

"Larry has asked me for my opinion," he replied, "and I feel he really wants to know what I have to say. That is different from the others."

"But they love and respect you and could learn so much if you would just share more of what you know."

"That," he said, "is not for me to do. I am not their teacher."

As Hameed turned more deliberately toward the realm of relationships, he was also focusing more attention on how he was relating interpersonally with his students. During our annual summer retreats, which were now centered on the diamond vehicles, he was pleased that many students were having deep experiences but saw that they were still seeing the world and themselves from a limited viewpoint. Knowing that their growth would be stunted if he acquiesced to their unstated but obvious desire that he join them in their perspective stimulated the development of his personal essence further. One of the gifts of the Pearl is the bridging of two human souls without either having to leave their inner domain. The strength and integrity of Hameed's personal presence, operating with increasing interactive skill, opened the jeweled vortex of the teaching with more and more grace.

By the fall of 1986, Hameed recognized how much personal love he was feeling for the individuals in his life—friends, students, and family. Although he still preferred his alone time or one-on-one conversation to social gatherings, he was much less likely to jump up and disappear in the middle of dinner parties. His teaching had filled out more thoroughly as well. He became more flexible in expressing the many qualities and dimensions of True Nature as exemplified in his presence as Hameed the Essential Man. He became a faceted, crystalline Pearl embodying the presence of all the aspects and the boundless dimensions through the Absolute. This, as Hameed has said many times, is possible for all human beings.

As with all the other dimensions, however, the Absolute was not a permanent destination. One foggy day in October, I heard Hameed's plunk-and-scuffle on the stairs of my tree house. I peeked out the window. His shoulders were sagging under the weight of his heavy mind. I dropped what I was doing and went out to meet him and offer a friendly hug. When I saw his solemn expression, emerald-green tenderness wafted from my heart and enwrapped him.

"What's up, Meedle?"

"I am not sure what is happening. I am feeling separate from the Absolute in a way I can't explain. I don't want anything else. I feel no need for anything else. But it appears that I am moving away from it."

It soon became evident that the Absolute as we had known it was beginning to recede—or at least this is what he was feeling. We wondered why this could be happening when the Absolute seemed so final and had been stable for a couple of years. Many teachers we had known or read about remain in the Absolute or in other boundless states for decades, even lifetimes, without disturbance. We thought for a while that an issue had caused this divergence, but that turned out not to be the case. Despite Hameed's wish to stay in the Absolute, and for no reason we could discern, a force he was resisting was moving him into new territory. The shift was marked by sadness and confusion.

I reminded Hameed that we always felt a loss when we were moving into new understandings, especially those that were taking us to a new state. But he wasn't feeling a new state, and he didn't want another to replace the Absolute. Even more puzzling was that the Nameless and Supreme were becoming forefront again.

The settled contentment of the Absolute is such an uplifting transcendence out of the conflicts of daily existence—it is like coming to rest in the haven you have always desired. Who wants to get evicted from that? A journal entry on October 15, 1986, shows Hameed's reluctance to leave that perfection for parts unknown:

> I did believe and did want it [*the Absolute*] to be my station always, although I have been aware of the fallacy of any conceptualization. If I had the choice, I would remain as it or annihilated completely into it.

We knew by now that what was happening could not be controlled. When we realized that attachment to staying in the Absolute was the source of confusion, the resistance subsided. A later entry that day:

> A certain perspective has been emerging regarding the soul in its relation to the Absolute. This perception got more definite after I learned about the journey of descent as it is understood by the Sufis. The idea is that after the soul reaches the Absolute and dissolves into it, and it becomes a station, another journey starts. It is a journey of limitation, descending down from the expanded height of the Absolute to the station of man—but a man endowed with the divine qualities.
>
> The ideal of Sufism is the complete man, who unifies the individual with the infinite and is equidistant from both. So the idea is not just to become the Absolute. The Absolute is the beginning of the journey of descent.
>
> This might be what has been happening to me since my clear experiences and my constant abiding in the Absolute. I have been

having to deal with the soul—its impurity and its inadequacies and its purification and its development! The most important thing now is to abandon the conceptualizations of the journey of ascent and let my mind be completely open to the Guidance so I may find out what actually is happening.

I am willing to descend from this station if it is what is supposed to happen.

Me? I was stubborn. Of course, my unwillingness to budge led to a whole new batch of issues. I was angry about having to leave the Absolute—which simply showed me I had already left! Rather than following the flow of the Guidance, I fought my way upstream, which spun me in the eddies of trauma. Memories of my sibs and me losing our home and one another when I was thirteen flooded me. The dark, peaceful Absolute had been my true home and baseline pulse, but I still had some serious inquiry and integration to do.

The hidden places in my soul opened up to reveal the suffering I'd had to push away at that time. The pain continued to unfold as a wound, which grew into a rift in my soul and extended like a slash through the whole universe. I was swimming in a hellish sea of anguish. Body, mind, and soul felt agitated, scratchy, raw, as though brimstone were burning through them. From within the pain streamed tears of sorrow from the depths—the Absolute itself crying for its babies. The suffering I felt was not just my own; I was overcome with grief for the pain of everyone and everything that had ever known pain—in the past, in the present, and forever, in all directions.

Within the helplessness and grief, brightness stirred. I was awash in a sea of compassion. My soul emerged as a brilliant green-and-gold wave. From then on, each person's joy became a celebration of my own heart, and their suffering my own visceral, exquisite pain.

This experience revivified my desire to help and to serve. I would struggle for years to distinguish the difference between the two. It would take a long time to realize that I was not here just to help other people in any and all ways. My assignment was to serve the Absolute in its mission to awaken the truth within as many beings as I could, which for me meant helping people to know that in themselves.

Even though this descent we were being nudged into meant departing from the beloved Absolute as we had known it, the reminder that the tribe we belonged to were nomads made us two explorers willing to vacate the zenith that we once believed marked the end of our long expedition and to begin the descent. We had no rope, carabiners, or harnesses. All we had was the usual tool of Inquiry, which was like the Swiss army knife of the inner landscape. That, along with big love and a well-nourished spirit of adventure, would provide what we needed.

Hameed began to understand how the journey of descent was manifesting itself as the Absolute, not the soul, descending into the dimensions it manifests. The Nameless, the Supreme, the Logos, and Divine Love were now comingling with the Absolute, bringing the understanding that what we had seen as terraces around the mountain were actually all part of one Absolute—not as a vertical hierarchy of reality but as an ontological and epistemological hierarchy of experience offering us different lenses of perception.

The interpenetration of the Absolute into all the boundless dimensions expanded and deepened our understanding of them. Sometimes, the Absolute showed itself as the source, core, and very nature of all forms and phenomena, physical or spiritual. At other times, it showed itself as the deepest layer of stacked dimensions of increasing subtlety, culminating in the rarefied absence of the Absolute. And sometimes the physical world appeared like a transparent holographic light show of virtual reality. I was rather enthralled by that one.

This process of descending into more immanence answered many vexing philosophical questions. In the first dimension, for example, phenomena turn out to be not illusory but rather illusion-like, for they appear as the variegated glimmerings of the radiant blackness of the Absolute. The illusion is the belief that they exist on their own, independent from each other or their source. In all the dimensions of descent, the Absolute remains as the inner and unchanging ground in which manifestation alters in appearance, depending on which dimension the Absolute is comingled with.

When the Absolute revealed itself as totally coemergent with the Supreme, or pure, boundless Being, we referred to it as "the Quintessence." Here there is fullness inseparable from the deepest emptiness, and knowledge inseparable from mystery. And transcendence and immanence are experienced as two sides of the same reality, though completely comingled; which one is dominant depends on the needs of the situation or the particular soul.

The soul's process was one of refinement and clarification on the journey of ascent, but when we reached the top of the mountain, we were under no illusion that all obscurations in the soul had been completely dispelled. We understood later, however, how important our experiences on the way up had been for tuning the soul and opening up the direction of the teaching to new realizations. As unique and unexpected as certain experiences were from this point forward, the relationship of the unmanifest to the manifest dimensions, and the ways these impacted our perceptions, brought out realities that are classic in many traditions.

The differentiations on the journey of ascent gave us a greater understanding of the possibilities of true Being than would have been possible if the five dimensions had not arisen as distinct from each other and the boundlessness of Being had appeared as undifferentiated. There would be no journey of descent without these differentiations. The Absolute shows the different relationships it has to manifestation—all the way to being coemergent with it. The movement of the Absolute from transcendence to immanence culminates in the understanding that the transcendent and the immanent are one and the same. The world and its nature are one and the same. There is not something that has a nature; there is only True Nature.

These understandings enabled us to go back down the mountain through the terrain we had traveled going up—but without leaving the perspective of the summit. Even to say "down" is inaccurate because this is a magic mountain where any sense of direction becomes irrelevant in usual dimensional terms. Imagine, instead, the mountaintop gathering all manifestation into itself and playing with it to see what combinations it can come up with, and you will move closer to sensing what this might be like.

It might have seemed to others that we had been in a deliberately thought-out, step-by-step process on the ascent, but what had actually been occurring was the shifting of forms of experience through the various layers. What at first appears to be a movement toward True

Nature, God, or the divine, for example, is only perceived as such from the perspective of someone moving in time and space. But even if we consider the journey in terms of movement in any sense, it cannot be forward or even inward; it is rather the unraveling of the manifold potential of the soul and the freeing of it to morph into novel forms.

I suspected that I'd never really moved toward anything and had never gone anywhere. The teaching that had been implicit all along, of being where we are as the next and only step—which ends up being no step at all—was delivered in the form of a diamond with a brilliant point inside at its center. We called it the Point Diamond. The faceted, elongated shape manifests the color of whatever essential quality is needed at a given time, displaying its knowledge of how to break free from the influences of mind and allow the natural force of Being to guide our unfoldment.

The Point Diamond shows the way to your true center, but not by moving you to some other place. The Point Diamond teaching is: Sink into where you are as completely as possible and understand it with precision; this will reveal each subsequent layer, quality, or dimension of your nature. And each next step is *your* next step, not someone else's and not toward an idea of where you think you should be. The perceived movement inward is actually your soul becoming more transparent to her inner nature, shifting you into new forms of experience.

Another stream, which Hameed called the subtle process, intertwined with our dipping into the absence of the Absolute. He saw this as spiritualizing the soul further, meaning that her very fabric was becoming more rarified as it transformed from a plasmatic, flowing presence to a more chiffon texture. It felt like an angelic presence, delicate and subtle. This rendered the soul so fine that it became subsumed into Absolute empty, crystalline absence, becoming a completely transparent lens for the Absolute.

The soul was now a selfless agent as "a prolongation of the Absolute," as Hameed put it. This is similar to a hand that does not need to be identified with the body in order to be in service to it—the hand is simply a part of the body with a specialized job to do. Thus, while the soul can totally blend with the transcendent absence of the Absolute, it can also appear in the space-time universe and do the bidding of the Absolute.

As Hameed became subsumed more and more into the Absolute, even the sense of being its organ disappeared at times. What remained was oneness of Being, where the soul could be implicit in the Absolute or else move more into the foreground as an individual consciousness. The boundless dimensions could arise, the individual soul could emerge and act, but there was no longer a static relationship between them.

Now that this was understood, each time that I said "I," it pointed to the unidentifiable, unknowable mystery that is the core of everything, even of my occluded selfish self. There was no other I. Just follow any I to its depth, and the only I is what you will find. But we recognized that the Absolute can be experienced not only as the final I but also as total selflessness, depending on one's vantage point. We understood "total selflessness" to signify not only selflessness in one's actions but also that everything is empty of self-existence.

This shows the annihilating potential of the emptiness of the Absolute, though nothing is actually destroyed or ripped apart. Instead, pure absence cuts through illusion, not by taking action but by simply revealing the nature of manifestation as the pure, empty absence of Being.

There is no nonbeing without Being—they are two sides of the same thing. The Absolute is total nonexistence in coemergence with existence. This paradox is a distinct experience but incomprehensible to the mind, causing it to sputter and then stop. As the emptiness of the Absence dominates, the heart rests into zero affect and dissipates. The body lightens into nonsensate darkness, the individual consciousness erased.

We came to understand that even though cessation of the individual consciousness is a passing experience, it has value on our path in each of the four ways it occurs. The first is the cessation of individual identity, which happens in the realization of the Point. The second is the disappearance of individual boundaries, when we understand that we are boundaryless and not separated from the ground of Being even when we are located; this is part of the Stupa teaching. The third is the cessation of the soul, when we deal with our identification with being a located individual consciousness. The fourth is the experience that not only one's consciousness but also the whole physical universe has vanished. Lights out everywhere.

As the totality of our individual consciousness is annihilated through the power of absence in the third and then the fourth cessation, all awareness completely ceases. All experience is gone for a period of time, usually while in a meditation, but awareness arises once again, refined. This can happen on any of the four levels, over and over again.

The role of cessation is appreciated in the Diamond Approach for several reasons. Through the experience of total absence of consciousness, we learn that as awareness begins to glimmer awake out of the dark nothingness of nonbeing, we are still an individual with our own experience, regardless of how expanded or located. Our individuality is the soul, which is not an illusion but a real phenomenon.

In addition, after one works through the visceral fear of annihilation that occurs in total cessation, the soul is now beyond the terror of its own demise and enjoys the freedom of not grasping on to any idea, feeling, or sensation. She can relax in the understanding that the disappearance of consciousness is not the same as physical death. Further, cessation can be a kind of a rehearsal for the soul's passing through the portal into the mysterious unknown when our bodily life is over. Through practice and over time, we can develop the trust that because True Nature is inherently benevolent and optimizing, even physical death is not as frightening as we once held it to be.

All along the path of realization, we discover that each death is a loss of another layer of self, freeing us from limitations that block a greater realization of *what* we are. Each new facet of essential reality that is integrated into the soul fortifies the maturation of the Pearl further, making us a more complete human being by actualizing the truth of *who* we are.

When our history is seen as only one facet of the overall being that we are, it still remains a part of us, but we are less at the effect of time, since we know ourselves as the timeless within which time and space occur. Our personal history feels further away from our center, so the expression of our personal essence is less filtered by it. When I review my own history, I often feel as though I were peering into another person's life. Sometimes it seems like another incarnation or even that I am a different species. That entity, whatever forms she may have taken, has died many times over the years, and each death has rendered her into a more ghostly image. But a trigger that is strong enough can revive her back to a more substantial form, offering another opportunity to practice.

As a personal essence, one has no thought or image about being a person, but the capacity to express Being in a spontaneous, personal way is natural and simple. This is a precious way to be of service. Becoming a more actualized vessel of True Nature does not necessarily mean becoming a teacher, however. It means that the wisdom we carry and that we share with others is part of who we are, and the spirit of the teachings is conveyed through our actions. Anyone who is sincere in his or her love for truth is a natural vice-regent of True Nature.

Integrating the dimensions during the journey of descent developed the personal essence further into what we named the Pearl, for it is the individualization of all aspects, dimensions, and vehicles experienced on both the ascent and the descent. Ibn 'Arabi calls this the state of the complete human being that is the totality of the spiritual universe as a personal presence.[4] As Hameed more fully embodied this state, he appeared as an immense faceted, dense, crystalline presence that exuded absolute royal simplicity. From his journal in the fall of 1986:

> There was a sense of individuation. The crystal oneness became the surface that was me, and the depth was the Absolute. One night, by myself, I felt some kind of integration, an end of a process. I felt finished, complete, not lacking or wanting anything. The Absolute felt as myself. I experienced myself as the Logos and Nameless Oneness that has the Absolute as the inner nature. I feel this now. When I sense the body, I become in touch with a crystalline surface, unfaceted and boundless.

By 1987, the nomads were heading for another universe of spaces that made boundlessness look conventional. We were zeroing in on the secret beyond the deep. It was closer than we knew.

29 ❖ Through the Jeweled Portal

DECEMBER 1987. I AM lying on my bed, watching a trio of squirrels playing tag and quarreling, creating a ruckus. I can see Mushka splayed out on her padded lounge on the deck, languidly watching the display. A few months earlier, she would have been on all fours, barking orders, but now she doesn't have the energy.

In recent months, Mushka's health had declined in tandem with the waning light of the sun as it meandered southward. Her arthritis was beyond the help of any remedy. Her hearing and sight were deteriorating, and she was now incontinent as well. I was troubled by the pressing question of the right thing to do for her. At sixteen, she had outlived her life expectancy by a half dozen years.

My thoughts shifted to the group meeting that would begin the next day. I was looking forward to a weekend of teachings. I needed to be held in the group field and do nothing but listen to Hameed expound and watch him work.

Morning came in lightly after a night of heavy sleep. Mushka seemed back to her old self, licking me awake and signaling that she was ready to go outside. I was glad to see her perking up. I let her out, threw on some clothes and makeup, slammed down a shot of juice, and stumbled down the stairs. As I entered the Ali house, the smell of hot iron and burning wood wafted out from the group room. The heat from the stove calmed me as I walked down the hallway.

Winter often initiated a period of inner hibernation for me, but this year it was different. Even before Mushka had started to decline, I had been feeling a new brand of ennui. Sometimes it seemed like a close relative of depression. My little buddy's distress was bringing up boatloads of sadness, but this other feeling was markedly different. I didn't know what to make of it.

I took my usual spot in the corner of the group room, propped myself up with couple of fat pillows stuffed into the crook, and contemplated my inner flatness. I was even beginning to wonder about quitting school, even though I was only a few months from completing my master's degree. "It feels like I've lost my passion for it," I muttered to myself. "Come to think of it, I don't feel enthusiastic about much of anything." But as more of my travel companions for the weekend arrived, a breezy mirth swept through my emotional flatland. Where had that come from?

Hameed arrived, looking casual and reserved. I noticed the suppleness of his movements as he took his seat near the stove. I couldn't quite read his state—it didn't look deep and it didn't seem particularly shiny either.

The gladness I'd felt only moments before gave way to a dispirited monotone in my soul. I was ready to just sit and be.

After a short break following the opening meditation, Hameed returned to his seat and picked up his beads. Removing the toothpick from his mouth, he reiterated the importance of not merely going for experiences but of letting living presence reconstruct us through its own laws. He referenced a statement that Jesus made about giving up one's personal life to follow him.[1] Reminding us of how easily we can get sucked into the vortex of ubiquitous details that derail us from our prime objective of attending to presence, he stressed once again that only a heart-based focus of will can support us to cleave to the inner life as we walk the outer one.

Hameed would not be teaching the boundless dimensions formally until the 1990s, but he was already speaking from their broader view to contextualize the various aspects and vehicles that many of the students were uncovering in their personal investigations. That evening, as Hameed worked with individual students, I witnessed them deepening into sweetness, love, and clarity, and I could see him filling with love nectars in response. After the group was over, however, he told me, "There was a way in which I was not fully experiencing the love and sweetness, even though the work was clear and effortless."

The following week, at a small group meeting where the work of the weekend could unwind within each person's own process, a woman I will call Marianne took the opportunity. When she expressed the desire to be one with Hameed, he deftly navigated the territory with her, again brimming with energetic love. Rich, honey-like golden presence flooded the whole group and moved us along with Marianne into a pool of sweetness. Everybody in the room was on their own lily pad on the lake of love, blooming as participants and witnesses to the intimate moment between the two. When Hameed closed the meeting, I noticed that he was back to the indescribable.

As he and I were reflecting on the work of the evening, he said, "Some sort of crystal arose tonight, Kran. It was solid, dense, hard, and sharp, but it had no affect of any sort."

"Yeah, from the outside, it appeared that you were totally responsive and sensitive to everybody, but it was hard for me to tell what state *you* were in. What was it?"

"I dunno. It echoed somewhat how we have been experiencing ourselves recently. 'Lack of interest' comes close. I felt present, but something was different about it. There was no freshness or feeling of clarity. The states that were needed for the inquiries seemed to arise . . ." His voice trailed off. "But the state was nothing I can quite define. Kind of neutral, really. Almost not a state at all—or at least not a state with distinct, defining characteristics."

Throughout the journey of descent, we had been experiencing the Absolute both as background and intermingling with other states. But with the arising of this new form of crystalline, pure awareness and presence that we simply referred to as "the crystal," we stopped feeling the Absolute as a constant presence in our experience. The odd thing was, we didn't miss it when it wasn't there, and we didn't desire it. But Hameed did not see what was happening as a departure from the Absolute. "I know that the Absolute is what I am," he said, "even if it isn't explicit in my experience."

This single crystal with no quality, affect, or discernable meaning remained dominant in our consciousness for months. Other states would come and go, bringing hints of insight about the crystal, but there was no big *aha*! It seemed to be outside the realm of presence or absence—it was both and neither. It was not a particularly pleasant or desirable feeling.[2] It felt rather uneventful, actually. Our first theory was that this crystal was like the others that had shown up on the journey of descent, and we simply did not understand its knowledge yet.

At first, it was sometimes a bit cloudy, for lack of a better word, like some types of natural quartz. But then it became a black, dense emptiness like the Absolute, and this seemed to verify our suspicion that it was most likely another of the wisdom gems we were finding on our way down the mountain.[3] One thing was noticeably different about this crystal, however: It had the Absolute inside it but not necessarily always around it. Another strange property was that it did not depend on the presence of the Absolute to exist, yet it still felt like a particular yet unbounded presence—though not boundless in the sense of being everywhere; it felt localized.

Some of the diamonds, or nonconceptual crystals, that arose during the journey of descent were similar enough to this crystal that we bypassed all the signals and concluded that it must be a form of the Absolute. At that time, we saw the Absolute as the source of everything, including the teaching, so we also called the crystal "the source crystal."

Upon further examination, we realized that rather than the dense emptiness of the Absolute, the density of the crystal was a kind of nothingness. This vague feeling of nothing was akin to the same nothingness space we had felt weaving in and out of our awareness over the prior months, but in this case, it was dense. We already had experienced the void of space as nothing when we first had encountered it years ago, followed by the emptiness of the Supreme as infinite nothing. Then the clear absence arrived, followed by the black absence, which brought even greater degrees of emptiness.

Each kind of space that had emerged along the way seemed more rarified than the one before. At some point, however, we saw that what we were experiencing now was a nothing space that was not more rarefied than the absence of the Absolute but rather another order of emptiness altogether. It had fewer features conceptually and experientially than anything we had known before. It was hard to describe in any specific terms except for . . . nothing. From that point on, we called this state "featureless nothingness."[4]

As Hameed and I were investigating this phenomenon, Mushka's suffering was increasing. After I sought advice from various professionals, friends, and even psychics, I made the difficult decision to end her life. The neutral feeling of nothingness that I was experiencing did not spare me from the feelings about what I was about to face. I even began to question whether I was doing the right thing.

On the chosen day, I spent the morning with Mushka, taking her to her favorite spots in the rose gardens. The traveling vet was due to show up at three. I started to shake inside as the time of his arrival drew closer. Mushka was lying on her blanket on the deck of our tree house; I sat beside her, cross-legged, with her head in my lap. Hameed had come to be with me and to bid Mushka farewell, and to do what we had done for other friends and students in recent years—hold her in our love and follow her soul on its journey.

I heard the vet ascending the stairs; with each step he took, my chest squeezed with apprehension. When he arrived on the deck, I gestured for him to come over to where we were sitting. A few words were exchanged about what to expect, and he gave us a few last minutes with her. Then he quietly asked for my permission to inject her. I nodded.

Mushka's head grew heavier in my lap as her breath slowed. In seconds, she was gone.

I saw her bright spirit becoming a butterfly. She was free now. I felt a palpable sense of benevolence. Hameed turned to me and patted my knee with a soft, kind hand. "I saw her leave her body as a point of light and turn into one of those pretty butterflies she used to play with," he said with a mild shade of sorrow.

Though my heart was aching, I knew that my beloved Mushka had had a good life. I could even feel that she was happy to be free from her hurting body. The tears would come later.

I sprinkled her ashes among Marie's roses, where she used to play with the butterflies.

Hameed and I, left to our expeditions without Mushka's panting company, continued to explore the enigmatic crystal interloper. It remained unchanged, with no discernable affect or apparent purpose. The Absolute was a frequent guest rather than the constant companion it had been for some years; the mysterious form of the crystal was our baseline at this time. The gems that had arrived before it seemed to have been more generous in telling us their story. I couldn't tell whether the crystal was being stingy or if we just hadn't come up with the correct invitation for it to display the resolutions to its riddles.

As Hameed and I began to accept the neutral quality of the nothingness, we felt it more as dispassion, and we discovered that we could fully engage with life while in that mode. (In hindsight, we understood that the dispassion is the correct inner posture of surrender for inviting the wisdom carried by the crystal.) We also noticed that the dispassion did not conflict with, or even affect, other feelings or states. States of all colors and flavors appeared and vanished again without a trace; ego or essence, ubiquitous or local—nothing altered the crystal in any way. In fact, it seemed to be the other way around.

The dispassion of the crystal evaporated our concerns about what condition we were in. Hameed lost any remaining interest in comparing his states with those of teachers and other people or even with states he had experienced in the past or had hoped for. This freed him up, which he felt happy about, but it was not an exuberant joy. More like a homeopathic dose—just enough of a heart clue that we were headed in the right direction. By May of 1988, we were living in the absence of judgment about, or ambition for, any experience—whether dual, nondual, ego, or essential. We even started to question what enlightenment meant.

Hameed began to call what we were experiencing a kind of nonconceptual freedom. He recognized this as the gift of the crystal, which he began to refer to as "the Freedom Crystal." The dispassion and its resultant freedom from ambition, however, did not shut the door on any new book, event, or other opportunity that might shuttle us onward in our understanding. We were still curious nomads, but it was like wandering in the wilderness in a snowstorm.

One day, Larry Spiro informed Hameed that the Dzogchen master His Holiness Penor Rinpoche, the head of the Nyingma sect of Tibetan Buddhism at the time, was coming to town. Larry had been active in the Buddhist community and studied with several Tibetan lamas in the '70s and '80s. He knew that Hameed had been reading Dzogchen texts and that we attended events together to further our education, so he asked if we would like to go with him to see the master. Curious about how the Rinpoche's understanding might inform the transcendent states we had been marinating in over the previous few years, we were grateful for the opportunity to attend the two-day event.

I was buzzed with anticipation as Hameed and I walked up the few cement steps to the entrance of the Dharmadhatu Center in Berkeley on June 18, 1988. We slipped off our shoes and added them to the montage of footwear in the foyer. Passing through the hefty wooden doors that opened into the big hall, we surveyed the room, which was dotted with neatly placed floor pillows. Down the aisle I padded, and Hameed plunked, until I spied three available cushions in a row on the right, about fifty feet away from the stage. We settled in and waited for Larry.

A small group of monks in red-and-saffron robes sat on the small stage at the front, awaiting the Rinpoche's arrival. They were stationed around a seat that was more like a square platform, about a foot high and topped with a red pillow. The Tibetan *thangkas* gracing the walls gave the surround a textured, exotic appeal.

Larry arrived, a toothy grin peeking through his lush, dark beard. He groaned like a large ship listing as he made his way to the floor, greeting us with his cheerfully nasal Boston accent.

The procession was about to begin from the back of the room. Hameed rotated to the left, looking back over his shoulder to get a view of His Holiness. Then, untwisting, he leaned toward me on his right and whispered through a cupped hand, "What do you see?"

I turned and saw a large-framed man, somewhat stout and hunched, ambling awkwardly down the passage. "A chunky guy that walks like a duck," I whispered back. I clapped my hand over my mouth, realizing how irreverent that might have sounded. I meant no disrespect, but I wasn't seeing or feeling anything special yet.

"Yeah. Bad knees from years of meditation," Hameed confirmed.

The Rinpoche wriggled onto his nest, pulled his knees into the cross-legged position, and began to chant in a monotone bass, with an occasional high note that would immediately slip back into the droning, slow syllables of Tibetan. After about twenty minutes of chants and prayers, he began to speak. A translator made sense of the words for us, since Penor Rinpoche didn't speak English. We wondered whether this might affect the transmission of the teaching, but within minutes, the depth of the nine yanas of the Nyingma sect of Tibetan Buddhism ballooned tangibly into the room.

In the middle of the second day, when His Holiness was describing the final three levels of the teaching, I entered a state of consciousness that seemed much like the Absolute that Hameed and I had being experiencing for a few years—a state in which everything is the ungraspable absence of Being, beyond definition. Darkness enveloped the space and absorbed all manifest reality into its vacuity, leaving only a glimmer of transparent shapes marking the virtual reality of the world. I looked around the room, and the forms appeared as glittering surfaces transparent to a smooth, dark clarity. My mind was dissolving. I began to feel consciousness disappear.

Everything in our consciousness and in our surrounds was erased in the Rinpoche's powerful transmission—with one exception. The only remaining dimension of our awareness that had not been annihilated by the Rinpoche's state was the same crystal presence that had emerged for us within the Absolute and had remained, unchanged, for many months, no matter what we felt or experienced in addition to it. Even the intensity of the Rinpoche's presence had not been able to dissipate it. Not only did it remain steady, it also became stronger and more faceted, as though it had been fortified by the transmission.

This caught our attention. The stunning fact that the crystal had maintained its existence even when the master had evoked what we experienced as the annihilating emptiness of the Absolute sent us probing with more urgency to discover whatever we could about the crystal.

After a couple of weeks of contemplation, Hameed arrived at some clarity concerning Dzogchen practices. He felt that they were valuable for students of Buddhism involved in practices geared toward states that can be activated and realized. But we had known for some time that it was no use for us try to move toward a specific state—and that even if we reached it, we couldn't choose to either stay in it or leave it. The Dzogchen path points the way to a deep realization, but it is not the orientation or practice for our Work and for us. As potent as Penor Rinpoche's empowerments had been, we were on another kind of journey. That said, the ever-curious Hameed continued to read all the books about Dzogchen and Mahamudra he could get his hands on to understand their perspective more completely.

I was still in school at that point and began to wonder if my depleted interest in it was similar to my lack of excitement about the spiritual domain. I didn't feel negative. I was merely neutral. So I got up and went to class, read books, and wrote papers. It just happened, and I made no effort to stop. Besides, it was logical to complete my degree, since I was only a few credits away from graduating. Hameed encouraged me to continue, if for no other reason than to follow through on my intention. "It will strengthen your capacity for inner support to stay the course," he said.

I took my last class in the summer of 1988. It was on sex education, of all things. It was supposed to help budding therapists question their own attitudes about sex and gender issues that might arise while working with clients. I grudgingly signed up for it.

I stood at the entrance of the brightly lit classroom on the first day and scanned for a spot to settle in. I was watching the room in motion as the other students milled about, choosing their seats, and my eyes stopped at a guy with a strong jaw and wavy brown hair, sitting directly across from me. I recognized him from a class I had been in the year prior. He was ruggedly handsome, slender, and looked like he was in his late thirties. I smiled and gave a wave of recognition.

He patted the table in front of the vacant chair to his left, so I made my way over and sat down, and we dived into an upbeat conversation after introducing ourselves. Like two teenagers, we chuckled, flirted, and passed notes during the lecture. It had been a long time since I'd felt this easy with a man.

I had known that something was still missing for me in terms of relationship. Meeting Greg sealed the deal on my next step in that world. We began to see each other frequently, and he seemed mature, thoughtful, and attentive. Soon our mutual appreciation and carefree delight grew into out-and-out love.

My crystal life now faced the challenge of straddling two worlds. But the signs were positive: My mother loved Greg at first sight. He liked Marie and Hameed—an added bonus, since they would always be family to me. And I was optimistic that Greg would be able to accept the indefinable, unconventional connection that Hameed and I shared. I had no illusion that the dynamics would be simple, but Greg and I were both therapists; we could work it out. And we had time. Still sensitive about my divorce from Perry, I was in no hurry to step into a formal commitment. I didn't move in with Greg until the end of 1989, and we married in 1992.

As the journey of descent progressed, Hameed and I constantly moved between the Absolute expanse and the crystal. I skinned my knees on lots of boulders on my way down the mountain, while his path seemed more like skiing gracefully downhill. When I was not tending to my scrapes or experiencing nonduality, I felt the simple presence of the crystal.

In early October 1988, Hameed and I engaged in another inquiry about the Freedom Crystal. Throughout the prior few weeks, it had been appearing as various colors and qualities of essence, and we had observed that we remained neutral amidst the presences that were manifesting. I had the insight that the crystal was freeing us from needing the essential aspects to manifest; now we knew that they were part of us whether we felt them explicitly or not. The next morning, Hameed wrote in his journal:

> Last night the freedom crystal got bigger and more intense. I became the crystal. I feel I am a boundless dense presence. There are not any separating boundaries, but there is also not infinite extension. I do not feel separate from appearance. The question of separation or boundaries does not figure in here.
>
> There is a dense presence, hard. It is concentrated at the location of the body. I am the presence. It is a dense consciousness. Simultaneously it is nothing. The sense of nothingness is not absence.
>
> I know I am the crystal, yet it has no sense of self and no quality whatsoever. No sense of emptiness, clarity, space, or freshness. Everything in the world appears ordinary.

We did not know at that point that the Freedom Crystal was a vehicle, but Hameed's experience that night should have been our first clue. This crystal needed a different kind of discriminating intelligence to penetrate its knowledge; we were getting close but were not there yet.

After Hameed's experience of becoming the crystal, many tensions arose in our body-consciousness, presenting us with an entirely new notion of boundaries, unrelated to psychological issues. We were still coming from the perspective of our prior experiential knowledge—that boundaries are all about being separate from other things, other people, and from Being. The habit of seeing ourselves as existing in a 3-D spatial universe, even in a spiritual sense of extending infinitely, is the air we all breathe. It took many forays into the Absolute and back again to grok that the type of boundaries we were currently experiencing had to do with the concept of space itself.

The Absolute had revealed itself as the deepest nature of the soul and of all manifest reality, and we had realized it as the ground of all grounds of Being. But our experience and knowledge of True Nature was still limited because we thought that anything that would be "beyond" the Absolute would have to be foundational to it. We had not yet realized that the teaching now emerging was a departure from that way of thinking. This conundrum would not become clarified for us until we understood more about the absence that is characteristic of the Absolute, and its erasure of the concept of space.

The nothingness we had been experiencing grew more interesting now. We felt it as a kind of space, but not in the usual, dimensional way. It was a spaceless space: The feeling of openness that accompanies any sense of space remained, but the sense of extension and expansiveness that usually accompanies it did not. Here there was neither depth nor surface, so any notions of going "deeper" or "beyond" were no longer relevant. We couldn't call it space, yet it was open—not closed or blocked in any way. This was an off-the-map segment of the journey that had us going sideways instead of deeper.

Our discovery that space is not a prerequisite for experience activated the animal soul, which is totally dependent on the perception of space for its existence. The spaceless dispassion we were experiencing unearthed passionate attachments and woke up other unknown creatures hiding under the rocks. Powerful desires and needs, agitation and aggression, and adherence to particular positions created an internal maelstrom.

In that situation, Hameed's character lent itself much better to emotional camouflage. Plus he was seated more firmly on the side of the neutrality. Me? Everything shows. I had to hold myself in check to keep from acting out the banshee inside, which could still wail out glib or spiky remarks, overcoming my better judgment. Yet a new kind of detachment was silently growing within us along with the whole agitated mess.

Amidst all the shifting sands, Hameed and Marie were buying a vacation home in Hawaii and spending more time there. He and I spoke on the phone when he was away, continuing to explore the Freedom Crystal, but it wasn't the same as having our casual daily contact. As our outer lives diverged, we experienced much of this period as a lull in the development of the Diamond Approach. For months, we kept waiting, and occasionally hunting for, what would be revealed next.

Hameed coined the term "the gray night of the soul" for our experience of the bland, featureless desert we were crossing. This passage was so unremarkable and uninteresting, even boring at times, that it was beyond lack of meaning. It dawned on us that the spaceless nothingness we were continuing to marinate in despite all our outward activities might not be intermediary to anything. Maybe this was all there was!

When we began years later to teach this part of the Work, we found that many individuals believe that if they fully allow the nothingness of the crystal in, they won't feel motivated to do anything and won't even care about anything. We have found that during this stage, students can veer off course, interpreting their overall lack of interest as an indication that they are not interested in the teaching anymore. "It has done its job," some will say, or, "I found another path that I think is more relevant to where I am now." Others may feel that they are finished with spiritual work altogether. Or they might feel that something is wrong with them because they don't have more drive, so they try to cultivate a passion for some other pursuit to escape the nothingness. This initial lack of interest in not only the usual activities of daily life but also in inner investigations is the dragon at the gate of the crystal secrets.

The nothingness we were living in felt like a loss of everything because reality no longer had features of any kind to cling to. Part of the test, as Hameed called it, of the gray night of the soul was to see how much we really loved the truth truly for its own sake. Truth—whatever that was now—seemed to be saying to us, "How much do you want to know me? How much are you willing to let go of? Are you willing to give up even your cherished Diamond Approach?"

The understandings that were arriving during these times, and those that would span the next decades, were so different from what we had known before that Hameed and I felt we had left the path of the Diamond Approach. As it turned out we *did* leave the map—but not the path. This leg of the journey defied all categories.

It was not easy for Hameed or me to discuss our new realizations with anyone. Though Hameed found slight resemblances to certain Zen teachings, we were very much on our own with these breakthroughs for the better part of twenty years. It was as if a muzzle had been implanted that would pop into place the moment I began to say something about the crystal. I could not say more than a few words—even to the few friends who had peripheral experiences of it—before going mute.

Insights slipped in quietly, like invisible wanderers sitting in the corner of our consciousness, awaiting our notice. But we were still using the flying manual for an outdated starship, and it was jamming the guiding mechanism of the new vehicle. We needed a better guidance system for navigating through and beyond space-time. Gradually, it became evident that the source crystal was conveying the wisdom of freedom from various angles that we had not thought about, experienced, or even known we wanted.

One day, during another exploration, we finally saw the connection between the nothingness and the inscrutable crystal: The crystal was the nothingness taking a form, compacting itself into a faceted crystal. And the qualities arising within this faceted nothingness brought understanding about our relationship to the aspects of essence from yet another new angle, as all our teaching vehicles do. This helped us to recognize that the crystal was another vehicle, so we began to refer to it as "the Freedom Vehicle." We needed this understanding to recalibrate our navigation instruments for the strange domain we were meandering around in.

It still felt as though nothing much was happening but, over time, recognition and understanding accumulated to reveal a more coherent picture. For instance, integrating the realizations about the nothingness and the crystal opened up unimaginable ways of seeing the relationship of one manifestation to another. Our discovery that there was no extension in the nothingness meant that everything occupied the same place—which ended up not being a place at all.

This no-place brings new and different kinds of union, as when Hameed and I felt ourselves interpenetrating with other people or things. More than once, we experienced each other as two dense fields overlapping, while we remained autonomous. This reminded me of my hand interpenetrating the wall in my dream without disappearing. Sometimes it was as though a whole universe existed within both Hameed and me, and we collided without losing our individual forms. Then there were the occasions when I felt that everything was within me or I was in everything. To up the mind-blowing factor another notch, I occasionally felt myself in everything and everything in me at the same time—like

Indra's Net,⁵ in which each diamond at each juncture reflects all other diamonds within the net. Or in a hall of mirrors that reflect one another infinitely—there appeared to be infinite extension, but in reality that was not the case.

The Freedom Vehicle makes it possible to have these types of unity experiences—we call them experiences of unilocal unity, or unilocality—with another person, a group, or the whole universe. Unilocality is the view of reality related to a nothingness that has no sense of space, extension, or distance. The experience of being in union in this nondimensional nothingness is unilocal unity. It can arise as the experience of two or more individuals sharing the same location, often experienced as being inside each other.

Unilocality is neither dual nor nondual. We are not talking here about an ocean of consciousness that unites all forms as they arise within it—the nonduality of the boundless dimensions; nor is it dual, when individual forms are separate and relating spatially. In unilocality, all forms exist within one another.

One day in the early 1990s, when Hameed and I were sitting across from each other in an inquiry, our perception of the spatial dimension disappeared, and we felt we were one crystal—not even two that were overlapping or interpenetrating or merging to become one. You could say that two becoming one crystal (one Freedom Vehicle) is a unilocal unity phenomenon, but it requires something more than any other type of unilocal experience: personal realization of the crystal. You must know the Freedom Vehicle as being *what you are*. This experience stunned us into the recognition that we had only scratched the surface of the potential forms of union, which pointed to the interminable openness of unilocality.

Hameed and I hit another gap when our strong commitments to our marriages and managing the mushrooming demands of a growing school greatly reduced our availability for Inquiry practice together. Hameed insisted that it was going to take the two of us to unlock the crystal's secrets, so we made the extra effort to make it possible.

During a session to jointly probe into our experience of the Freedom Vehicle one afternoon, Hameed and I felt the impulse to look at each other straight on. As we sat, hands on knees, linked eye to eye, we were drawn as though by a tractor beam to bow forward toward each other.

Our foreheads got brighter as we moved closer. The moment they connected, a spot lit up like a pulsar at the bridge of our noses. The burst of energy was indescribably alive and electrifying. We remained motionless for an eternal minute. Then we sat back and took in what happened.

"Wow. What was that, Hameed?"

"An explosion," he answered, and lapsed back into silence. His attention was wrapped in the experience itself.

Over the following weeks, this experience began to evolve for each of us. The whole ocular area opened, and both eyes merged into one opening. Then the potent star at the bridge of the nose migrated to the heart center and detonated a quasaric energy.

Now that the crystal cruiser as a space-unfolding mechanism was humming along smoothly, the teaching evolved with more fluency. The explosive quasar, with its densely packed divine energy, bumped the Freedom Vehicle up to warp speed, which revitalized and clarified the teaching, as Hameed had suspected it would. The thrilling energy of the cosmos hurtled us through portals that were beyond any concept we had, not only of duality and nonduality but of unilocality as well. What we had been experiencing as vagueness and a hiatus in the teaching turned out to be simply a lack of the right fuel for our ship to continue on its voyage.

The crystal showed us that it was not in the business of uncovering psychological issues but rather of revealing the limitations of our ontological and epistemological views—our basic notions of reality. The Freedom Vehicle was, and is, a mind-twisting experience—a radical nonconceptuality in the sense that there can be concepts, no concepts, or both when you are in its realm. It is neither timeless nor in time. Or you could say that because it is outside of all physical dimensionality, it has all of time and space as its potentials. It is not self and not no-self. You can't call it spiritual or mundane—and even the concept of True Nature doesn't apply. The Freedom Vehicle is utter simplicity without any ideas about it.

Of course, the Freedom Vehicle is not a physical conveyance that moves through space, but it reveals space as one potential of the multidimensional manifold of the cosmos. From this perspective, every experience, and even every thing, is a potential wormhole to another universe of experience.

Imagine, if you will, that the fleshy density of your body has dissipated. In its place is you as a gemstone of any shape, with a completely faceted surface. As you feel into it, you notice that you are also total openness—more substantial than mineral rock but more open than the feeling of limitless sky. Now you notice that each facet is like a transparent window to another universe of experience. You are a geodesic structured gem of complete transparency. The view from each window is not contiguous with the one next to it; each view opens to another way of knowing reality.

As Hameed looked back on all of these experiences, they seemed to him to fall into a particular order. Many Buddhist schools use the terminology of the "turnings of the wheel of the dharma" as a framework to describe the progression of their teachings. Hameed borrowed this means of categorizing experience, and we now refer to the four turnings of the Diamond Approach teaching to denote the paradigm shifts within the Work. Subsequent turnings do not negate the truth of prior understandings; they contain them from a more inclusive perspective. These divisions help us conceptualize the progression of the teachings and understand the experiences we have as we practice.

The first turning is the work on the soul and individual realization: the lataif, the Pearl, the Point, and the diamond vehicles. The second is the journey up the mountain through the boundless dimensions, followed by the journey of descent. The third turning is marked by the realization of the Freedom Vehicle, featureless nothingness, and unilocality. The realization of the Freedom Vehicle as our true being opens the door to the fourth turning in which a succession of ways of viewing and experiencing reality become available that are radically different from anything that came before.

The fourth turning reveals the nonhierarchical view, which frees us from the need to qualitatively compare various views of reality—or even the experiences and awakenings that give rise to such views—since each has is its own truth and validity. It shows that we do not have to characterize the spiritual journey as a movement from one state to another, progressing toward subtler and more fundamental realizations. The nonhierarchical view, however, is also only one perspective, one way of looking at reality. The hierarchy of a progressive path is also a valid view.

Another central feature of the fourth turning is the view of totality—the openness to all possible real ways of knowing and experiencing reality. The view of totality allows for all views to coexist, including their inconsistencies and incompatibilities. One can hold one view, several views simultaneously, or no view at all.

Every spiritual teaching has its view of reality that originates in and depends upon a particular kind of awakening. And each path is different in what it considers the final truth. The freedom of totality is that no reconciliation is needed between views that differ. The various states of realization are different ways that True Nature manifests. There are not many True Natures; True Nature is indivisible as well as ineffable.

Reality and consciousness are much more mysterious and rich than what can be experienced and known in any one realization, regardless of how comprehensive or liberating it is. There is no single, final, ultimate truth waiting to be discovered. Being keeps revealing new ways to experience and know reality; if we are not attached to finding some ultimate condition, we will have the privilege of experiencing truth in its endless display.[6] Our curiosity, our heart's wish to know the truth, and our willingness to surrender to the gift of where we are in this moment, with the unknown as our companion, will keep us completely open and open-ended. These qualities naturally set us on a path of unending discovery and runaway realization.

Such was the impact of the quasar. The valence that had brought Hameed and me together when we exchanged our first smile and said our first hellos had once again manifested the right conditions to further the teaching, as it had done all along the way. Partnership, friendship, even relationship—all evaporated. What remained was one crystalship, continuing to peel back space-time to new realms of experience, in endless realization.

One evening, after a retreat meeting that Hameed and I were teaching together, I began to have strange sensations. I turned to Hameed. "Something is happening on my forehead that is really weird."

"What is it?"

"It feels like somebody is scribbling on it with a magic marker . . . made of bright light!"

"What do you feel there or see there? What does it say?"

At first I had no idea what it was—pictures, maybe? Symbols? Finally, I was able to respond. "I don't know—but I think it looks like another language."

I picked up my pen and made a mark or two on a paper.

Hameed looked at the paper and then at my brow. "It's Arabic," he said with surprise.

"What the hell . . . why Arabic?" I felt my face twist with annoyance. Why hadn't it been written in a language I could understand?

"Maybe I am supposed to read it," Hameed ventured. He paused, then zeroed in on my brow.

"Well, what does it say?" I asked, more than a little curious.

"The capable. It says 'The Capable.'"

Over the following days, more words came unexpectedly: one phrase at a time, always on my forehead, and with the same fluid presence of brilliancy. I didn't know whom these messages were meant for. I would just tell Hameed when they appeared, and he would read them:

> The Maker of Images
> The Friendly Loving One
> The Alone
> The Only
> The Free

Perhaps the questions that are alive in your own capable heart are beckoning you to follow the Friendly Loving One, and inviting you into the Alone with the Alone. If your soul has been touched by what you have read in this book, you may encounter the Only in the mysterious depth that unites us all. And if you remain true to your heart's desire, you will exit the universe of the known . . .

through the jeweled portal

to

freedom.

Afterword

After traveling with me through the first fifteen years of the journey, you now have a hint of the crystal universe that Hameed and I have been immersed in for the nearly three decades since the Freedom Vehicle made its first appearance.

The crystal remains the main revelatory conduit of the Diamond Approach teachings, and much of our current teaching is either directly related to the third and fourth turnings or is cradled in their perspective. Only a fraction of the varied realizations we know of that have emerged through the fourth turning have been unpacked, systematized, and taught, and the fourth turning continues to unfold new and different realizations, filling out the view of totality.

A mystery will keep its secrets no matter how much one says about it; and the riddles remain until the right conditions arise for them to be solved and their meaning can be apprehended by a soul seasoned to hear it. Thus, each student's unique unfoldment determines when and how the details of the Freedom Vehicle—and all the other teachings—are revealed and applied.

The teaching has always taken care of itself, choosing the right times, places, and people through which to express itself. It also finds new ways to extend its golden threads so that those who feel drawn to the heart of our work can find us. Some of the teaching is now becoming available through the World Wide Web, providing an intriguing parallel to the way the Diamond Approach has developed. From some invisible spiritual internet of knowledge—I mean, have you ever *seen* an internet?—the teaching is continually being downloaded.

The magnitude of spiritual knowledge that forms any body of teaching generally takes centuries to develop; in our case, the teaching has been downloaded with great accuracy and speed, with Hameed as its principal diamond server, decoding the raw bits of information and creating a language understandable to Earthlings.

The presence of the teachings on the web echo a kind of unilocal unity through its connecting force but will never fully replace the old-fashioned, face-to-face relationship between teacher and student; we have discovered that the most profound and personalized understandings occur within the context of private sessions.

The Ridhwan School continues to have two brick-and-mortar centers. The center in Boulder was the first footprint of the Diamond Approach and has remained in its original location since it was purchased in 1981. We bought the Byron Street center in Berkeley in 1994, which gave us a firm footing in the world now that we were in two locations. In 2008, we relocated to the Eunice Street building. The Berkeley center serves as the main hub of the Diamond Approach, housing the staff necessary for overseeing an international organization. Both centers are the home for the Academy groups, overseen by Hameed and Karen, as well as other activities of the School. Teachers all over the world use additional venues while remaining protected under the Ridhwan umbrella.

There are now about four thousand Diamond Approach students worldwide, with sixty-six groups in ten countries, covering the United States, Canada, Europe, Asia, and Australia. We see the School as a global beehive where all function as worker bees, with every bee having a place and providing their realization and expertise. The task of the entire organization is to discover how to best collect and store the honey of the teaching in the soul vessels of each member of the hive.

Our understanding that interdependence is the key to functional unity led to a new development. After an illness in the '90s that rendered him quite weak, Hameed was inspired to establish a governing body for the future of the School. He formed a council of elders and called it the Synod. Its purpose is twofold: to ensure that the legal and administrative structures of the School function in alignment with the principles of the teaching and to provide spiritual leadership for the teacher body and the students. Its functions have expanded to include more interfacing with the students and teacher body in order to clarify communications and probe into issues that impact all members of the School.

The first Synod meeting took place in the spring of 1998. The original members, chosen by Hameed with my input, were Bob Ball, Jessica

Britt, Karen Johnson, Linda Krier, Deborah Ussery Letofsky, Morton Letofsky, Sandra Maitri, Duncan Scribner, Scott Layton, and Jeanne Hay Rosenblum. Currently, half of the membership is voted in by the teacher body, and the other half is selected by Hameed. All of these fine people continue to be among my most cherished friends and all continue to serve in the school in some way. (See our website for a listing of current Synod members.)

Hameed and I no longer serve on the Synod, though we continue to be consulted about various matters. Hameed also left his post as president of the Ridhwan Foundation in 2005, and Morton Letofsky was elected by the Synod to take on that role. Our stepping back from governance seemed a wise preparation for Hameed's and my eventual departure from the physical world, so that a healthy, functional organism would remain. Hameed is still considered to be the spiritual leader of the School.

As of the turn of the century, Hameed and I began to colead some groups within the School. Together and solo, we have given talks at conferences on consciousness studies and at various public events, bridging the Diamond Approach to other areas of discourse. Along with other teachers of the Diamond Approach, we also have been interfacing with other organizations to provide online teachings.

Marie and Hameed have been happily married for thirty-seven years at the time of this writing, December 2016. He continues to have contact with his daughters Rima and Saludeen, as well as with his siblings and extended family in Kuwait, and he has seven grandchildren. His nephew Mishall Abdul Muhsen lived with Hameed while attending college in the '90s and is now a member of the first Diamond Heart group in Europe. Hameed's nephew Saad Alkhalfan is also a participant in that group. Hameed's mother, Hameeda, left the earth plane in 2014. He is grateful for all she gave him in this lifetime and sees her in a beautiful place now.

Hameed and Marie's daughter, Tanya, is not part of a Ridhwan group but continues to appreciate the positive influence of the Work on her life. Tanya has a degree in early childhood education and is employed by a private organization in Oakland. The relationship among the three of them remains strong.

My mother, June, left this world in 2010, and I am deeply grateful for her having been the conduit for me to enter this world and for the catalyst she was for me in so many areas of my life. I have a loving relationship with my older brother, David, and younger sister, Kristin. Sadly, my younger brother, Erik, passed away unexpectedly in 2014.

Perry and I have maintained intermittent contact over the years, and Richie is still one of my closest friends. Greg and I are still family after separating at the end of 2015, when I made the decision to devote the rest of my life to the development and optimization of the Diamond Approach. I want to support the teachers, the teaching, the students, and the structures through which the Diamond Approach is shared with the world, and my householding days are no longer compatible with this calling. A small parsonage is being built at the Eunice Street property, where I plan to spend my last days serving in any way I can.

As for Hameed and me, we continue on as a crystal gyroscope, riding the oscillating edges of the known and the unknown.

Mushka has never been replaced.

In Grateful Acknowledgment

There would be no relevant teaching or tale to tell without human beings who value it. Each individual who has been touched by the Diamond Approach is an implicit part of our unfolding story. You have given of yourself as you have come to know yourself. Infinite thanks for all your gifts.

I feel immensely blessed to be part of the mandala of all those who served *The Jeweled Path* from inception to birth. My deep gratitude to Elianne Obadia, my Writer's Midwife. You cheered me on when I felt I couldn't take another step, guided me firmly to discover my writer's voice, and helped me to tell the story that was alive inside me with honesty, courage, and vulnerability—and we had so much fun in the process.

A bow of respect and love to my best friend and comrade, Hameed Ali, for your generosity and support during this endeavor. You shouldered work for me and provided financial support that afforded me spacious time to write. You knew when to keep me company and when I needed to go it alone. Thank you for your faith in me to tell the story of the Diamond Approach, and for entrusting me with your most precious material possession—your journals.

Boundless appreciation for my trusty word warriors, the manuscript readers who traveled through the pages of this book and offered their time and sage advice brilliantly and beautifully: Linda Krier, my best girlfriend ever, I am so very thankful for our unwavering companionship on this journey and for your thoughtful, incisive reflection that kept my writing on point. Geneen Roth, I am touched by the sparkling time we spent together and for wielding your diamond-edged sword, keeping the freshness of the lived moments of the narrative crisp and galvanizing a new level of friendship. Byron Brown, your editorial feedback and fact-checking is always so precise and clear. Thank you for the great service of birthing the Diamond Approach into published form and nurturing it from its inception.

Many thanks to you, Deborah Ussery. You stood by me as friend and generous spirit with your vast memory banks, which I drew from repeatedly for an accurate accounting of the times, places, and people involved over many years.

Hameed Qabazard, your talent expresses the beauty of your generous spirit throughout the physical environment of our center, in our publications, and media.

Warm thanks to Liz Shaw and the editorial board at Shambhala Publications for recognizing the value of the Diamond Approach teaching and supporting it by publishing our books since 2002. A special nod to the fabulous editorial staff: assistant editor Audra Figgins, copyeditor Jill Rogers, and proofreader Emily White, as well as to the Shambhala design staff.

If it weren't for you, Kristina Grondahl and Marie Ali, I wouldn't have been as well fed during these last two years of writing. Your meals, heartful friendship, and literary feedback nourished me in heart, mind, and body.

Much love to you, Jessica Britt and Sharon Binder, for your caring support that kept me on track through the turbulent life events that paralleled this book's creation.

Hameed and Jodi Qabazard, and Scott and Kelly—thanks for welcoming me into your hearts and homes, offering me space to write in solitude.

Domo arigato to you, Jeanne Hay Rosenblum and Paul Ruyten Rosenblum, for your supportive enthusiasm for this book when it was simply a colorful idea forming itself in my consciousness. Jeanne, your generosity toward teachers, students, and strangers alike embodies the selflessness of service that this Work teaches. And a shout-out to all of you on the Ridhwan staff who personally supported me during my many pinwheel-eyed days of writing.

Thank you, Gregory Edgell, for tending so generously to the endless tasks of practical life while I was struggling to find time to write this book, and for our marriage that helped me to grow.

Deep gratitude to you, Scott Layton, for your phone call to Hameed that beckoned him back to Boulder, initiating the original group of guinea pigs that led to the teaching as we now know it.

I feel such appreciation for you, my buddy Duncan Scribner, for the ways you supported the School to develop through the eighties and nineties, and for helping light up the European flame for the Diamond Approach.

Sandra Maitri, you are the first friend I ever had who felt like a kindred spirit in the search of the mysterious miracles of the inner universe. I am so very glad for what we have shared. And I am forever indebted to you for introducing me to Hameed Ali and inviting me to move to Colorado with you.

Richard Gordon, my soulful ally, I feel the depth of my heart's recognition of the incredible gifts you have given me—teaching me to speak my mind; opening me to so many ways of exploring spirit; telling me the truth no matter the cost. You have helped me to venture into my blind spots and stood by me until I could see.

Susan Aqille, you stood by me and helped me find my way in the world when transitions from relationships and growing edges left me homeless and adrift. Thank you.

My salutations would not be complete without a nod to each member of the Obsidian Synod, in all of its permutations, as the leadership of the School. You work tirelessly in loving service to safeguard our spiritual values as they inform our in-the-world structures. I hold deep regard for our stalwart Ridhwan Foundation Board members as well—past and present—who have given of their time and skillful intelligence to ground our organization in the practical details of functioning in harmony with various cultures and legal requirements around the world. I see you all here in these pages, even though all your names do not appear in black and white.

A bow to you, Morton Letofsky, the first teacher and Synod member to take on the position originally held by Hameed as president of the Ridhwan Foundation—and the mensch I am pleased to call friend.

Bob Ball, my heart is moved by witnessing and being the recipient of what you give of your time, energy, and love to individuals and to the teaching as you serve as vice president of the Ridhwan Foundation.

I am more grateful than I can say for all the behind-the-scenes support —the work of many people on the staff of the Ridhwan organization who keep our citadel functioning in the world. This has taken a great deal of time and talent over the years, with each person standing on the shoulders of those who came before:

Thanks to Sarah Hurley for being the first office manager for Diamond Books and the DHAT office . . . to Janel Ensler, our executive administrator until 2006, who took on the task of office management when Sarah's job expanded beyond the original job description . . . to Rob Newmarch, our first executive director, who served with great care throughout the arduous tasks of establishing the systems for Ridhwan to become an international organization . . . to Dana Harrison, our first associate executive director, who, in turn, is moving into Rob's position, and is an inspiring addition in this time of the School's growth and development.

Much gratitude to you, my siblings, for loving me through all of my unconventional adventures, even when you didn't understand what I was up to.

And finally, for Russ and June: Though you passed long ago, you are never far away from my heart. Thank you for a second chance at life when you became the parents of my soul and held my hand as I took my first steps toward freedom.

Notes

CHAPTER 1: THE JOURNEY BEGINS

1. I do not think that psychic experiences necessarily lead to or are an indication of spiritual capacity or freedom. As the reader is probably aware, there are many less glamorous reasons for these kinds of occurrences. Children tend to see reality in a much less filtered way than the adults around them do.

CHAPTER 2: GROWING UP IN KUWAIT

1. Among Shiite Muslims, "ayatollah" is a title in the religious hierarchy achieved by scholars who have demonstrated highly advanced knowledge of Islamic law and religion. From the Arabic *āyat allāh*—"sign of God." For more information go to www.dictionary.reference.com/browse/ayatollah.

CHAPTER 3: ACCIDENTS AND OPPORTUNITIES

1. *Heart Dweller,* pamphlet copyright 1973, A. Hameed Ali, first published in 1995 by Diamond Books/Almaas Publications in Berkeley, CA.

CHAPTER 4: FLEDGING

1. The Sanskrit word *darshan* literally means "seeing" and refers to a meeting with a spiritual teacher or guru—most often but not always in a group—to receive spiritual teachings or transmissions. *Shaktipat* is described in the yogic texts as an initiation that activates an inner unfolding of awareness, leading to progressively higher states of consciousness. Shaktipat is given as an infusion of energy through grace of the guru, often in a darshan setting, as in this story. The term *Shakti* refers to the primordial cosmic energy, or generative, manifest power that creates the universe. For more information you can go to www.siddhayoga.org/shaktipat.

CHAPTER 5: OUT OF THE BLUE

1. The Fischer-Hoffman Process has had various incarnations, changing its name to the Hoffman Process and later to the Hoffman Quadrinity Process, by which it is now known. The Hoffman Institute website (www.hoffmaninstitute.org) gives this brief history:

> Hoffman's basic insight came to him in 1967. For the next five years he collaborated with psychotherapists and psychiatrists to help individuals on a one-to-one basis. In 1972, he and noted psychiatrist Claudio Naranjo, MD, began presenting Hoffman's method as a 13-week course in a group setting. He called it the "Fischer-Hoffman Process" in honor of the late Siegfried Fischer, MD.

CHAPTER 6: IN THE LAP OF LOVE

1. Hameed's curriculum for the SAT classes he taught included the Enneagram—which he, as well as Sandra, had been trained in and had taught in one of Claudio's earlier groups—as well as Sufi stories, journaling, and working with students using many of the techniques and practices he had learned over the years from various teachers.

CHAPTER 7: THE GOLDEN COG

1. A few years later, Alia would change back to using her maiden name, Johnson. She brought much to the School by editing Hameed's books.

2. The first Returning Process group was led by Hameed and Sandra, the second by Sandra, and the third by Hameed. In the seed group in Colorado, formed thirty-nine years ago as of this writing, it was required that anyone who wanted to join but had not completed one of these first three groups participate in a Process group led by a facilitator trained by Hameed. Eventually, this gave way to the Diamond Heart structures (DH1, DH2, and so on) in which a number of people began to study the teachings together and advanced year by year with the same group of students.

3. Hameed steadily attended an evening group that Henry led for four years. The group had a strong Gurdjieffian influence, and Henry also used his extensive psychological knowledge to confront students with their patterns. During the work periods that took place on Sundays, Henry taught some of the seminal practices regarding the embodiment

of presence that we continue to use in the School today. The small-group format that Hameed uses is fashioned after his experiences with Henry as well. The art of defending against the superego lives on in the School and is a crucial step in freeing consciousness to go beyond conventional inner experience.

4. In simplest terms, transference is the redirection of positive and/or negative feelings and desires—especially those unconsciously repressed and retained from childhood—toward a person in the present time.

5. Hameed never intended to live in Colorado; he committed only to doing the Process groups there. His involvements in California, such as completing his Reichian training and the possibility of being with Marie in a more committed way, kept him based there.

CHAPTER 8: CRACKING THE COSMIC HEAD

1. The Karmapa is the head of the Karma Kagyu, the largest sub-school of the Kagyu, one of the four major schools of Tibetan Buddhism. In the Black Hat ceremony, also known as the Black Crown ceremony, "His Holiness puts on the Black Crown and enters into a meditative state in which his mind is merged with the mind of Chenrezig, the Bodhisattva of Compassion. It is said that attending the ceremony brings great benefit, and even seeing an image of it can make a real connection between our minds and the benevolent mind of the Karmapa." The sixteenth Karmapa, from whom Hameed received the Black Hat transmission, died in 1981. For more information go to www.dharma-haven.org/tibetan/karmapa-crown.htm#Showing.

2. "Dharmakaya" is a Sanskrit term that means "body of truth" or "body of reality." "Mind itself, totally pure by nature, is spontaneously present as the ground aspect of Buddhahood-dharmakaya, suchness itself without any transition or change [the Diamond Approach views this as the boundless dimensions] for it occurs naturally and primordially without being created by some agent." Longchen Rabjam, *A Treasure Trove of Scriptural Transmission* (Junction City, CA: Padma Publishing, 2001), 8.

3. "Tarthang Tulku is renowned as a visionary, independent thinker and also as an innovative teacher. Educated in the Buddhist tradition in Tibet, he has been writing and teaching in America since 1969." From the back cover of *Knowledge of Time and Space* by Tarthang Tulku, Oakland, CA: Dharma Press, 1990.

CHAPTER 9: WHEN THE STUDENT IS READY . . . ESSENCE DELIVERS

1. The Fourth Way is an approach to self-development described by George Gurdjieff, which he developed over years of travel in the East. It combines what he saw as three established traditional ways or schools: those of the mind, those of the emotions, and those of the body; or of yogis, monks, and fakirs, respectively. It is sometimes referred to as "the Work," "work on oneself," or "the System." The fact that Fourth Way schools take place "in the world" and as part of ordinary life is a central difference from any of the three ways by themselves.

2. Sensing, Looking, and Listening is a practice of both concentration and mindfulness that is first done in the morning—optimally, just before getting up—and then throughout the day. It is an ancient practice whose efficacy for grounding in presence during daily activities becomes increasingly evident as one becomes more refined in the practice.

3. "Lataif" is an Arabic word that means "subtle/subtleties" or "delicate" and is pronounced la-TAI-if; the singular is "latifa" (la-TEEF-a).

4. For quite a while, we used the Gurdjieffian terminology "personality" instead of "ego" when we wanted to distinguish ego from essence. This changed when we realized that Gurdjieff used the term "essence" differently than we do. For him, it seems to refer to what we call the individual consciousness, which Hameed and I began to refer to as "soul" in the mid-'80s. In the Diamond Approach, essence is the nature of the individual consciousness, or soul.

CHAPTER 10: AND NOW WE ARE THREE

1. Hameed Qabazard is a master photographer and videographer. He has been involved all along in creating cover designs for Hameed's books, including graciously allowing us to use some of his photographs on several covers in the Diamond Books series. He also brings his artistry to the School by taking publicity photos for us, providing audiovisual materials and overseeing all AV functions for the retreats, and creating other visual materials as needed.

CHAPTER 11: DIAMONDS ARE A GIRL'S BEST FRIEND

1. The name "Meedle" was given to Hameed when he was in a SAT commune in Oakland. After I heard him called that, it became one of the nicknames I used for him.

2. A rare color of sapphire.

3. "Qualia" is a philosophical term that denotes the qualities, or textures, of experience—the taste, the feel, and so on.

CHAPTER 12: IN THE HEART OF PARADISE

1. Hameed and I explore our experiences in a variety of ways. Sometimes it happens in a dialogue of inquiring into our experience, which we formalized much later as a dialectic practice simply referred to as Dialectic Inquiry. This method was born of our mutual interest in the questions that were presenting themselves in our day-to-day conversations. At other times, we do our explorations in sessions that are more structured but still informal, where one of us is the subject and the other the "guide." Here the focus is not on mutual process but rather on one of us working on a burning personal question.

2. The Arabic word *sohbat* means "conversation." Some Sufis use it to describe conversation and spiritual companionship between people who are on the path together and regard each other with love and trust.

3. In taking an aim we make a commitment to carry out a specific intention. This spiritual practice became a common way in the Diamond Approach to work on ourselves. Hameed learned about taking aims from Henry; it is a feature of Gurdjieff's work, and it still is how we approach some issues today when on-the-ground action is needed because Inquiry alone is not shifting a certain behavior. Decisively taking an aim, however, goes against the inner tide of habits and unconscious motives, so following through can reveal feelings or attitudes that might not surface otherwise. These simply become more grist for the mill during the Inquiry process.

CHAPTER 15: DIAMOND BUDDIES

1. For further information about Odiyan, go to www.odiyan.org.

2. Around this time, during a trip to Tucson with HQ and Faisal to visit HQ's brother, he wrote a fair amount of *The Void* by hand in his small room. This would be his third written contribution to the spiritual discourse of the day, appearing in print in 1986, the same year as *Essence*. His first book, *The Elixir of Enlightenment*, was published in 1984. *Elixir* and *Essence* were both published by Samuel Weiser; in 1998, they were combined by Weiser into one volume: *Essence with The Elixir of Enlightenment: The Diamond Approach to Inner Realization*.

3. This openness of mind is not an abstract concept; it can be experienced directly. It is most palpable when we feel it directly, first as space in the head and then as it descends into the body.

4. The Diamond Vehicles:
   1. The Diamond Guidance
   2. The Markabah
   3. The Citadel
   4. The Diamond Dome
   5. The Stupa
   6. The Diamond Will
   7. The Water Chandelier
   8. The Diamond Pearl
   9. The Point Diamond
   10. The Freedom Vehicle

5. Idries Shah, *Thinkers of the East* (Baltimore, MD: Penguin, 1972), 66–67.

Chapter 16: Unsettled in California

1. Jessica would be instrumental in revitalizing the breathwork in the School at the turn of the century.

2. This is a list of the first students in the California group to become trained teachers ordained around 1986 by the Ridhwan Foundation. Many of these teachers went on to serve the School in various important ways.

   Marie Ali
   Jessica Britt
   Janel Ensler
   Kristina Grondahl
   Alia Johnson (passed in 2010)
   Jeanne Hay Rosenblum
   Joan Kenley (no longer active in the School)
   Hameed Qabazard
   Sarah Stanke
   Michael Torreson (no longer active in the School)

Chapter 17: My Guardian Angel Flies Away

1. The sound of the celesta—or celeste, meaning "heavenly" in French— is similar to that of the glockenspiel, but it has a more subtle timbre.

One of the best-known works showcasing the celesta is Tchaikovsky's "Dance of the Sugar Plum Fairy" from *The Nutcracker*. For more information go to https://en.wikipedia.org/wiki/Celesta.

CHAPTER 18: THE PROOF IS IN THE PLEASURE

1. The Mobius is a center in the subtle body that interfaces with the physical body at the xiphoid process, which is a small extension of the lower part of the sternum, or breastbone. We gave it the name "Mobius" because we saw an infinity symbol in it when it opened. The opening of this center is required for any state of consciousness—including the realization of the boundless dimensions—to imbue the whole body.

2. Hameed explained that he had heard of a teaching in the mystical Jewish tradition with a similar name, "merkava," but there is no resemblance between that and his teaching of the Markabah.

3. An infant experiences two very "different" mothers; one is the good/loving/nurturing mother that is a pleasurable experience and the other is the bad/uncaring/inadequate mother, which the baby associates with the condition of not getting his needs met and with the resulting feelings of frustration. The baby is not developed enough to experience these as being the same mother. In the Markabah teachings, this pleasurable, loving mother is the main area in the psyche that we zero in on to decouple Mother from the intrinsic pleasure of our own being.

4. Before Faisal and Patty married, she found a house on the outskirts of Boulder, which Faisal and Hameed bought together. After the ownership shifted to Faisal and Patty, Hameed initially stayed there as their guest whenever he was in Colorado.

CHAPTER 19: BEING IN BOOT CAMP

1. Platinum is the essential quality we refer to in the teaching as universal will. It opens up the larger context of the individual will in proper relationship to others and to our surroundings and circumstances. It enables one to hold a bigger picture and pulls the individual will into alignment with it as a support for the real life.

2. These days, the Citadel teachings are often presented immediately following those on the personal essence in order to bring in the support for it. The students learn that when presence is functionally rooted in us, then beauty, proportion, and balance grace our life and that when we

nurture our inner life and perform our daily tasks with a foundation of self-respect settled in the certainty of the ground of Being, we become the vessels that carry the reality of the divine into the world.

3. Idries Shah, *Tales of the Dervishes* (New York: E. P. Dutton, 1970), 21.

CHAPTER 20: MARCHING TOWARD THE LAND OF TRUTH

1. The following is a list of the first Colorado teachers, ordained in 1980. Many of them went on to teach groups, become board and Synod members, and take on the responsibilities of being program directors in the School.

> Jerry Alexander (passed in 2014)
> Lauren Armstrong (in California since 1981)*
> Bob Ball
> Carol Carbon*
> John Davis
> Linda Krier
> Scott Layton (in California since 1991)
> Deborah Ussery Letofsky*
> Morton Letofsky*
> Patricia Walker Rice*
> Duncan Scribner*
> Deane Shank
> Pompe Strater (no longer active in the School)

*The first teachers to receive training to lead the Returning Process, who then participated in the first teacher training.

Please see our website for a complete list of active teachers and their activities.

2. Some of the original teachers in the School feel that before becoming a teacher, or even before participating in a Diamond Heart group as a student, a person should take the Returning Process, but it is no longer offered as part of the curriculum. Instead, an in-depth application process that includes writing about one's personal history is required for entering the School.

One can view this development in different ways. We found that developing the capacity to deal with aggression and maintain a disciplined attitude during the Returning Process highlighted both limitations and strengths in ways that filling out an extensive application including details of one's personal history do not. One had to be very strong and committed almost from the get-go to make it through the gate back then. On the other side of the coin is the advantage of having many in the School now who are deeply immersed in and appreciate the Diamond Approach, even though some have less tolerance for strict adherence to discipline. But steadfastness is still required, since our groups and teacher training programs today are more extensive because more knowledge has been added or needs to be further unpacked. In addition, continuing education is required for all teachers.

CHAPTER 21: LOVE AND PEAS

1. The dull dome is the personality counterpart and major barrier to the emergence of the bright and transparent mind of Being. As our conviction in the reality of learned knowledge surfaces, the dull dome can be experienced directly. As we examine our positions and our adherence to mental knowing as it is used to define the self, the crude leaden heaviness is transformed to gold and light.

2. As the placement of this vehicle around the head suggests, it is a level of mind related to its spiritual nature. Sometimes I view it as a fourth layer of brain/mind (beyond the reptilian and mammalian and the neocortex) that incorporates presence, a natural evolutionary step for the human being.

3. All of the vehicles would show up in their main center of operation—belly, heart, mind, or above the head, which is the fourth center located outside of the body but within our personal consciousness. Then they would often make their way through each center before encompassing the body entirely. Each of these ways of experiencing the vehicles brought more maturity.

CHAPTER 22: A STAR IS BORN

1. Nisargadatta Maharaj (1889–1981) was an Indian guru of Shiva Advaita. After realizing himself as the Absolute and receiving an inner revelation some years afterward that he should teach, he began to initiate and work with visitors and disciples in his home beginning in 1951, giving discourses twice daily until his death.

2. James F. Masterson (1926–2010) was an internationally recognized psychiatrist who helped inaugurate a new approach to the study and treatment of personality disorders, including borderline and narcissistic.

3. Heinz Kohut (1913–1981) was an Austrian-born American psychoanalyst best known for his development of self psychology, an influential school of thought within psychodynamic/psychoanalytic theory that helped transform the modern practice of analytic and dynamic treatment approaches. Self psychology has burgeoned into one of the most significant analytic theories since Freud first introduced psychoanalysis to the scientific world in the early twentieth century.

Hameed wrote in his journal, "Kohut gave us language to describe what we had been observing. We had not seen the way all these manifestations were connected until we had this way of connecting them. He offered us concepts that were applicable to our experiences and observations, so I began to pull the threads together, and that became the Point teaching in the School."

4. Otto Friedmann Kernberg is a psychoanalyst and professor of psychiatry at Cornell University Medical College who is most widely known for his psychoanalytic theories on borderline personality organization and narcissistic pathology. His integrative writings were central to the development of modern theory of mind that is perhaps the theory most widely accepted among modern psychoanalysts.

5. See Hameed's book *The Point of Existence* for more details about narcissism and self-realization within the context of the Diamond Approach.

CHAPTER 23: THE VIEW FROM BEYOND

1. Hameed called this witnessing state "Brahman" because he had been reading about some Hindu schools that call it either that or "the universal witness," and what we were experiencing seemed similar to him. Some schools call it "the Ultimate" or "the Absolute," indicating that it has additional properties besides vast witnessing.

Without understanding the implications, Hameed had a glimpse of something that would take the teaching beyond a hierarchical view years later: "The Brahman is an exit from any notion of a hierarchy of spiritual realities," Hameed wrote in his journal, "and it is ultimate not because it is deepest but because it can coexist within any dimension of experience."

2. When we talk about the boundless dimensions in the Diamond Approach, we are not only referring to the underlying unity of the vastness; all manifestations within the boundless dimensions arise as a form of

each particular ground. For example, in the boundless dimension of love, we see everything as made of love; in awareness, everything arises as the clear light of awareness.

3. Divine Love is a dimension of boundless Loving Light. It is often first felt as a golden-yellowish, soft, rich, flowing sunlight in which everything is love and lovely. It can also arise as an ocean of tender green compassion, or pink fluffy sweetness, or even as a strong, sturdy, or powerful presence. It can be infused with pearly presence and feel vast and personal simultaneously. As we recognize this love as our nature from which we separated as we grew into an Earth creature of ego, we can resettle into the natural atmosphere of love that nurtures, satisfies, and heals that rupture.

4. When safety and trust became an issue, the work of Donald Woods Winnicott on the relationship of the holding environment to the development of the infant became relevant for our unfolding understanding on this path. See Winnicott's book *The Maturational Processes and the Facilitating Environment: Studies in the Theory of Emotional Development* (Madison, CT: International Universities Press, 1985).

5. It was around this time that Hameed began to use the term "True Nature." This is because he recognized the formless ground as the nature of our individual consciousness and of all manifest reality.

CHAPTER 24: TAPIOCA SUPREME

1. Another person who provided important support for Hameed in thinking through the establishment of the various structures and their functions was Susan Lea, Hameed's friend and tax attorney in the 1980s. Through her encouragement, Hameed started the DHAT Institute, which eventually became the educational wing of Ridhwan.

2. At this point in the unfoldment of the teaching, we had not discovered the more basic level of awareness that we refer to as the Nameless—awareness discriminated from knowing.

3. At first we saw the Brahman as a permutation of the Absolute, which we called the Ultimate. The Absolute as the depth and mystery of Being would reveal its more complete understanding within the context of the Diamond Approach a couple of years later. As this book was being written, we recognized the Brahman as its own state apart from the boundless dimensions. We initially had no way to determine this fact

since we had not imagined that there were any experiences beyond duality and nonduality. The state of the Brahman as we now teach it in the School is understood as one of the experiences of the fourth turning of the teachings that are discussed in later chapters.

4. For more information go to https://en.wikipedia.org/wiki/Jnana_yoga.

5. DHAT, established prior to the Diamond Heart Programs, was the educational arm of Ridhwan until 2015, but it no longer exists. For many individuals, the term "Diamond Heart" has become synonymous with the Diamond Approach as the name of the teaching, but the formal name for the teaching is the Diamond Approach. "Diamond Heart" refers to the program structures of the groups that bear that name. Under the Ridhwan umbrella, the Academy runs the Diamond Heart groups and seminary programs. Hameed and Karen are the directors of the Academy. The term "academy" was borrowed from Plato, who established his as a gathering place for those interested in pursuing knowledge and discovering truth.

The initials *D H A T* also form the name of a character in some Sufi tales, Prince Dhat, an individual born of royal blood who is sent on a journey to rescue the Princess Precious Pearl. He becomes lost and goes to sleep eating the fruits of the world. Finally, he finds the pearl he is looking for.

CHAPTER 25: WHAT DID YOU SAY THE NAME WAS?

1. Each boundless dimension arises with its particular presence and emptiness. In the Supreme, for example, there is the teeming fullness of Being whose emptiness is the no-thing-ness of Being. Absence is the emptiness side of the clear light of awareness.

2. Heinz Kohut's understanding of transferences in childhood and early object relations aided Hameed in conceptualizing the set of issues related to the undifferentiated self and how those manifest in adult relationships.

CHAPTER 26: THE ABSOLUTE END

1. The Diamond Will is sometimes referred to as a mountain due to its massive feeling of presence and support. It manifested to support the realization of the true essential self with the wisdom of nondoing. In the boundless dimensions, this new level of the Diamond Will arises

as the wisdom of boundless realization. On the Supreme level, it is first revealed as the merged Diamond Will because it is the resolution/letting go of the fused, internalized early object relations with the good mother that form the basis of our positive identification of self. This is critical because any identification, positive or negative, is an impediment to realization. In the Nameless and Absolute dimensions, the Diamond Will emerges again as support for the nonconceptual identity.

2. The Arabic word *monajat* refers to a heartfelt longing for and loving connection with the Beloved/God, but the term can also be extended to mean a spiritual inquiry between individuals who share a bond of love and trust. Rumi's poetry is an example of monajat. His relationship with Shams is also an expression of it, in the sharing of their love for the Beloved.

CHAPTER 27: SOUL DANCING

1. William Ronald Dodds Fairbairn (1889–1964) was a Scottish psychoanalyst and an important figure in the development of object relations theory. He offered an alternative viewpoint to Freud's view of the libido as pleasure-seeking. Fairbairn saw the libido as object-seeking, with the aim of creating relationships with others. See his classic book *Psychoanalytic Studies of the Personality* (London: Routledge, 1952).
2. To put it simply, a Riemannian manifold is related to the folding of space.
3. In some Eastern traditions, "nonconceptual" refers also to pure consciousness or pure presence because it is beyond subjective mind and prior to naming. We see this as the Supreme ground of knowing, since it is the innate self-knowing without the self-reflection and recognition of form that is basic to all knowing.

CHAPTER 28: DOWN WE GO

1. At this time we saw the Absolute as the true nature of everything and used the terms "Absolute" and "True Nature" interchangeably. The latter term as we use it today refers not only to the Absolute but also to any way we can experience our nature, which includes experiencing it beyond nonduality.
2. The first Diamond Heart Program (DH1) began in both California and Colorado in 1988, starting with the basics as Hameed had taught them. (He continued to lead the group that he had begun in 1978.) As of this

writing, there have been ten Diamond Heart groups in California—DHI through DH10—and nine in Colorado. Some of these have blended over time, due to attrition and the development and changing needs of the students.

3. Hameed's publisher at the time, Samuel Weiser, encouraged Hameed to choose a pen name. Hameed decided on "A. H. Almaas" because *almaas* means "diamond" in Arabic, and he felt it was an accurate reference to the true author of his books—the Diamond Guidance—which was responsible for the wisdom coming through him. He has always said, "I am not the source of this knowledge."

4. One of the unique teachings of the Diamond Approach is that each dimension must not only be realized, it must be personalized as well. The development of the soul into a true individual occurs on six levels, which involve various experiences of merging, integration, expression, and physical embodiment, culminating in the Microcosm Pearl. The following is a brief synopsis of the levels of the development of the soul into true individuality:

   White Pearl: Princess Precious Pearl—the first pearl to arise
   Fleshy Pearl: the physical embodiment of the personal essence
   Complete Pearl: the integration of all the aspects
   Diamond Pearl: the integration of the first six diamond vehicles
   Crystal Pearl: the integration of the boundless dimensions
   Microcosm Pearl: the integration of all dimensions of ascent and
      descent

CHAPTER 29: THROUGH THE JEWELED PORTAL

1. Hameed saw Christ as the Pearl, the personalization of God in the world, a view we had come to many years before. Hameed used many of Christ's teachings about the dimension of Divine Love, in which love, faith, hope, and surrender of the soul to the larger presence of Being is pivotal in understanding the heart of True Nature.

2. Some individuals experience the crystal as being like a rock or meteor when they first encounter it.

3. The crystals that brought the wisdom of the nonconceptual realms of Being were less crisp and transparent than the diamonds of the conceptual realms. They served to take us not only beyond concepts but also beyond mind.

4. The feeling of nothingness that the crystal brings is often conflated with narcissistic emptiness, but it is more amorphous than the distinct characteristics that we usually associate with that painful condition. In this state of featureless nothing, there is nothing to be recognized as one's self.

5. Indra's net, also called Indra's jewels or Indra's pearls, is a metaphor used to illustrate the concepts of emptiness, dependent origination, and interpenetration in Buddhist philosophy. For the story of Indra's net, see www.uua.org/re/tapestry/youth/bridges/workshop7/indra.

6. Every view from the realized condition is valid, but that is not the perennial philosophy that every pathway leads to the same place.

About the Author

Karen Johnson began her journey into the spiritual universe at the age of fourteen. After graduating from art school at twenty-three, she met Hameed Ali (A. H. Almaas), which set her on a new trajectory. They eventually became colleagues, codeveloping the Diamond Approach as it is taught in the Ridhwan School today. Karen holds a master's degree in psychology and trained in dance as well as art. Working alongside each other for the past forty years, she and Hameed continue the wild and thrilling ride through the endless realms of our miraculous nature.